ELEMENTS OF
C

FOUNDATIONS OF COMPUTER SCIENCE
Series Editor: Raymond E. Miller
Georgia Institute of Technology

ELEMENTS OF C
Morton H. Lewin

PRINCIPLES OF DATA SECURITY
Ernst L. Leiss

UNDERSTANDING LANGUAGE: Man or Machine
John A. Moyne

ELEMENTS OF
C

MORTON H. LEWIN

Rutgers University
Piscataway, New Jersey

SPRINGER SCIENCE+BUSINESS MEDIA, LLC

Library of Congress Cataloging in Publication Data

Lewin, Morton H.
  Elements of C.

  (Foundations of computer science)
  Bibliography: p.
  Includes index.
  1. C (Computer program language) I. Title. II. Series.
QA76.73.C15L49   1986   005.13′3   86-4910
ISBN 978-1-4612-9271-5   ISBN 978-1-4613-2155-2 (eBook)
DOI 10.1007/978-1-4613-2155-2

To Suki,
who brings a sense of humor
and joy wherever she goes

PREFACE

Statements in C, like statements in any other programming language, consist almost entirely of expressions and special reserved words. Declarations in C, *unlike* declarations in other languages, *also* contain arbitrary expressions. Thus, studying the means by which C expressions are constructed and evaluated is especially important—particularly since the number of permissible C operators is so large.

Since all of the operands in a C expression (excluding constants) must be properly *declared* before they are used, and since declarations themselves contain expressions, the teaching of C involves the following chicken-and-egg problem: Should one begin by considering only *elementary* declarations, in which case the topic of expression construction and evaluation cannot be fully treated in one place, because the operators that pertain to the more complex objects—like pointers and structures (whose declarations have not yet been introduced)—have not yet been covered, or should one postpone entirely the issue of how declarations are written (merely *assuming* that all of the objects under discussion have been properly declared) in order to fully treat *all* types of operands and operators in one comprehensive discussion?

If the student is encouraged to begin writing programs immediately, the former choice is mandatory, because even the most elementary programs must contain proper declarations. Thus, most C textbooks postpone the discussion of objects like arrays, structures, and pointers (and of the operators that pertain to them) until the second half of the book is reached.

In this book, I have chosen the latter approach—in order to fully cover all of the "jargon" of C in one place. The price that is paid for this choice is that the point at which actual programs are written is the thing that is postponed. However, the all-important topic of expression construction and evaluation, which is the key to understanding the C language, is *completely* covered in one chapter. *All* of the objects that can be manipulated by C programs are introduced there.

Since the student is not yet writing programs, he/she is given practice in expression construction and evaluation by way of 100 short problems (call them expression "puzzles") that appear at the end of the "Operators and Expressions" chapter. These problems are specifically designed to provide the kind of practice that would normally be received during the coding of a large number of elementary programs. Solutions to all of the problems are provided in the back of the book.

To demonstrate that it is possible to explain how an object is used in an expression *even before* all of the detailed properties of that object (e.g., how it is formally declared and how it is initialized) have been discussed, consider the treatment of pointers. There is no reason to postpone their discussion (which is so important) to a late chapter. Once you learn that a pointer has a name, and that the value of a pointer is an address, it is relatively easy to accept the notion that the value of an expression like

*pointer__name

is the *contents* of that address.

As the above example implies, this book is written for those who have had some previous exposure to assembly language programming and basic hardware principles. Specifically, it is assumed that the reader is either a professional who is converting to the use of C, or a "second- or third-year" engineering-oriented student or hobbyist. Some experience with at least one high-level programming language is also assumed.

Thus, this book is *not* intended for a beginner. A certain amount of maturity and previous background is assumed. To ensure that the prospective reader is "in tune" with the book's level of presentation, the first chapter is intentionally designed to carefully spell out, first, what is expected of the reader, and second, what the reader can expect from the book. In particular, one introductory section describes in great detail the technical background of the "ideal" reader. Another section provides a preview of the some of the key concepts that will be highlighted in the book, and the final introductory section explains how the topics that will be studied will be *sequenced*. As the above discussion implies, the order in which the material is presented is somewhat unorthodox. For example, many objects are first introduced in an *informal* or *intuitive* manner, assuming that the reader has already seen similar objects in his/her previous experience.

It is also emphasized in the Introduction that this is *not* a book on programming *technique*, using the C programming language as a vehicle. Rather, the book is designed to explain the characteristics of the language itself. Since it is well known that students learn a programming language by writing programs in that language, how do I justify an approach that defers the point at which the coding of complete programs actually begins? I do it by citing examples to demonstrate the disadvantages of providing information to students only on a "need to know" basis. For instance, when students begin coding too soon, using only elementary declarations, they are often not prepared for the complexities of the constructs employed in the declarations of so-called "derived" object types. Most students, *and professionals*, who were very comfortable with declarations like

$$\textbf{int count};$$

which declares **count** to be of type **int**eger, are nevertheless totally unprepared for and completely thrown by a declaration like

$$\textbf{char} \; *(*\textbf{fcn\_name}())[] ;$$

which declares **fcn_name** to be a function returning a pointer to an array of pointers to **char**acters.

There are other disadvantages to writing programs too soon. Since you begin immediately to use standard I/O library facilities, you are often not made aware of the distinctions between the native C language—as provided by the compiler—and its library extensions. You also generally attribute too much importance to the **main** function, which appears in all C programs, and you may develop erroneous ideas about the contents of the standard header file **stdio.h**, which is included in virtually every program that you write.

In this book, the coding of complete programs does not begin until four chapters of fundamentals have been presented. Instead, during this time, I provide appropriate exercises and problems at the end of each chapter—to help the reader practice the fundamentals that were discussed in that chapter. When all of the rudiments have been covered, exercises of the form "write a program to . . ." are finally given (in an integrated sequence of 25 problems at the end of Chapter 5).

Since the *entire* C language is not so complex, it is possible to present virtually *all* of it first, before discussing any real programs. While students who want to start "practicing" immediately may be somewhat frustrated by this "standard textbook" approach, it does materially reduce the amount of naivete (and wasted time) that accompanies jumping into the water before you have learned to swim. My experience with this approach has been successful, although, admittedly, the price paid is that the number of complete program examples that are presented in this book is less than that found in other C texts.

Although several references are made to the UNIX operating system (UNIX is a trademark of Bell Laboratories), this book is specifically designed to be operating-system-independent. It also limits its attention to the widely accepted "standard" definition of C, as described in Appendix A of the book by Kernighan and Ritchie (*The C Programming Language,* Prentice Hall, 1978). Virtually all of the existing C compilers, at the time of this writing, support *no more than* this version of C. In particular, extensions that are expected to be added, when the ANSI version of C is ultimately adopted and documented, are intentionally omitted. It is expected that they will be easily assimilated by users familiar with the present version.

Special features of this book include a problem solutions chapter that contains solutions to *all* of the end-of-chapter problems and two appendixes that contain easy-to-use capsule summaries of the most common standard library functions. Each one-line summary presents the format for the *call* of a function, briefly describes the operation executed by that function, and specifies what that function returns. It clearly implies how both the function and its arguments should be declared.

CONTENTS

Chapter 3   Program Structure

Chapter 4   The C Preprocessor

Chapter 5   Flow of Control

Chapter 6   Advanced Topics

Chapter 7   The Standard Library

Solutions to Problems

Appendix A   Table of ASCII Codes

Appendix B   C Keywords and Their Uses

CHAPTER 1   **INTRODUCTION**

1.1 The Significance of C

In 1970, it was estimated that about 90% of all "serious" programming (i.e., that done by professional programmers) was done in assembly language—even though many of the high-level programming languages that presently exist were available then. (A predecessor to C was just being developed at that time.) This state of affairs was accounted for using the explanation that most of the programs under development were system programs, which, if coded in a high-level language, would occupy too much space or would be too slow. In those days, the proliferation of microprocessors was virtually inconceivable.

The rapid development of microprocessors in the 1970s had little effect on this situation, initially, because most high-level languages were not supported in early microcomputer development systems. Only relatively recently has the need for *machine-independent* systems programming been seriously recognized.

This is one of the reasons why C has assumed its present level of importance. There are several others. Certainly, the wide popularity of the UNIX operating system, which is written in C and which offers broad C programming support, is chief among these. In addition, the language was fortunate to have had a lengthy shakedown period of active, in-house use where it was conceived (at Bell Laboratories) before many of the members of the computing community were introduced to it. Furthermore, at about the time when its popularity began to grow, an excellent document (the book *The C Programming Language* by Kernighan and Ritchie, Prentice–Hall, 1978) was available to act as a standard definition of the language.

It has been claimed that perhaps the most prominent reason for C's wide acceptance is that a typical C program is portable. It may be run on different computers with little or no change. This is true principally because the single, standard definition of the language (the book cited above), which has been in force over a wide spectrum of processors, specifically took portability issues into account. It did so chiefly because of experience gained, in the late 1970s, in the porting of the UNIX operating system from one computer to another.

Another prominent reason for C's growing popularity is that, because C is a relatively low-level language (i.e., it provides the programmer with facilities and constructs that are normally associated only with assemblers), programs written in C generally execute faster than those written in other high-level languages.

These two characteristics, portability and execution speed, are the main reasons why many more programs are written in C today. With the proliferation of microprocessors, the life of a program written in an assembly language (i.e., a language specifically tailored to a single processor) is severely limited. Invariably, the next generation of processors, offering many new features and performance improvements, is incompatible with the previous generation. Therefore, to protect one's software development investment, it is necessary to devise programs that are not only fast but also transportable. They should not have to be rewritten when the improved processor arrives.

Other reasons for C's wide acceptance include its support for separately compiled modules (so that large programs may be subdivided into relatively independent parts, each possibly assigned to a different programmer) and its provision of convenient constructs not only for flow of control but also for structuring of data. We will see examples of these presently.

1.2 Prerequisite Summary

The Preface noted that this book is written assuming a reader who is primarily an assembly language programmer—either a professional who is converting to the use of C or an experienced engineering-oriented student or hobbyist who has already had a sufficient introduction to computer organization and assembly language programming. Some experience with at least one high-level programming language is also assumed. Even though assembly language experience is the main prerequisite, a reader who is primarily a high-level language programmer may also benefit from the book's approach. Since this approach is somewhat unorthodox, it is worthwhile digressing here to spell out, in some detail, those concepts that are assumed to be known by the reader. This will ensure that when we begin our study, in the next chapter, we will all be "on the same wavelength."

This book is written making the same assumptions as are normally made in the development of a typical Programmer's Reference Manual. Specifically, the reader is assumed *not* to be a beginner. Further, the purpose of this book is *not* to teach programming *technique* using the C programming language as a vehicle. Rather, it is meant as a text that explains the characteristics of the language itself.

Rather than merely list those topics to which it is assumed the reader has already been "exposed," a brief summary of the key concepts in each prerequisite area will be given. If you find that your background on a given topic is weak or nonexistent, it is recommended that you take the time to review the fundamentals in that area, using an appropriate source.

The assumption of assembly language experience carries with it the assumption that you are already familiar with the following hardware principles:

A register stores a string of bits. A memory is an ordered collection of identical registers, each having associated with it a number called its address. A processor fetches and executes coded instructions that are part of a program stored in a memory to which the processor has access. These instructions may be generally categorized as data movement instructions (including input and output), arithmetic and logical instructions, and transfers of control. The operands that are manipulated by instructions vary in length. They include bit fields, bytes or characters, words, double-words, and so on.

A signed numeric operand is normally represented in two's-complement form. The upper bit is the sign bit. A short signed integer is normally converted into a longer one (e.g., into double-precision form) by sign-bit-extension, in which the sign bit is copied into all higher bit positions. A floating-point number is usually represented as two signed numeric fields—a mantissa and an exponent.

Logical instructions include NOTs, ANDs, ORs, EXCLUSIVE ORs, and arithmetic and logical shifts. Transfers of control are normally conditional on the results of previous arithmetic and logical operations. The most important transfers of control are subroutine CALLs and their companion RETURNs.

A stack is a "last-in–first-out" set of registers. The last item pushed on a stack is the first item available from it. A subroutine CALL executes by pushing a return address on a stack. Its companion RETURN executes by popping that same address. Thus, subroutine calls may be *nested*. Typically, a subroutine call involves passing to the called routine input arguments that the called routine uses in its computation. The called routine often returns results of its computation back to its caller. While these input arguments and results may be passed via processor registers or via fixed memory locations, they are often passed via a stack. A stack is also very useful as a source of temporary registers for "scratch-pad" computations.

A memory byte is often employed to store a character. A contiguous sequence of bytes is used to store a string of characters. The 8-bit code that represents a single character may be written in binary, octal, decimal, or hexadecimal form. Simple rules exist for converting between these alternative numeric representations. The most common standard code for representing characters is the ASCII code. It includes not only codes for the most common printing characters but also codes for nonprinting control characters. A control character is one whose reception causes some special nonprinting control action, like carriage return or backspace.

The assumption of previous programming experience (not only in an assembly language but also in at least one high-level language) carries with it the assumption that you are already familiar with the following software principles:

A programming environment includes a means to create and modify source files (containing source programs), to compile or assemble these source files into corresponding object files, and to load and link these object files in order to run them. It is important to distinguish between those operations that are executed at *compile time* and those that are executed at *run time*. The fact that a program passes the compilation or assembly process (without any error messages from the translator) simply means that the program was found syntactically correct. It does not necessarily mean that it will run properly. When it does not run properly, debugging techniques are used to isolate those portions of the program that are not behaving as expected.

A typical source program contains comments, declarations, directives, and statements. Comments are ignored by the compiler or assembler. They are very important, however, in documenting the program, and good programs contain profuse comments. Most directives and declarations do not directly cause object code to be generated. Rather, they guide the compiler or the assembler by providing information that helps it to do its job. For example, an EQUate directive, in an assembly language program, directs the assembler to substitute, for all subsequent occurrences of a given symbol, a specific constant. Such a directive is important because it permits all occurrences of that constant, normally appearing in many places throughout the source program, to be changed with only one modification to the program—namely, in the directive that defines that constant's value. Experienced programmers recognize that even the most universal of constants has a way of later requiring modification.

As it runs, a compiler or assembler maintains a symbol table for its own use. Every time a new symbol or name is encountered in the source program, it is recorded in the symbol table. Associated with each symbol in the symbol table is a value. Typically, this value is an address. For example, the symbol may name a variable, in which case the address is the memory location where the value of that variable is stored. Alternatively, the symbol may label the entry point of a subroutine (i.e., it is the name of that procedure), in which case the address that is associated with the symbol is the value that is inserted into every CALL instruction that references that subroutine. Normally, the programmer selects a symbol so that it suggests the role that that symbol plays in the program.

Statements in a typical high-level language contain reserved words (like **if**) and expressions. One of the most common statements is the assignment statement. Generally, it has the form

$$\mathbf{variable \ = \ expression}$$

and it executes by assigning to the named variable the value of the specified expression.

An expression contains operands and operators. For example,

$$\mathbf{A \ * \ (B \ + \ C)}$$

is an expression containing three operands and two operators. An expression is evaluated by applying the operators to the values of their respective operands, in the proper order, to derive a single value, called the value of the expression. Typically, the code that a compiler generates to evaluate an expression utilizes a stack. In the above example, this code would (at run time) do the following: First, the values of **B** and **C** would be pushed on the stack. An addition operation would then replace the top two stack operands with their sum. Next, the value of **A** would be pushed on the stack, and finally, a multiplication operation would replace the two top stack operands with their product—leaving the value of the expression on the top of the stack.

Operators are generally either unary—requiring a single operand (e.g., the "-" in **-D**)—or binary—requiring two operands (e.g., either the "*" or the "+" in the example above). A relational operator, like "<" or ">=", is a binary operator. The value of a relational expression is either *true* or *false*. Typically, a relational expression is employed in a decision-making statement (e.g., an **if** statement) that affects the flow of control in a program. Most of the high-level language statements that mechanize program loops employ relational expressions to define the loop *exit* conditions.

A typical assembly language program contains both macros and subroutines. A simple macro is a package of source statements, grouped together under a single name. This package is inserted verbatim into the source code stream at any point where the macro name appears. Thus, the assembly language programmer has a choice for each small computational package. Either a macro may be inserted, in line, or a subroutine call may be employed. Macros generally execute faster, but consume more memory space because each invocation requires a new block of inserted code. A subroutine, on the other hand, exists in only one place in memory.

A typical object program contains a code area (where the instructions, which are to be executed at run time, reside) and one or more data areas for the variables that that program manipulates. A given variable in a data area may be initialized in either of two ways: First, the compiler or assembler may be directed to output the appropriate data value in that variable's memory space. In this case, the variable is automatically initialized when the program is loaded—even before the run begins. Second, an appropriate assignment operation may be executed, at run time, to give the variable the proper initial value.

This brief summary was not intended to be an equivalent of the statement: "You will understand what is presented in this book provided that you know it already." Rather, it was meant to more clearly define the initial state of the ideal reader. Several of the concepts that are briefly summarized above will be reiterated at those points in the book where it appears appropriate.

1.3 A Preview of C

An expression, in any programming language, contains operands and operators. It is evaluated by applying the operators to their corresponding operands, in the proper order, to develop a single value—called the value of the expression.

Since virtually every line in a C program contains at least one C expression, one's initial impression of the language is often based on one's first glance at a real C expression. Consider, then, the following expression:

```
--(p)->_cnt  >=  0  ?  *(p)->_ptr++  &  0377  :  _fillbuf(p)
```

which was extracted verbatim from one of the lines in an actual C source file. [This file, named **stdio.h** (described in detail later), is an essential part of every C programming environment.]

The purpose of this rather intimidating example is to illustrate that C provides a very large number of special operator symbols. They make it possible to express very intricate computations in an extremely concise manner. In the next chapter, *all* of these new notations will be explained. Periodically, we will return to the expression above to decipher another small part of it. When all of its pieces have been separately explained, we will reexamine it as a whole to find that it indeed describes, in one line, a rather complex sequence of operations—one that is normally represented, in other programming languages, by many lines of source code.

Although you may meet all of the qualifications for the ideal reader—as described in the last section—it is still quite likely that you have not been exposed to a "typed" language—one in which each program object (e.g., a variable) must be properly *declared* before it is referenced. A declaration of an object not only defines a *name* for it, but also specifies that object's *type*. Simple types are integers and floating quantities. More complex types are arrays, pointers, and structures. The C compiler employs such declarations to ensure that every programmer-defined object is not used in an "improper" manner. This process is known as *type checking*. For example, the compiler will reject any attempt to use an expression whose value is a floating-point quantity as an index into an array (which should be integral). Similarly, the compiler will reject any attempt to perform a logical operation (e.g., a shift) on a pointer value (which is a machine address). If you are familiar with a language like Pascal, then you already know about type declarations.

C is relatively unique in that, in addition to the fact that all of its statements contain arbitrary expressions, its *declarations also* contain arbitrary expressions. For example, as you will soon find out, while a declaration like

int count;

declaring **count** to be the name of a variable of type **int**eger, is relatively easy to grasp, a declaration like

char *(*fcn_name())[];

declaring **fcn_name** to be the name of a function returning a pointer to an array of pointers to **char**acters, takes quite a bit more time to digest.

Thus, learning how to decipher C expressions is clearly the most fundamental key to learning the language. It is for this reason that all of the possible operators and operands that may appear in C expressions are explained in detail in the next chapter. Once you become conversant with the way in which C expressions are constructed and evaluated, you will have little difficulty mastering the other properties of the language.

As alluded to above, while you study the next chapter, you will encounter many new C notations. For example, you will find that most C programmers increment a variable, **a**, not by saying **a = a + 1**, which you may have been used to using (and which, by the way, is perfectly legal in C), but by saying **a ++**. You will find that a relational test for the equality of two variables (in an **if** statement, for example), which you may have been used to expressing as **if (a = b)**, is instead written in C as **if (a == b)**. In each case, you may ask for a justification for the new notation. There are several that may be given.

First, you will find that virtually every new notation is a useful shorthand for an often-used construction. While its use may not necessarily improve the readability of a program, it will make for very concise source code. (Whether C programs are more or less readable than programs in other languages is difficult to measure. One can argue that *no* program, in *any* language, is really "self-documenting," i.e., easily read. That is the reason why the profuse use of *comments* has always been encouraged.)

Second, in many cases, the use of a special operator symbol may permit the compiler to generate more efficient code than would otherwise be possible. While it is difficult to prove that this will always be the case, the following intuitive argument should be adequate for our purposes: Since a compiler may be tailored to generate optimized code for every special operator that it encounters, a language having more such operators (assuming that they correspond to commonly used programmer constructs) should yield more efficient output code. Essentially, a small additional burden on the programmer, to learn the new constructs, yields a more efficient object program.

Third, in several cases (== is an example), the new operator is merely C's version of an operator that is already traditional in other languages. In particular, some of C's operators (e.g., its pointer operators) have counterparts chiefly in *assembly* languages.

Finally, if none of the above justifications satisfies you, we can resort to the ultimate justification, as provided by Kernighan and Ritchie while discussing a specific line of C code: "Although this may seem cryptic at first sight, the notational convenience is considerable, and the idiom should be mastered, if for no other reason than that you will see it frequently in C programs."

You will find shortly that the atomic data elements that are manipulated by C programs are **char**acters, **int**egers, and **float**ing-point numbers. (The **bold** portions are their keyword abbreviations.) All other types of objects that may be declared must be "derived from" or "anchored to" one of these atomic data types. For example, when you declare a *pointer*, you must specify to what *type* of object that pointer *points*. When you declare an array, you must specify the *type* of the objects *comprising* the array. If this type is not one of the *atomic* types, then further information in the declaration must be given until one of the atomic types is finally specified. Thus, there are potentially an infinite number of possible object declarations that may be made. For example, there are "pointers to arrays of **int**egers." There are also "arrays of pointers to **char**acters." There are also "arrays of pointers to arrays of **float**ing-point numbers" and "pointers to pointers to **char**acters". And so on.

Similarly, a C function (i.e., a subroutine) is declared as one "returning" a *type* of object. This returned value is the result of that function's computation. You will shortly find that a function *call* is specified in C by writing down the name of the function, followed by a list of expressions for the input arguments that the function expects—enclosed in parentheses. For example,

power (a, b)

represents a call on a function named **power**, passing to it the values of two
variables **a** and **b**. Such a call construct may be embedded within an arbitrary
expression. When this expression is evaluated, the occurrence of the call sub-
expression is effectively replaced by the value that is returned by the function
in response to the call. Thus, for example,

c * (power (a, b) + d)

is evaluated by adding the value of **d** to the value returned by the **power**
subroutine (which may be, for instance, **a** raised to the **b** power) and then by
multiplying that result by the value of **c**.

   If you have had previous exposure to a Pascal-like language, this notation
is not new to you. On the other hand, if you are an assembly language programmer, the expression above might be the equivalent of code like

```
PUSH  A
PUSH  B
CALL  POWER
PUSH  D
CALL  ADDER
PUSH  C
CALL  MULTIPLY
```

assuming that all of the subroutines that are called process the top two stack
entries, leaving their results on top of the stack. (For simplicity, all arguments
are assumed to be of the same length, namely, that of the operand of a PUSH
instruction.)

   Finally, if most of your programming experience involves programming
languages that employ only *global* names (e.g., high-level languages like BASIC,
or *any* of the assembly languages), then it is likely that you will find C's
mechanism for limiting the *scope* of a name to be a new and very useful facility.

   The scope of a name is that part of a program over which that name may
be referenced. The scope of a global name is the entire program in which it
appears. C makes it possible to define *local* names, which are "known" or
addressable only within a portion of a program—e.g., only within a specific
function. This facility makes it possible for a given segment of a computation
to employ *private* registers that cannot be accessed, either inadvertently or intentionally, from other parts of the same program. The registers are effectively
invisible to the other parts. Such a facility can be used to materially simplify

the *interface* that a typical function presents to a system—because the registers that it employs are not visible outside the function.

Similarly, C makes it possible to allocate storage to variables either on a permanent basis or on a *temporary* basis. Global variables are allocated permanent storage, while local variables are normally allocated temporary storage. However, you will also find that C makes it possible to limit the scope of a permanently stored object—so that, even though it *exists* in storage, it becomes temporarily inaccessible.

The ability to limit the scope of a variable not only makes it possible to simplify function interfaces, but also substantially reduces the likelihood of program errors—specifically, those that are caused by the fact that a portion of a computation merely *had access* to variables that should have been unavailable to it.

1.4 This Book's Approach to C

The best way to learn the details of a programming language is to write a sufficient number of *programs* in that language. However, writing programs before you have learned all of the fundamentals has some distinct disadvantages—particularly in C. You may develop some misconceptions about the language that may take some time to correct.

In a typical C textbook, particularly one meant for beginners, you are encouraged to start writing programs immediately. The book begins by introducing the simplest objects, namely, variables and constants. More complex objects (like arrays, functions, pointers, and structures) are introduced in the later chapters. Consequently, the treatment of the operators that *pertain* to these more complex objects is *also* postponed. Thus, you are exposed to the C operators, and to the objects to which they apply, in a *gradual* manner, chapter by chapter.

As a result, there is no *single* unified treatment (in one chapter) of *all* of the possible operands and operators that may appear in C expressions. One disadvantage of this approach is that students who were quite comfortable with beginning declarations like

$$\textbf{int count;}$$

are nevertheless totally unprepared for and completely thrown by declarations like

$$\textbf{char *(*fcn\_name()) [];}$$

(The meanings of these declarations were given in the previous section.)

I believe that the reason for this is that insufficient time is spent in a concentrated study of all types of C expressions, at the outset—before real programs are written. It is for this reason that I have chosen to postpone the point at which complete programs are discussed in this book. Such an approach is feasible provided that the reader has a background similar to that described in Section 1.2. That is, if you have already seen a sufficient number of elementary program examples in other languages, you are more likely to appreciate a presentation of the key aspects of C (in the introductory chapters) using only short examples of the constructs involved. It is when you have *less* experience that you are more likely to need more support in the form of *complete* program examples, each of which demonstrates one new construction.

For example, in Section 3.4, we define a *compound statement* or *block* as an arbitrary sequence of C statements enclosed in braces "{" and "}", and, for convenience, we represent such a construct with the notation

```
{
 .
 .
 .
}
```

even before strict definitions of all of the possible types of C statements have been given. If you already have some idea about what a typical "statement" looks like, in any language, then you should be satisfied with this definition. On the other hand, if the concept of a statement is new to you, you may be confused. Thus, a novice will not be happy with this book's approach. It assumes a certain amount of programming maturity.

We can treat all types of C expressions at the outset (in Chapter 2) only if we postpone explaining how their operands are formally declared. (Since declarations *themselves* contain expressions, it is simplest merely to *assume* that all of the operands under discussion have been properly declared.) Since the issue of declarations is not discussed until Chapter 3, and since real programs must contain proper declarations, the presentation of full program examples must be similarly postponed.

Thus, in Chapter 2, we will begin with *informal* (i.e., intuitive) definitions of many objects—that is, with sufficient descriptive information to permit us to *reference* these objects in expressions. Their *formal* declarations are then discussed in Chapter 3, at which time more detailed descriptions are provided. By attacking the most formidable hurdle first, we make it easier to handle several subsequent issues—e.g., the syntax of formal declarations. By the time you complete Chapter 3, you will know not only about all types of C expressions but also about virtually all C declarations and about how the scope of each declared object name is determined.

In order to write realistic programs, you will still need to learn about at least two other issues: first, the way in which symbolic constants are defined in C, and second, the way in which the flow in a typical C program is controlled. Since symbolic constants are handled by a special program—known as the C preprocessor—it appeared logical to describe *all* of the properties of that program in one place (namely, in Chapter 4). Then, in Chapter 5, all of C's control flow statements are described.

Again, while it would have been possible to give you only a *few* of the properties of the C preprocessor first, and to describe only a *few* of C's control flow statements first, in order to provide you with sufficient information to get you started in writing programs immediately, it appeared logical (since you already have some experience) to assume that you would be sufficiently patient to digest the whole story on each of these topics, before beginning to generate code.

Reiterating, then, this book is written under the assumption that you are *not* a novice (who may need to write at least one elementary program to practice each new construct before going on to the next one). Rather, you are assumed to have sufficient background so that all of the facets of a given topic may be presented to you before that subject is actually practiced.

By the time you finish the study of Chapter 5, you will have learned virtually all of the "native" C language, i.e., that portion that does not make use of functions available from the Standard Library. It is at this point that you will actually begin to write complete programs—using an integrated sequence of 25 programming problems at the end of Chapter 5.

To ensure that you are able to employ, in real situations, all of the constructs introduced in Chapters 2 through 4, each of these chapters ends with a sequence of problems specifically designed to give you the kind of practice that would normally result from the coding of many elementary programs. In particular, Chapter 2—on Operators and Expressions—ends with 100 short problems that deal only with expression evaluation.

A solution to *every* end-of-chapter problem is given in the back of this book. It is assumed, of course, that you will check a solution only after having made a diligent effort to develop your own.

To further clarify this book's approach, it is worth reiterating that its purpose is *not* to teach you programming *technique* (i.e., how to write programs). Rather, it meant to be a text that describes the characteristics of the C language. Thus, the number of complete program examples that are presented in this book is less than that found in most other C texts. Even though programming by example is not the primary thrust of this book, those examples that are given are chosen to demonstrate the author's conception of good programming practice.

As was pointed out earlier, this book adopts an engineering or assembly language approach to C. While the "pure" high-level language programmer may not be curious about certain low-level details (e.g., about how data structures are aligned in storage or about how arguments are passed to functions), and may indeed be grateful to be relieved of such concerns, we will nevertheless consider some of them.

We proceed then to study the ingredients of C expressions. As is normally done, we will start with the most elementary objects, namely, constants and identifiers, and will build from there.

CHAPTER 2 **OPERATORS AND EXPRESSIONS**

2.1 Constants

A *constant* is an explicit data value written by the programmer. Thus, it is a value known to the compiler at compile time. The compiler may deal with this value in any of several ways, depending on the type of constant and its context. For example, the binary equivalent of the constant may be inserted directly into the output code stream. The value of the constant may be stored in a special data area in memory. The compiler may decide to use the constant's value for its own immediate purposes—e.g., to determine how much storage it should allocate to a data array.

C permits *integer* constants, *floating-point* constants, *character* constants, and *string* constants.

An *integer* constant consists of a sequence of digits. It is normally interpreted as a *decimal* value. Thus, **1**, **35**, and **23456** are all decimal integer constants. However, an integer constant beginning with the digit *zero* is considered as an *octal* number. Thus, the integer constant **0377**, in the example in Section 1.3, is an octal number. An integer constant having a leading **0x** or **0X** is considered as a *hexadecimal* number. For example, **0x4F** is a hexadecimal integer constant having a value equivalent to a decimal 79.

Whenever an alphabetic character appears within a numeric constant (the "x" above is an example), it may appear either in uppercase or in lowercase form. Thus, a hexadecimal constant may include the digits **a** or **A** through **f** or **F**. Similarly, a floating constant in scientific notation (described below) may include either an **e** or an **E**.

A *floating-point* constant consists of an integer part, a decimal point, a fractional part, and an exponent field containing an **e** or an **E** followed by an (optionally signed) integer. Both integer and fractional parts are digit sequences. Certain portions of this format may be missing, as long as the resulting number is distinguishable from a simple integer. For example, either the decimal point or the exponent field, but not both, may be omitted. Similarly, either the integer part or the fractional part, but not both, may be absent.

Examples of floating constants include **3.14159**, **4567e-5** (which is the same as 0.04567), and **0.89E3** (which is the same as 890.). To express an integer value as a *floating* constant, we merely include a decimal point. Thus, **3.** and **3.0** are both floating constants, each having a fractional part whose value is zero.

Problems at the end of this chapter will give you some practice in distinguishing between decimal, octal, and hexadecimal integers and floating-point numbers.

A *character* constant normally consists of a single character enclosed in single quotes. Thus, for example, **'b'** and **'$'** are both character constants. Each takes on the numeric value of its character in the machine's character set. Unless we state otherwise, we will henceforth assume exclusive use of the ASCII (American Standard Code for Information Interchange) code, a table for which is provided in Appendix A. Thus, for example, writing down the character constant **'A'** is equivalent to writing down the hex value 41 or the octal value 101. The **'A'** form is preferable, of course—first, because its meaning is unmistakable, and second, because it is independent of the actual character set of the machine.

In C, certain special characters, in particular, nonprinting *control* characters, are represented by special, so-called "escape" character sequences, each of which begins with the special backslash (\) escape character. (A backslash is normally not interpreted as a regular character. Rather, it indicates that the character or characters that follow it are to be interpreted in a special way.) Most of these escape codes are designed to make visible, on paper, any of those characters whose receipt by a printer or terminal causes a special, nonprinting control action (e.g., backspace or carriage return). The table below enumerates the most important of these:

Escape code	Character represented
\n	Newline
\t	Horizontal tab
\b	Backspace
\r	Carriage return
\f	Form feed
\\	Backslash
\'	Single quote
\"	Double quote
\ddd	Character whose value is octal ddd
\0	Null character (i.e., \000)

Notice that each sequence—containing two or more characters—really names a *single* special character. The first few escape codes represent the most common nonprinting control characters. Since a single backslash has been given a special ("escape") meaning, the sequence \\ is necessary to represent the regular backslash character. The **\ddd** construct permits representing any arbitrary character value—for instance, a rare control character not in the list above. Thus, for example, **\007** is the ASCII bell character, whose reception rings the terminal bell. Note, in particular, that the *null character*, whose value is all binary zeroes, is represented by the special escape sequence \0. Observe also that **\101** and **A** are the same objects. So are **\060** and **0**. (Recall that the ASCII code is assumed throughout, unless stated otherwise.)

You should bear in mind that each of the sequences in the table above is the "name" of a special character. It may be used to represent that character in any *string* of characters. For example, the string of characters

abc \bd\tefg\n

actually represents the following string of 11 characters:

a b c space backspace d horiztab e f g newline

in which case, after printing, the **d** has been positioned immediately after the **c**.

When a special character is used as a character *constant*, it must (like any other character) be enclosed in single quotes. Thus, '\t', '\0', and '\007' are all character constants. Notice, in particular, that \n is a *single* character that causes a printer or terminal to start a new line at the left margin. The actual value that represents '\n' in the character set may vary from system to system.

In many C environments, \n happens to be represented by the ASCII line feed character. Observe also that ' 0 ' and '\0 'have totally different values. ' 0 'is the same as a hex 30 (in ASCII), while '\0 ' is the same as a hex zero. Finally, note that the escape sequences \' and \" were both defined to permit, respectively, a single quote character constant (i.e., '\' ') and a double quote within a string constant (e.g., "a \"quoted\" word").

A *string* constant is a sequence of characters enclosed in double quotes. Whenever the C compiler encounters a string constant, it stores the character sequence (omitting the surrounding double quotes) in an available data area in memory. It also records the *address* of the first character of this array. This address is called a *pointer* value. In addition, the compiler appends to the stored sequence one additional character, the null character \0, to mark the end of the string.

The length of a character string is the number of characters in it (again, excluding the surrounding double quotes). Thus, the string "message\n" has a length of 8. The actual number of stored characters is one more than this value—to take into account the appended \0 delimiter. Notice that the *null string*, written as "", has a length of zero. It is converted, by the compiler, into a pointer to a single \0 character in memory.

2.2 Identifiers

An *identifier* or *name* is a sequence of characters, invented by the programmer, to identify or name a specific object. The kinds of objects that may be named in C are numerous. By describing them, we may learn something about the character of the language, since they are the elements that C permits the programmer to define and manipulate.

As you might expect, variables, arrays, and functions may be named. A *variable* is a data object in storage. An *array* is a collection of data objects of the same type. A *function* is a callable action—an executable entity. It is sometimes called a procedure or a subroutine. An important nameable object, that plays a major role in C programs, is the pointer. A *pointer* is an object whose value is the *address* of another object. A *structure* is a collection of data objects, generally of different types, but all related in some way. The elements that comprise a structure are called its *members*. A *union* is similar to a structure in many respects. Structures and unions are also nameable objects. Their individual members must be named as well. Even the internal *composition* of a structure or of a union may be given a name. Among other objects that may be named are macros, macro and function arguments, and program labels. All of these elements will be studied in greater detail as we proceed.

An identifier is a sequence of letters and digits, beginning with a letter.

The underscore character "_" is also permitted in a name. It is considered as an additional allowable letter. It permits multiword readable names (e.g., **max_size**).While any number of characters may be specified by the programmer, the compiler retains only the first eight. In other words, two names having the same first eight characters are considered as identical. Uppercase and lowercase letters are regarded as distinct.

Examples of permissible identifiers include: **velocity**, **count3**, and **time_of_day**. Illegal identifiers include **3_WAY** and **NET_$**. You will see, as we proceed, that it is conventional to use *lowercase* names in C programs, with uppercase names reserved for special objects—e.g., symbolic constants (discussed later). While it is legal to adopt some other convention that satisfies the rules given above (e.g., by using mixed names like **Max** and **INput**), such practice does not conform to the most common C usage.

It is good programming practice to choose names that suggest the roles that the named objects will play in the program. Notice that a name beginning with the underscore character, like **_read**, is legal. Again, common C practice is to reserve such identifiers for use in system programs—e.g., programs in the "standard I/O library" (discussed later). Such a convention ensures that these names will not collide with (i.e., duplicate) user-defined names. Note that most of the identifiers that appeared in the example in Section 1.3 (i.e., **_cnt**, **_ptr**, and **_fillbuf**) are of this type.

Virtually all of the identifiers in a typical C program are processed only by the compiler. However, a few names—called *external* names (defined later)—may be subsequently processed by system programs other than the compiler (e.g., by the loader or by the linker). It is conceivable that these programs may further restrict the maximum number of characters that guarantees uniqueness in a name. For example, the loader may truncate all of the names that it handles to six or seven characters. Similarly, the linker may not distinguish between uppercase and lowercase characters in the names that it processes. This issue is system dependent. You should check on the specific characteristics of your own programming environment. They may dictate that only the first six or seven characters in external names should be considered significant, or that uppercase and lowercase versions of the same characters in external names should be treated as identical. (A truly portable program takes these potential system restrictions into account.)

Whenever the C compiler encounters a new identifier, it places it in a *symbol table*, which it maintains for its own purposes. Each entry in this table contains a name (also called a "symbol") and other information about that name. Specifically, this other information includes a code specifying the *type* of object that the identifier identifies. This information is derived from the way in which the program *declared* the identifier in the first place. (Declarations are discussed in detail in Chapter 3.)

Each entry in the symbol table also contains a value that the compiler has assigned to the name. Typically, this value is a memory address. Of course, the C programmer is normally oblivious of such address values, since one of the primary purposes of using identifiers in the first place is to free the programmer from any concern about where the objects that the program manipulates are actually stored.

2.3 Operator Precedence

An *expression* contains operands and operators. It is *evaluated* by applying the operators to their corresponding operands, in the proper order, to develop a single value—called the *value* of the expression.

The operators in an expression are represented by special symbols, like " + " and "*". An operand in an expression may itself be another expression. That is, expressions may be nested, in the algebraic sense. When an expression is an operand, it must be evaluated before its value may be used in a subsequent operation.

For example, in the evaluation of the expression $3*(4+5)$, the internal expression $4+5$ is evaluated first. As this example illustrates, internal expressions may be circumscribed by *explicit* parentheses. Alternatively, inner expressions may be *implied* (in the absence of explicit parenthesization) by operator *precedence* rules. If a choice exists between which of two or more operators should next be applied in the evaluation of an expression, the operator of highest precedence is the one selected. For example, we will soon find that the precedence of the arithmetic multiply operator "*" is higher than that of the add operator " + ". (The "*" operator is said to "bind more tightly" than the " + ".) Thus, an evaluation of the expression $3*4+5$ would begin with the evaluation of the inner expression $3*4$. Notice that the application of an operator precedence rule is equivalent to employing an *implicit* pair of parentheses. In this example, they are positioned explicitly as follows: $(3*4)+5$.

When all of the operators in an expression have *equal* precedence, an "associativity" rule is applied. There are two such rules that are possible: One is a *left-to-right* rule. The other is a *right-to-left* rule. Every set of operators, at the *same* precedence level, has its own associativity rule. For example, we will soon find that the divide operator "/" and the multiply operator "*" have equal precedence. Furthermore, they associate left to right. Thus, to explicitly show how the expression $3*4/5$ is evaluated, we may include the *implied* parentheses, producing $(3*4)/5$.

The operator precedence table (see Section 2.18) summarizes the precedence and associativity rules for all of C's operators, each of which is defined individually in the sections that follow.

You are reminded that, while a detailed knowledge of all of the precedence rules helps you to write down expressions that employ the smallest number of inner parentheses, in some cases it is useful to include redundant parenthesis pairs in an expression just to make it more readable. For example,

$$(a * b) + (c * d)$$

is probably more readable than

$$a * b + c * d$$

Other similar examples will arise later.

Before introducing the collection of C operators, however, we describe a few elementary C expressions that we are already in a position to discuss. First, notice that an expression need not contain *any* operators. It may consist entirely either of a single constant or of a single identifier. In the former case, the value of the expression is the constant's value. In the latter case, the value of the expression is the current value of the object that the identifier identifies. Second, observe that *all* of the operands in an expression may be constants. Such an expression (called a *constant expression*) is evaluated by the compiler, at *compile* time, and not during actual execution of the program (i.e., at run time). The resulting value is disposed of, by the compiler, in the same way that any simple constant is treated. For example, it may be used as the initial value of a variable.

2.4 Function Calls

A *function* is an executable action—a procedure, a subroutine. For this discussion, it is not necessary to know in detail how a function is *defined*. The steps involved in this process will be covered later. It is sufficient, for our present purposes, to explain that every function has a *name*, that it expects a specific number (possibly zero) of *arguments* to be passed to it, and that, when it returns, it often, but not always, returns a *value*.

A function call in a C expression consists of a function name immediately followed by a list of arguments *enclosed in parentheses*. The arguments in the argument list are themselves expressions. They must be separated by commas, and, typically, the number of arguments supplied must match the number of arguments that are *declared* for the function in its definition.

For example, **square_root(x)** is a call on a function named **square_root**, supplying the single argument x. (We assume that the function is defined as one expecting a single argument value.) Similarly, **justify()** is a function call supplying no arguments. (The parentheses must always be present, however, to denote a *call*.) Finally, `maximum(a*b,c+d)` is a function call supplying two arguments, each of which is itself an expression involving two or more operands. Whenever an argument is specified, the expression comprising it is evaluated and the resulting value is passed to the function.

An expression may consist of a single function call. In this case, if the function returns a value, the value of the expression *is* that value. If the function returns no value, then the effect of the "evaluation" of the expression is merely to execute the named subroutine. No returned value is expected. Such a procedure is common. For example, the action executed by the function call `justify()`, above, may be to rearrange a collection of characters in a globally known array, with no meaningful value returned. An expression containing only the call merely asks for *execution* of this action.

The parentheses surrounding the arguments in a function call format are considered as *operators*. They evoke a specific operation, namely, the execution of the function named by the immediately preceding identifier. They are distinguishable from other parenthesis pairs (e.g., those used to delimit internal operands in an expression) because they *immediately follow* a function name.

When a function call is only part of an expression, and that expression is evaluated, the value *returned* by the function, after it is called, effectively *replaces* the appearance of the call in the expression. Thus, for example, the evaluation of the expression

$$\texttt{square\_root(x) + y}$$

involves calling the `square_root` routine (passing to it, in the process, the value of **x**), then replacing the call in the expression by the value returned by the function, and finally adding this value to the value of **y**. The call is executed first because the function call operators "(" and ")" are defined as having a precedence that is *higher* than that of the add operator " + ".

Notice that when a function call is only part of an expression, the function named *must* return a value. This value is used in subsequent evaluation operations. Observe also that the call `_fillbuf(p)`, in the sample expression in Section 1.3, meets all of the format requirements for a function call.

You may be under the impression, based on your previous programming experience, that when an expression is evaluated, the values of all of the operands that participate in the evaluation do not change. For example, evaluating the expression A + B*D does not change the current values of variables **A**, **B**, and **D**. However, in C, there are many conditions under which the process of expression evaluation may indeed change the values of the participating operands. We call such effects *side effects* and will point them out as we encounter them.

As an illustration, consider a C expression that contains a call on a function whose execution alters the value of some global variable. Evaluation of the expression will invoke execution of the function, which will, in turn, change the stored variable value.

For example, one would normally expect that execution of the **square_root** function, mentioned above, would not produce any special side effects. Suppose, however, that in the process of execution it happened to alter the value of the variable **y**. In this unlikely event, the value of the expression

$$\text{square\_root}(x) \; + \; y$$

would indeed depend on the order of the evaluation operations (i.e., Is the value of **y** picked up *before* or *after* the call is made?)—because a side effect is involved.

The definition of the C language makes no restriction on the order in which function arguments, supplied in a call, are evaluated. Normally, the order of evaluation is not important, so long as the values ultimately derived are directed to their proper argument positions. However, the order of evaluation may be important, and may affect the predictability of the computation, when side effects (as defined above) are involved. For example, suppose that the side effect of one evaluation clears a specific variable, while that of a second evaluation increments the same variable. Clearly, a clear followed by an increment yields a different result from an increment followed by a clear.

2.5 Indirect Access via Pointers

A *pointer* is an object whose value is the *address* of another object. The declaration of a pointer in a program (described later) not only *names* the pointer, but also specifies the type of object that the pointer *points* to. (Recall that this information is retained in a symbol table that is maintained by the compiler.) Thus, *every pointer is type specific*. It should not be employed to address an object type other than that specified in its definition. For example, if a pointer is originally declared as a pointer to integers, it should not be used to address floating-point numbers.

A pointer is employed to access an object *indirectly*. This mechanism of indirect addressing is very familiar to assembly language programmers. When an expression containing a pointer is evaluated, the appearance of the pointer name is replaced by the pointer's value (an address). To indicate a reference to the object *pointed to* by this value, C uses the unary operator "*". That is, if **ptr_name** is the name of a pointer, then the value of the expression

$$\text{*ptr\_name}$$

is the value of the object *addressed by* the value of **ptr_name**.

For example, if **ptr_name** is known to point to a character, and if the value of **ptr_name** happens to be address 3000, then the value of ***ptr_name** is the value of the character variable stored at memory location 3000. On the other hand, if **ptr_name** is declared as a pointer to floating-point numbers, and if its value happens to be address 5000, then the value of ***ptr_name** is the floating quantity stored at memory location 5000.

You have, no doubt, noticed that the operator "*" has two possible meanings. It may used to represent either multiplication, which is a *binary* operation (i.e., requiring two operands), or an indirect access, which is a *unary* operation (requiring only one operand). C distinguishes between these two possible meanings by examining the context of the expression in which the "*" appears.

In several assembly languages, the symbol "@" is used for the same purposes as is the unary "*" in C.

It is often necessary, in a C program, as it is in most assembly language programs, to write down an expression that represents the *address of* an already-defined (i.e., already-named) object. Typically, such an address value is either assigned to a specific pointer (e.g., to initialize it) or passed, as an argument, in a function call. It may also participate in an expression that performs some pointer arithmetic (discussed below). C uses the symbol "&" to represent the unary "address of" operator. Thus, for example, the statement

$$\texttt{ptr\_name = \&var\_name;}$$

assigns to the pointer **ptr_name** the address of the variable **var_name**. (Notice that every C statement normally terminates in a semicolon.)

For example, if **ptr_name** is a pointer to an integer and **var_name** is an integer whose value is stored at memory location 6000, then execution of the statement above will *point* **ptr_name** at integer **var_name**. In other words, **ptr_name** will take on the address value 6000.

As another example, if **read_int** is a function that reads an integer from the keyboard, and deposits the value read into the memory location specified by an argument in the call, then

$$\texttt{read\_int(\&var\_name)}$$

will set **var_name** to the integer read. Notice that omission of the "&" would merely pass the *value* of **var_name**, not its location in storage, to **read_int**. If a function is to alter the value of a variable *where it resides in storage*, that function must be passed a *pointer* to that variable.

In some assembly languages, the expression **A(anyname)** has a value equal to the address that was assigned to the identifier **anyname**. In such cases, the "A(...)" operator is equivalent to C's unary "&" operator. While the value of A(**anyname**) is always calculated at assembly time, the value of **&expres-sion** may be calculated either at compile time—in which case it is a constant that may be used, for example, to initialize a pointer–or at run time—if the value of the expression to which the "&" operator is applied is not known at compile time.

For example, as we will learn in the next section, element **i** in an array of identical elements named **array_name** may be represented by the expression

array_name[i]

Once such an array has been defined with an appropriate declaration (discussed later), storage for it is allocated by the compiler. Once this has been done, the value of an expression like

&array_name[3]

is known at compile time, because the address of the origin of the array is known and because the size of all of the objects that comprise the array is *also* known. (Whenever an array is declared, the *type* of all of the objects *comprising* it is also given.) On the other hand, the value of an expression like

&array_name[i]

is *not* known at compile time, because the value of **i** will vary as the program runs.

In most cases, the "address of" operation is performed at compile time.

It was mentioned earlier that every pointer declaration (described later) not only names a pointer, but also specifies the *type* of the object to which the pointer points. The compiler uses this information in several ways that are convenient for the programmer. Specifically, whenever a pointer is *incremented*, the actual address value of the pointer is, in reality, incremented by the *size* of the object to which the pointer points. Similarly, any decrement or, more generally, any addition or subtraction of an arbitrary integral value, is properly *scaled* by the size of the pointed-to object.

Thus, pointer arithmetic depends on the size of the referenced objects. This is done specifically to facilitate the positioning of a pointer into an *array* of identical objects. The programmer is freed from all concern about the actual size of the objects involved (which, in general, will vary from machine to machine). Thus, if **ptr_name** points to an object in an array, **ptr_name + 1** points to the *next* object, while **ptr_name-n** (**n** an integer) points **n** objects back. These properties are *independent* of the sizes of the objects involved.

If you remember that the value of a pointer is an *address*, you will have no trouble recognizing that the number of possible relational and arithmetic operations on pointer operands is limited. Specifically, two pointer values may be compared (for equality or for any type of inequality) only if they point to objects of the same type. For example, they may be pointing into the same data array, and one may be advancing until its value reaches that of the other. In addition, one pointer value may be *subtracted* from that of another—again, only if they point to the same object types. Notice that all of these permissible pointer operations are meaningful only when the two pointers are pointing into the *same* contiguous data area. Since pointer values are machine addresses, it clearly serves no useful purpose to add or to multiply two pointer operands. No C compiler will accept such operations.

Thus, for example, if the middle address between the two pointers **low_point** and **high_point** is desired, the expression (**low_point+high_point**) /2 is *not* the proper one to compute it. You should use instead the expression **low_point+ (high_point-low_point)** /2.

One final note about pointer values: Under normal conditions, you will not care about what absolute values your pointers will have. (Recall that one of the conveniences of a high-level language is the relief from all concern about where the objects manipulated by your program actually reside.) Indeed, the actual address values that *are* assigned to pointers are clearly machine dependent. (First, different machines have, in general, different word lengths, different address lengths, and different addressing modes. Second, even if this were not the case, different C compilers will, in general, use different address assignment algorithms.) C does, however, guarantee that *one* pointer absolute value will *never* point to a legitimate object. This is the value *zero*. Thus, for example, if a function is designed to *return* a pointer value, a returned value of zero may be used to indicate some type of exception condition. As this statement implies, an "equal" or "not equal" comparison of a pointer value with the constant zero is the only meaningful comparison between a pointer value and a constant.

In the same way that every pointer is defined to C as a pointer to a specific object type, every *function* is defined to C as a function *returning* a specific object type. That is, *every function is also type specific.* (We deal later with the special case in which no value is returned by a function.) Specifically, a function may be defined as one that returns a *pointer* value. Similarly, a pointer may be defined as being a pointer *to a pointer*. Thus, for example, if **fcnpoint** is the name of a function that returns a pointer to an integer, then

$$\ast\texttt{fcnpoint}()$$

is that integer. (It is assumed, for simplicity, that **fcnpoint** requires no input arguments. The "()" function call operator has a precedence that is higher than that of the "*".)

Similarly, if **pptr** is defined as a pointer *to a pointer* to a floating-point number, then

$$**pptr$$

is that floating-point number. (The unary operator "*" associates right-to-left.)

2.6 Array Elements as Operands

An identifier in an expression is recognized as the name of an *array* (which is a collection or sequence of objects, all of the same type) if that name is immediately followed by an arbitrary expression enclosed in *square brackets* (i.e., "[" and "]"). Further, the *value* of the bracketed expression signifies *which* element in the array is referenced. That is, the value of the bracketed expression is the subscript or index of the selected element. In C, the first element in any array has an index value of *zero*. Thus, the construct **vector[2]**, in an expression undergoing evaluation, is replaced by the value of the *third* object in the array named **vector**. Similarly, **vector[i+j-k]** has a value equal to the specific element, in the array named **vector**, whose subscript or index is the value of the expression **i+j-k**.

Notice that the construct **name[...]** implies a reference to an element in an array, in the same way that the construct **name(...)** implies a function call. In an expression undergoing evaluation, the former is replaced by the value of the selected array element while the latter is replaced by the value returned by the function.

The objects that comprise an array may be arrays themselves. This is one of the ways by which C permits the construction of multidimensional arrays (discussed later).

In C, the value assigned to an array name is the *address* of the initial element of the array. In other words, an array name is equivalent to a *pointer* to the array's first element. C also assigns to this pointer, as its pointed-to object type, the type of the objects that *comprise* the array. Thus, an array name is *indistinguishable* from a pointer to the array's first element. This means that

$$array\_name[0]$$

always has the same value as has

$$*array\_name$$

or, more generally, that

array_name[i]

and

*(array_name + i)

are *entirely equivalent expressions*. The parentheses are necessary, in this last expression, because, as the operator precedence table shows, the precedence of the unary "*" operator is higher than that of the " + " operator. Without the parentheses, the value of this expression would be the value of array element zero, incremented by i, instead of the value of array element i.

An array is also an object that is type specific. That is, like "pointer *to*—" and "function *returning*—," we also have "array *of*—," where "—" represents almost any other object type. In particular, an array of pointers is a very common data structure. Thus, for example,

*array_name[i]

has the value of the object pointed to by the $(i + 1)$st element of the array (of pointers) named **array_name**. (The array subscript operator "[]" has a precedence that is higher than that of the "*" operator.)

2.7 Some Derived Object Types

As we will see later, C fundamentally permits *two* types of elementary data objects: integers and floating-point numbers. Several variations on these themes are permitted. In particular, there are "long," "short," and "unsigned" integer types, and there are also "long" floating types. A *character* is considered as belonging to the integer class. Typically, it is even shorter than what is called a "short" integer. Details regarding each of these data types are given below.

From this introduction to pointers and arrays, you can appreciate that a character *string* in C is, in fact, an *array* of characters. Specifically, every string *constant* is stored as a character array (including the appended \0) whose *name* is an internally recorded *pointer*.

Some of the expression evaluation rules discussed earlier may be summarized as follows: Whenever an expression containing a name is evaluated, that name is replaced by its *value*. If the name represents a simple variable, then the value of that variable replaces it. If the name represents a pointer, a function, or an array, then the value that replaces it is an *address* (as derived from the compiler's symbol table). If the name is *preceded* by the unary "*" operator, as in

*name

then the address value is, in turn, replaced by the value to which it points. If the name is immediately followed by a left square bracket, as in

name [expression]

then the address and the following bracketed expression are both replaced by the value of the selected array element. Finally, if the name is immediately followed by a left parenthesis, as in

name (. . .)

then the address value is interpreted as the *entry point* to a *function*, which is then *executed*.

We have been using the term "object type" sufficiently often that it may be worthwhile digressing here, to review some of the examples that have already been presented and to introduce a few new variations.

You will recall that, in the discussion on identifiers (in Section 2.2), we enumerated some of the types of elements (or objects) that C permits a programmer to name. Now that a few of these (e.g., pointers, functions, arrays) have been discussed and their type-specific properties (e.g., pointer *to*—, function *returning*—, array *of*—) have been explained, we may consider objects whose descriptions combine two or more of the basic types. Each has a so-called "derived" type. Several examples have already been introduced.

A function may return a *pointer* value instead of a variable value, in which case

*name (. . .)

is the object to which the returned pointer points. A pointer may point not only to a data object but also to *another pointer*, in which case

**name

is the object to which the pointed-to pointer points. Notice, in particular, that an *array of pointers* is a very important data structure. Among its many uses, it is one means by which multidimensional arrays (discussed later) are realized.

A function argument may be not only a data value but also a pointer value. Consider, for example,

fcname (&variable)

which gives the called function direct access to a specific location in memory. The pointer argument may, in fact, be a pointer *to another function* (i.e., its entry address). Such a process permits a calling routine to specify which function the *called* function should *itself* call, at one particular point in its computation.

Since a function may return a *pointer* value instead of a data value, functions may effectively return *all* of the kinds of objects to which pointers may point. For example, a function may return a pointer to a message (i.e., to a character array).

Many other variations will become evident as we progress. We will find, for instance, that the elements of arrays may be not only variables, pointers, or other arrays, but also structures. Further, the *members* of structures may themselves be any of the objects mentioned above. Thus, for instance, it is entirely feasible, and useful, as subsequent examples will demonstrate, to define an array of structures—each of which has at least one member that is itself an array.

Some exceptions to the combinations that are conceivable are to be expected. Most of the constructs that are illegal in C are also illogical. For example, as might be anticipated, it is illogical, and illegal, to define an array of functions, or to have a function as a structure member. However, it *is* legal, and sometimes useful in these cases, to use *pointers* to the functions in place of the functions themselves.

2.8 Structure Members as Operands

A *structure* is a collection of objects, generally of different types, but all related in some way. They are grouped together, under a single heading, for convenience in processing. (In some programming languages, structures are called records.) Each object in a structure is called one of its *members*. Typically, all the members (or *fields*) of a structure represent different attributes or properties of a single element. For example, each item in an inventory may be described by a structure. The members of such a structure may individually specify such attributes as item identification code, manufacturer, size, color, physical location, number on hand, next delivery date, and so on.

Clearly, the members of a structure are generally objects of different types. In the example above, some may be integers, some characters, and some character arrays.

As you might expect, a structure is allocated storage member by member. However, the total size of a structure may be *greater* than the sum of the sizes of its individual members, because some objects may be required to meet certain *boundary* requirements when they are positioned in memory. For example, if member **i** ends in the middle of a memory word and member **i + 1** must begin at the next word boundary, then an unused memory segment (or "hole") will exist between them. Notice that each member of a structure has a specific *offset* or *displacement* from the *origin* of the structure.

Every structure in storage has a *name*, which was declared when the structure was originally defined in the program. (Formats for structure declarations are covered later.) This name is the heading mentioned earlier. If the structure is part of an *array* of structures, then its name is the name of the array, followed by the index value of the structure, in square brackets.

The *members* of a structure are the objects whose values are normally manipulated in expressions. (If a member is itself an array or another structure, then some further "inner" addressing or selection may be necessary to derive a value that *may* participate in the evaluation of an expression.)

Every member of a structure must have its *own* identifier. Thus, in addition to the fact that an entire structure has a name, every one of its members *also* has a name. For example, the name of the structure, in the inventory illustration given above, might be `item`, and each of its members might be named, respectively, `id`, `mfgr`, `size`, `color`, and so on.

A member of a structure is identified in an expression by use of a construct of the form

structure_name.member_name

The "." operator's function is to separate the portion that identifies the entire structure from the part that selects a single member. For example, using the same illustration again, the member named `size` of the structure named `item` is identified with the expression

item.size

Alternatively, if this structure happens to be element *n* in an *array* of structures named **inventory**, then the same member would be identified with the expression

inventory[n].size

A member of a structure may itself be an array or another structure. Continuing to use the same example, and assuming that the structure member named **mfgr** is itself a structure containing the members **name** and **phone_no**, the construct

item.mfgr.phone_no

isolates one of the inner data objects. Since the structure member operator "." associates left to right, no parentheses are necessary in the above expression.

A member of a structure is frequently accessed by way of a *pointer* to the structure. In particular, since structures are often configured in arrays, the pointer access mechanism is most natural. (Recall that the declaration of a pointer to a structure, which will be described in detail later, informs the compiler of the *size* of the structure, which may be considerable. Thus, increments and decrements of this pointer actually move it from the origin of one structure to the origin of another.)

If **pointer** is a pointer to a structure, then ***pointer** *is* that structure. Therefore,

$$(\texttt{*pointer}).\texttt{member\_name}$$

is another way to refer to a specific one of its members. Again, the parentheses are necessary because, as the operator precedence table shows, the precedence of the operator "." is higher than that of the unary operator "*". (Without the parentheses, the expression would have meaning only if there existed a *structure* named "pointer", having a member, named "member_name", that was *itself* a pointer. This was clearly not intended here.)

Since structure members are accessed via pointers so often, and since the expression above is a bit unwieldy to write down repeatedly, a shorthand for it was invented. A new operator "–>" was defined and given a meaning such that the expression

$$\texttt{pointer->member\_name}$$

identifies the named member of the structure pointed to by the named pointer. In other words, this expression is entirely equivalent to the expression **(*pointer).member_name**, given earlier.

The "–>" operator also associates left to right. This means that if the structure pointed to by **pointer** has a member named **sptr**, which is itself a pointer to *another* structure, then the construct

$$\texttt{pointer->sptr->mem}$$

selects the member named **mem** of the *latter* structure.

Referring, once again, to the sample expression given in Section 1.3, notice the two inner expressions **p->_cnt** and **p->_ptr**. (The parentheses around each p may be ignored for our present purposes. They will be explained later.) These inner expressions lead us to conclude that **p** must be a pointer to a structure having (at least) two members, named **_cnt** and **_ptr**, respectively.

Summarizing, if **pointer** is a pointer to a structure whose name is **structure**, and if **member** is a member of that structure, then the two expressions

> `pointer->member` and `(*pointer).member`

are entirely equivalent. Similarly, the two expressions

> `structure.member` and `(&structure)->member`

also have identical meanings.

2.9 Relational Operators and Expressions

A *relational expression* is one whose value is either *true* or *false*. Following a practice employed in some other languages, C represents the conditions "true" and "false" with *numeric* values. Specifically, a value of *zero* represents "false" and a value of *one* (or, in fact, any other *nonzero* value) represents "true."

Whenever C *tests* an expression for its truth or falsity, it merely examines the value of the expression and determines whether that value is zero or *nonzero*. Most of C's "control flow" statements (`if` statements, `while` statements, and so on) test such conditional expressions. For example, the simple `if` statement

> `if` *(expression) statement1*

executes *statement1* only if the value of *(expression)* is nonzero. While the expression that is tested is normally an unmistakable relation (e.g., **a>b**), having a value 1 if true and 0 if false, C actually permits it to be *any arbitrary expression*— even one that does not appear to be relational.

This has two important implications. First, an incorrectly written but legal expression, which was *meant* to be relational, may be the source of a program bug. For example, if the relation **a>b** is erroneously entered as **a>>b**, the C compiler will not complain, because (as we will soon find out) the new construct is a legal right shift expression. At run time, the "condition" will be "true" so long as the result of the shift (which is the *value* of the expression) remains nonzero. Second, a programmer may legally use a variable name in place of a relation, as a shorthand, if it is known that all of that variable's nonzero values correspond to "true" conditions. For example, if **char_ptr** is a pointer to characters, then the expression ***char_ptr** has a zero value only when **char_ptr** is pointing at the \0 (null) character. This property may be employed to distinguish the members of a character string and from its terminating delimiter [using, for example, a construct such as `if (*char_ptr)...`].

A *binary relational operator* makes an appropriate test, on the values of its two operands, and delivers either a value 1 (if the result of the test is true) or a value 0 (if the result of the test is false). The delivered value replaces both the operator and its operands in the expression being evaluated. Notice that each of the operands may be itself an arbitrary expression.

Following the tradition of most other programming languages, C uses the relational operators ">", "<", ">=", and "<=", all of which (as might be expected) have equal precedence. They have their customary meanings. For example, **a>=b** is true (has a value 1) only if the value of **a** is greater than or equal to the value of **b**. Otherwise, it is false (has a value 0).

In C, the *equality* relational operator is represented by the double equals sign "==". This follows a practice, already established in other languages (e.g., Fortran, Pascal), of distinguishing between the equality relational operator and the assignment symbol (a single equals sign in C). Most novice C programmers take some time getting accustomed to this special relational symbol. It has its classical meaning. That is, **a==b** is true (has a value 1) only if the values of **a** and **b** are the same. Otherwise, it is false (has a value 0).

C also uses a new symbol, the exclamation point "!", to represent the logical negation (i.e., NOT) operator. This is the only *unary* relational operator. It operates by *reversing* the truth value of its following operand. That is, it converts a 0 into a 1 and a *nonzero* into a 0. Thus, for example, the two relations **!(a>=b)** and **a<b** always have the same values. [The parentheses in the first expression are necessary because the precedence of the "!" operator is higher than that of the ">=" operator. Without the parentheses, the expression is true only when **!a** (which is 1 or 0, depending on whether **a** is zero or nonzero) is greater than or equal to **b**.]

Some C programmers will use the expression **!var_name** in place of the relational expression **var_name==0**, particularly when **var_name** is being used as a *flag* variable (having one of two possible values). For example, if a flag variable **done** has a value 1 when some other process has been completed, and 0 otherwise, then the construct **if (done)...** executes the "..." portion only when that process has completed, while the construct **if (!done)...** (reading "if *not* done") executes the "..." portion only if the process has not yet completed. The latter notation "reads" better than **if (done==0)....**

The "is not equal to" operator, which is represented in some languages by the "<>" symbol, is represented in C by the "!=" symbol (since "!" reads as "not"). Notice that this is a *single*, two-character operator, not a sequence of two operations. Observe also that the two expressions **a!=b** and **!(a==b)** have the same values.

The *logical connective* operators, "&&" for AND and "||" for OR, are also part of the class of relational operators. Each is a binary operator having its "classical" meaning. Thus, *expr1&&expr2* has a value 1 only if *both* operand expressions are true (i.e., nonzero). Otherwise, it has a 0 value. Similarly, *expr1||expr2* has a value 1 if *either* operand expression is nonzero (i.e., true). As the operator precedence table shows, "&&" has a higher precedence than

"||", and the precedence of each is lower than that of any of the other relational operators. This means that compound logical expressions like

$$\textbf{expr1\&\&expr2} \quad \| \quad \textbf{expr3\&\&expr4}$$

and

$$\textbf{a>b \&\& c<d}$$

or

$$\textbf{a>b} \quad \| \quad \textbf{c<d}$$

may be written parenthesis-free. However, keep in mind that explicit paren-thesization is only discouraged when it clutters an expression, making it less readable. Under many conditions, you will employ explicit parentheses either because you have forgotten a specific precedence rule or because they, in fact, improve an expression's readability.

The definition of C guarantees not only that expressions connected by "&&" and "||" are evaluated left to right, but also that *evaluation stops as soon as the truth or falsity of the compound logical expression is known*. This means that the evaluation of an AND expression (in which internal relational expressions are connected by &&'s) stops when the first *zero* internal relational value is found. For example, in evaluating

$$\textbf{a>b \&\& c<d}$$

if **a>b** is found false, then **c<d** is *never* evaluated.

Similarly, the evaluation of an OR expression (in which the internal rela-tional expressions are connected by ||'s) stops when the first *nonzero* internal relational value is found.

Normally, this evaluation-sequencing rule should not affect the behavior of a program. Certainly, the value of the compound logical expression being eval-uated is correctly derived. However, if the expressions undergoing evaluation generate any *side effects* (in which one or more operand values may themselves be changed during the evaluation process), then it is clear that the results *will* depend, in general, on *which* inner expressions are, in fact, evaluated. (The side effects issue was introduced and first discussed in Section 2.4.)

2.10 The Conditional Expression

Consider the situation in which there are two or more alternatives for an expression, with the one selected depending on conditions that will exist at the point.in the computation at which the expression is used. Such a situation arises frequently in programming. For example, depending on existing conditions, there may be two or more alternative expressions for the value to be assigned to a specific variable. There may be two or more alternative expressions, based on existing conditions, for the value to be returned by a specific function. There may be two or more alternative expressions, again based on existing conditions, for the value of a specific argument in a function call.

C's *conditional expression* is specifically tailored for such situations. It has the following simple format:

$$expr1 \quad ? \quad expr2 \quad : \quad expr3$$

It executes (i.e., is evaluated) by first evaluating *expr1* (which is normally a relational expression) and then evaluating either *expr2*, if the first result was *true*, or *expr3*, if the first result was *false*.

For example, the value of the expression

$$(\mathbf{a}{<}\mathbf{0}) \quad ? \quad \mathbf{-a} \quad : \quad \mathbf{a}$$

is the *absolute* value of **a**. Similarly, the value of the expression

$$(\mathbf{c} \; {>}{=} \; {'} \; {'}) \quad ? \quad \mathbf{c} \; : \; {'}\#{'}$$

is the value of the character **c**, if it is a printable ASCII character (see the ASCII table in Appendix A), or '#', if **c** is an ASCII *control* character. That is, every control character is converted into a visible "#".

Note that only one of the last two expressions in the construction is evaluated, depending on the results of the first evaluation. Observe also that the individual characters in the single operator "?:" are in non-adjacent positions, to permit separating the three operand expressions that are involved.

Use of the conditional expression frequently shortens the amount of source code that must be written. For example, a lengthy function call, which has several argument expressions—one of which is conditional— needs to be written only once.

The conditional expression is not only a shorthand. It may also result in less object code than would be generated by other alternative means (e.g., by use of one or more **if** statements).

Problems at the end of this chapter will give you some practice in the use of the conditional operator. Notice its use in the sample expression in Section 1.3. Observe also that parentheses are normally not needed around the expressions that are separated by the characters "?" and ":", because, as the operator precedence table shows, the "?:" operator has a very low precedence (i.e., it is usually applied last).

2.11 Increment and Decrement Operators

Although C permits statements of the form

$$var \ = \ var \ + \ 1;$$

and

$$var \ = \ var \ - \ 1;$$

(which we assume you have seen before), most C programmers prefer instead to use the special unary operators "++", for incrementing a variable, and "--", for decrementing it. For example, the construct **i ++** increments **i**.

There are several reasons why these new operators are preferred. First, each yields a more concise notation, particularly when the object being incremented has a long name or appears in a lengthy expression. For example, in **structure. inner_str. member ++**, the name of the object being incremented is written only once. Second, the compiler may be optimized to generate simpler code on seeing the special operator. For example, it may employ special auto-advance features that are available in the hardware. While you might argue that any compiler should be able to recognize the equivalence of **a = a + 1** and **a ++**, there are many constructs, having embedded "++" and "--" symbols, that are not as easily written using the former notation. Examine, for instance, the original sample expression in Section 1.3.

Third, the new notation has an expanded feature that permits either a *pre*-advance or a *post*-advance. If the "advance" operator appears to the *left* of its operand (i.e., before it), then the operand is advanced *before* its value is used in the evaluation of the expression. On the other hand, if the operator appears to the *right* of its operand (i.e., after it), then the advance takes place *after* the value of the operand is used in the evaluation.

The flexibility offered by these alternative *prefix* and *postfix* notations is particularly appealing. For example, if **char_ptr** is a pointer to characters, the expression ***char_ptr ++** not only has a value equal to the character pointed to by the pointer, but also *advances* the pointer, so that it points to the *next* character, after having delivered the previous character. Similarly, the relational expression **--count> = 0** decrements the count before testing its value. ("--" has a higher precedence than "> =".)

The operand to which an increment or decrement operator may be applied must be an "lvalue". An *lvalue* is any expression that refers directly to an area of storage whose contents may be changed. The term "lvalue" was coined because any expression on the left-hand side of an assignment (discussed later) must obey the same rule. Specifically, a variable or pointer name is an lvalue. So is a construct of the form ***(ptr_expression)**. Examples of *non*-lvalues include constants and expressions such as **-a** and **a + b**. Notice that an array name, even though it behaves like a pointer, is *not* an lvalue—because its *value* may not be changed (since the position of an array in storage is not alterable).

Observe also that *lvalue*++ and *lvalue* = *lvalue* + 1 do not *always* yield the same results. In the former case, the lvalue expression is evaluated *only once*. For example, **array[expression]** is an lvalue. If its evaluation causes side effects, the results for the two forms above may be different.

The application of the operators " ++ " and "– –" clearly causes side effects. The fact that these operators appear in so many expressions is one reason for the statement, given earlier (in Section 2.4), that there are many conditions under which expression evaluation changes the values of the participating operands. Problems at the end of this chapter will examine this issue further.

2.12 Bitwise Logical Operations

C makes available to the programmer virtually all of the logical bit manipulation operations that one would expect from a typical processor. All of these are *binary* operations (in the sense that each requires *two* operands), except one, which we cover first.

The unary operator "~" takes the one's complement of its following operand. That is, it complements every bit in it. Thus, for example, if a variable **mask** has a value 0377 (i.e., its lower 8 bits are all 1s and all higher bits are 0s), then the value of ~**mask** is 077..7400 (i.e., its lower 8 bits are all 0s, while all higher bits are 1s). Notice that, since the number of bits in an operand is machine dependent, a preferable means to specify a mask value that, when ANDed with an operand, will clear its lower (say) 8 bits, leaving all higher bits alone, is to use the value ~0377, all of whose upper bits are 1s, *independent* of the length of the operand.

The three binary operators "&", "|", and "^" yield, respectively, the logical AND, the logical OR, and the logical EXCLUSIVE OR of their respective operands. That is, each executes a bitwise elementary logical operation on two equal-length arguments. For example, if variable **a** has a value 0xAB, while variable **b** has value 0x56, then **a&b** has a value 0x02, **a|b** has a value 0xFF, and **a^b** has a value 0xFD. Typically, an argument is used as an AND mask to *clear* a specific field in another operand. For example, if **mask** has a value 0xFF, then **a&~mask** clears the lower 8 bits of **a**, leaving its other bits alone. (As the operator precedence table shows, the unary "~" operator has a higher precedence than the binary "&" operator.) Similarly, an argument is used as an OR mask to *set* a specific field in another argument to all 1s. Thus, **a|mask** sets the lower 8 bits of **a** to all 1s, leaving its other bits alone. An argument is used as an EXCLUSIVE OR argument to *selectively invert* specific bits in another argument. For example, **a^mask** inverts the lower 8 bits of **a**, leaving its other bits alone.

Notice that the "&" operator also has two possible interpretations. As a *unary* operator, it is pronounced "address of" (as discussed in Section 2.5). As a *binary* operator, it means bitwise logical AND. C distinguishes between these two possible interpretations by examining the context of the expression in which the "&" appears.

It is important that you carefully distinguish between the single-character operators "&" and "|", each of which executes a bitwise logical operation (as described above), and their double-character counterparts "&&" and "||", which are logical connective *relational* operators, each delivering a value of either 1 (true) or 0 (false), based on the truth or falsity of its operands.

The binary operators ">>" and "<<" execute right and left *shift* operations, respectively. Specifically, **a**<<**b** shifts operand **a** left by the number of bit positions specified by the value of operand **b**. Zero bits are shifted in, in which case each left shift is equivalent to a multiplication of the left operand by two. Thus, for example, **a**<<**3** multiplies **a** by eight. Similarly, **a**>>**b** shifts operand **a** right by the number of bit positions specified by the value of operand **b**. If the **a** operand is an unsigned number (normally the case), zeroes are shifted in. If it is a signed number, the result is machine dependent. In some environments, zeroes are shifted in unconditionally (i.e., "logical" right shifts are performed), while in other environments, a copy of the sign bit is shifted in (i.e., an "arithmetic" shift is performed) for each right shift.

Again, it is important to distinguish the double-character shift operators from their single-character counterparts "<" and ">", which are *relational* operators, yielding only the values 1 (true) and 0 (false). Problems at the end of this chapter will help you distinguish between operator symbols that have two possible meanings and between different operator symbols that look alike.

We should emphasize that most of C's operators (e.g., the arithmetic, relational, and bitwise logical operators) operate on operands stored in *temporary* registers—typically on a stack and in use only during expression evaluation. In other words, these operators operate on *copies* of variable values. They do *not* directly change the values of these variables where they reside in memory. [The "++" and "−−" operators, and the "assignment" operators (discussed later) are exceptions to this rule.] In particular, the shift operators "<<" and ">>" and the one's complement operator "~" do *not* directly change the permanent copies of their operands in storage.

2.13 Interpretation of Section 1.3's Sample Expression

Although we have not yet covered all of C's operators, we have come sufficiently far to begin to make some sense out of the sample expression given in Section 1.3. Again, for convenience we will ignore the parentheses around the first two **p**'s. (They will be explained later, when we discuss the subject of macros and macro arguments.)

By noticing the positions of the "?" and ":" operator symbols, we are led to conclude that the expression must be a *conditional* expression. The first portion (before the "?"), which is indeed a relational expression, is evaluated first. Recall an earlier conclusion, at the end of Section 2.8, that **p** must be a pointer to a *structure* having at least two members, named **_cnt** (short for "count") and **_ptr** (short for "pointer"), respectively.

The priorities of the operators in the first expression are as follows: "−>" first, "−−" next, and "> =" last. The count value is decremented first (because the "−−" operator is in a *prefix* position), and that result is then tested, yielding true (1) if it is nonnegative or false (0) if not. The count thus appears to be a positive integer that decrements for every evaluation of (or execution of) the entire expression. As long as the count's exit value remains nonnegative, the value of the second expression (the one between the characters "?" and ":") is the value of the entire expression.

In evaluating the second expression, we can tell, by context, that the "&" represents the bitwise AND operation. It has the lowest precedence of the set of operators in this expression. Since the "−>" has the highest precedence, the value of the pointer **p−>_ptr** is fetched first. The "∗" causes the value of the object that it *points to* to be fetched. Since the " ++ " operator is now in a *postfix* position, the pointer is incremented *after* its value is used. Notice that the unary operators " ++ " and "∗" have the same precedence (see the operator precedence table in Section 2.18), and that they associate right to left. This means that the post-increment applies to the *pointer's* value, and *not* to the value that it *points* to. The subsequent AND operation with the constant 0377 leaves the lower 8 bits of the final fetched value unchanged, but clears all of its upper bits.

There is some information that is not available in the sample expression. This information is provided in declarations that are found elsewhere in the program. For example, to what type of object does the structure member **_ptr** point? For simplicity, we will merely state that **_ptr** is a *character* pointer. We will state further that character values are automatically expanded into integers during expression evaluation, and that it is conceivable, for certain non-standard characters on certain machines, that this expansion may *set* all of the bits above the character. (All of these issues are covered in more detail later.) It is for these reasons that the AND with 0377 takes place.

In summary, it appears that the pointer **p−>_ptr** points into a character *buffer*, that it is incremented each time the character to which it points is fetched, and that the value of the expression is normally the value of this character. It also appears that the count keeps track of the number of characters remaining in the buffer, because, when it reaches zero, an alternative expression is evaluated.

This conclusion is supported by the name of the function called in the third expression (the one after the ":"). It would appear that, when the buffer is empty (i.e., when the count reaches zero), the purpose of the function call _fillbuf (p) is to refill the buffer with a new set of characters and, in the process, to reinitialize the count and pointer parameters. That is the reason why the function must be passed, as an argument, a pointer to the structure that contains these objects. (_fillbuf also returns the first character of the new buffer, decrementing p—>_cnt in the process.)

2.14 Arithmetic Operators

It is most likely that you are already familiar with virtually all of the arithmetic operators. Some were introduced earlier, in Section 2.3. Each is a binary operator (i.e., requiring two operands), except one, which we cover first.

The unary "-" operator *negates* the value of its operand (clearly, a signed number). A numeric constant is assumed positive unless it is preceded by this negation operator. That is, there is no unary " + ". It is implicit. (You are reminded that -x does not change the value of x where it permanently resides in memory.)

The binary arithmetic operators " + ", "-", "*", and "/" all have their customary meanings (i.e., add, subtract, multiply, and divide). They possess a few additional properties, however, that deserve some comments.

First, the specific run-time response to an *erroneous* arithmetic operation (e.g., one that generates an overflow or an underflow) is machine dependent. A program should check its operands before executing an arithmetic operation that may cause such an exception condition (e.g., before dividing by too small a quantity).

Second, integer division discards the fractional portion of the result. To retain this data, it is necessary to explicitly express the operands as floating quantities, possibly by using "casts" (explained later).

Third, you will notice that C follows the tradition of using the same symbol ("-") to represent both the unary negation operator and the binary subtraction operator. The context of the expression in which the operator is found determines its interpretation.

Fourth, C does not specify the *order* in which the operands of a commutative operation, like " + " or "*", are evaluated. Recall that the operands may themselves be arbitrarily complex expressions. Normally, of course, the order of evaluation makes no difference. However, if side effects are involved, it may.

The last arithmetic operator, called the "modulo" or "modulus" operator, is represented by the symbol "%". Its value is the *remainder* of the division of its two operands (which must be integers). That is, i%j, pronounced "i mod j," is the remainder of i/j. For example, **10%3** has a value of 1. Thus, given that integer division discards the fractional portion of the result, if i and j are integers, it is always true that

$$(i/j)*j + i\%j \text{ has a value equal to } i$$

provided that **j** is not zero.

2.15 Assignment Operators

The assignment statement is normally considered the most fundamental one in any programming language. Its traditional definition is as follows: The statement

$$var\_name = expression;$$

executes by computing the value of the expression and assigning that value to the named variable. (In some languages, the "=" symbol is replaced by the ":=" symbol.)

The assignment symbol, even if called an "operator," is normally not considered to be in the same class as any of the other expression evaluation operators. That is, a typical assignment is not *itself* considered as an expression (which may, in turn, be used as an operand in an even longer expression). Rather, the assignment is considered as a "terminal" process, after the expression on its right side has been evaluated.

This is not the case in C. C's assignment symbol, "=", is just another member of the large class of expression evaluation operators. It is given a very low precedence, as the table in Section 2.18 indicates, so that it may be used in the conventional manner. However, in C, an assignment (consisting of two operands separated by an equals sign) *itself has a value*, namely, the value that is being assigned. This value may participate, as an operand, in a subsequent operation. In other words, *an assignment is an expression*. In fact, it may be an inner expression in a still larger expression. For example, a common practice in C is to combine an assignment with a relational test, as in

$$if ((var = expression) >= test\_val) \ldots$$

Notice that the assignment, once inside its own explicit pair of parentheses, may participate in an expression's evaluation at any inner level. In the above example, the "..." portion represents what is executed if the relational expression inside the outer parentheses is found true. This expression compares the value assigned to variable **var** with the value of **test_val**. Observe that what is represented by the word "expression", in the above example, may be arbitrarily complex.

Another consequence of the fact that an assignment itself has a value is the multiple assignment statement, whose form is

$$a = b = c = number;$$

which is often used to initialize a set of variables to the same value. Since, as the precedence table indicates, assignment operators associate right to left, the above expression is evaluated by first assigning the value of **number** to **c**. The value *of this expression* is then assigned to **b**, and the value of *that* assignment is then assigned to **a**.

This last example also demonstrates the most common form for a C statement, namely, *an expression followed by a semicolon*. Its execution consists merely of the *evaluation* of the expression.

One unfortunate result of the fact that an assignment is itself an expression with a value is that a programmer may incorrectly write down an assignment instead of an intended equality relational test. For example, the intended relation in

$$if \ (a = 0) \ \ldots,$$

which should have been written as **(a == 0)**, will *always* be found "false." Similarly, the intended relation in

$$if \ (a = b) \ \ldots,$$

which should have been written as **(a == b)**, will always yield the value of b, and will thus be "true" most of the time.

Since an assignment of the form

$$variable = variable \ op \ expression$$

where *op* is a binary operator (such as "+", "<<", or "&"), occurs so often, C has a shorthand for it, namely, the construction

$$variable \ op= \ expression$$

For example, **a *= 3** multiplies **a** by 3. The permissible *op*s in the shorthand form are

$$+ \quad - \quad * \quad / \quad \% \quad << \quad >> \quad \& \quad \char94 \quad and \quad |$$

The new notation is justified not only because the compiler may be optimized to generate more efficient code for it, but also because it is more concise, particularly for long variable names, that have to be written only once. Some programmers claim that it "reads" better as well. That is, the expression **var** / = 3 may be pronounced as "divide **var** by 3." The new form also retains all of the properties of the original assignment operation. Specifically, the value that is assigned, which is the value of the entire expression, may be used as an inner operand in a more complex expression. Notice that an assignment expression, by definition, generates side effects.

The expression to the left of an assignment operator (" = ", " * = ", " += ", "& = ", and so on) must be an *lvalue*. An lvalue was originally defined and discussed in Section 2.11. lvalues include not only simple variables but also array elements, structure members, pointers, and storage locations referenced by pointer expressions. While it is normally the case that

$$\texttt{variable } op= \texttt{ expression}$$

and

$$\texttt{variable } = \texttt{ variable } op \texttt{ expression}$$

are equivalent (where **variable** represents any lvalue expression), it is important to observe that, in the former case, **variable** is evaluated *only once*. Under certain conditions (e.g., when **variable** has the form

$$*(pointer\ expression)$$

which is an lvalue, and when evaluation of the pointer expression causes side effects), the two forms may yield different results.

2.16 The Comma Operator

It is sometimes desirable to partition a single expression into a sequence of two or more related subexpressions, each of which is to be evaluated (or executed) *in turn*. Whenever C expects you to supply a single expression, at a certain point in your program, and you find it convenient to package a sequence of two or more subexpressions in its place, because each part is a distinct but related ingredient of the same process, you may separate the component subexpressions with commas.

For example, every **for** statement (discussed later) includes a provision for a single initialization expression, which is executed once, before the **for** loop is entered. Typically, this initialization expression is a simple assignment. Suppose, however, that the preloop initialization that is required really consists of a sequence of *two or more* such assignments. They may all be written, side by side, separated by commas, in place of the one expression that was expected.

The component expressions are evaluated, in turn, *left to right*, and the value of the entire expression is that of the rightmost component. Essentially, the "," operator just asks C to discard the expression value just computed and to restart its evaluation process over again.

An example of the use of the comma operator appears in a problem at the end of this chapter. We should emphasize that the commas that are employed as *separators* between the items in a *list* (e.g., a list of function arguments or a list of variable names in a declaration, covered later) are *not* comma operators. The order of evaluation in a *list* is not guaranteed to be left to right.

As the precedence table in Section 2.18 indicates, the comma operator has the *lowest* precedence of all of C's operators—even lower than that of an assignment. This means that if the comma operator is employed in an expression whose value is later *assigned* in some manner, the entire expression whose value is assigned should be enclosed in parentheses. For example, if the expression for a function argument, in a list of arguments, contains a comma operator, then that argument should be enclosed in parentheses. Thus, in the call

$$\textbf{funct(a, (t = 5, t + 4), c)}$$

the second argument has a value 9.

2.17 Data Conversions, Casts, and the `sizeof` Operator

Very little has been said, in the preceding sections, about the *types* of the objects that participate in an expression's evaluation. We have been implicitly assuming all along, first, that two object values, when combined via a binary operator, are always of the *same* type, second, that every operand's type is appropriate for the operator that operates on it, and third, that the type of the result of an expression evaluation always matches its intended use. For example, we have not considered what happens when an integer is combined arithmetically with a floating quantity, or what happens when a logical operation is attempted on a floating quantity, or what happens when a floating result of an expression evaluation is employed as an index into an array. These "what if" questions come up frequently in the study of every programming language. We will attempt to answer some of these questions here.

C offers both *implicit* data conversion, in which the value of an operand is automatically reexpressed, in another form, to accommodate an impending operation, and *explicit* data conversion, in which the *programmer* specifies the type into which an object's value is to be recast. The latter mechanism is known as a "cast." That is, under direction from the programmer, the value of an object is reexpressed, or *cast*, or "coerced" into another form. Before describing either of these conversion mechanisms, we offer a few words of advice.

The automatic or implicit data conversions executed by C are meant as a *convenience* for the programmer, to save some coding time in certain instances when these conversions appear to be called for. For example, if you attempt an arithmetic operation between an integer and a floating quantity, C will automatically reexpress the integer in floating form to accommodate you, assuming that you had sound reason for defining the integer operand as an integer in the first place, but that you want to use it temporarily as a floating-point number.

It may be that this is indeed the case, in which case you will be grateful that C was able to perform this function for you, *implicitly*, without the need for any special intervention on your part. On the other hand, it may be that the specified operation was, in fact, an *error* on your part, which C promptly ignored, deciding instead to automatically provide you with a convenience that you really did not want.

As a general rule, one should be very careful about mixing operand types in expressions. It can lead to surprises that may be difficult to diagnose. Some experts claim that it is best to avoid *all* arithmetic with operands of mixed types.

C's implicit conversion rules are meant to execute conversions that appear logical. C is also designed to reject operations that are clearly illogical. We cover a few of these first.

As pointed out in Section 2.5, operations using pointer operands are limited to additions and subtractions of integer constants, all types of comparisons between pointer values, and the subtraction of one pointer value from another. Clearly, the operand, to which the unary "*" operator is applied, must be a pointer. Although, on some machines, a pointer may be treated as if it were an unsigned integer, in the interests of portability, one should be careful to distinguish between pointers and integers. The two objects are distinct, having, in general, different lengths and different properties.

As indicated in Sections 2.11 and 2.15, the operand to which an increment or decrement operator is applied, or the operand to the left of any assignment operator must be an *lvalue*—identifying a manipulable storage region. C will reject other operand types.

All bitwise logical operations (described in Section 2.12) must operate on *integral* operands (i.e., all data types that are members of the integer family— including characters, and long, short, and unsigned integer forms). For example, it is clearly illogical (and therefore illegal) to shift a pointer value or to AND two floating values together.

There are many other illogical conditions that are also illegal. For example, the identifiers on either side of the "." operator must identify appropriate structure elements (see Section 2.8). The operand specifying a shift distance must be a positive integer. Similarly, an array index expression must evaluate to an *integral* quantity. And so on.

Having enumerated some of C's restrictions on operand types in expressions, we now describe certain implicit data conversions that C performs for you (whether you like it or not). We emphasize that these conversions are made to the *copies* of the values that C is using during expression evaluation. The objects whose values are being reexpressed are generally not changed where they reside in memory (except when side effects are involved).

As pointed out in Section 2.7, C fundamentally permits two elementary data object types: integers and floating-point numbers, with at least two data length variations permitted in each of these categories. During expression evaluation, to facilitate the process, a "standard" length is automatically employed for each data class. Specifically, all characters and "short" integers in an expression are implicitly expanded into integers (mentioned in Section 2.13) and all floating quantities are automatically expressed in *double*-precision form. We emphasize that these conversions are executed automatically, *even when not needed*. Then, if a nonfloating operand participates in an operation with a floating operand, it is first converted into double-precision floating form. Similarly, if a regular integer participates in an operation with a "long" integer, it is first converted into the long form. Thus, the general rule that C adheres to is that, when two objects of different types participate in an appropriate operation, the *shorter* one is reexpressed in the form of the *longer* one.

Since a function call is an expression evaluation process, the expressions comprising function *arguments* are also implicitly converted using the rules described above. In particular, all character arguments are automatically expanded into integers and all floating arguments are automatically reexpressed in double-precision form.

One property of C to note is that the expansion of a character into an integer may be machine dependent. Specifically, C does not specify whether this expansion should be executed by padding all higher bit positions with zeroes or by sign bit extension—in which the upper character bit is copied into all higher bit positions. While it is guaranteed that all characters in the machine's standard character set are positive (upper bit of zero), so that *either* form of expansion will yield the same result, the expansion of certain nonstandard, special control characters (having upper bits of one) may be machine dependent. This is the reason why certain lines of C code that involve character values (e.g., the sample line in Section 1.3) may include an AND with the constant 0377. Such an operation makes the code machine independent.

Implicit conversions include not only expansions but also contractions. Specifically, an *assignment* coerces the value of the expression being assigned to fit into the space available to the object on the left side of the assignment expression. Generally, compression occurs by *truncation* of higher-order bits. Longer integers are converted into shorter ones (e.g., into characters) by truncation. Double-precision floating values are converted into single-precision values by rounding, and a floating value is converted into an integer by first *discarding* its fractional part, before any truncation begins.

While it is important that you remember these general data conversion rules—especially to help explain results that you might not have anticipated—you should also remember that good programming practice dictates that, wherever feasible, you maintain a single data type across an entire expression.

Occasionally, it is helpful to *explicitly* force a data conversion at a given point in a computation. For example, two integers may be explicitly converted, temporarily, into floating quantities in order to execute a division that will retain the result's fractional part. Similarly, it may be found desirable to redefine the data type to which a specific pointer points. Under certain conditions, it may even be useful to explicitly *document* an implicit data conversion.

C makes available a construct that forces the value of an arbitrary expression to be reexpressed in the form of a specified data type. The operator, in this case, consists of an expression for that data type, enclosed in parentheses, *just preceding* the expression whose value is to be converted. This construct, called a *cast*, has the format

$$\textit{(type-name)}\ \texttt{expression}$$

It forces the value of the expression to be converted into the named type. Again, no changes are made to the permanently stored versions of the operands in the expression. Only the value of the expression, employed in the current computation, is modified.

Summarizing: a type-name, surrounded by parentheses, is one of C's *unary operators*. It is called a *cast*.

A *type-name* is a special kind of expression, normally used to *declare* a specific object type (described later). In its simplest form, it merely consists of a single C data type keyword, like **int** or **float**. (Other such keywords, and more general type-name expressions, will be introduced in Chapter 3.) For example,

$$\texttt{(float) i/j}$$

where **i** and **j** are integers, will retain the quotient's fractional part. Since the cast operation has the higher precedence (see the operator precedence table), it takes place first (i.e., **i** is converted to floating form), thereby automatically forcing the conversion of **j** to floating form, before the division is executed.

Notice that **(float) (i/j)** is inadequate, since the fractional part is discarded before the cast takes place.

In this regard, we should mention that an integer *constant* (see Section 2.1) may be cast into the form of a *long* integer, if it is immediately followed by "L" (upper- or lowercase). For example, **4567L** causes **4567** to be expressed in double-precision form. Such a cast is executed by the compiler, at compile time.

The last operator in the C repertoire is the **sizeof** operator. Normally, a C programmer is oblivious to the sizes of the objects manipulated by his/her program. In fact, the whole point to writing a machine-independent program in C is *not* to be concerned, in the slightest, not only about where these objects reside but also about how much space they occupy. (Both of these properties of a program are highly machine dependent.) However, occasionally, this information is needed, particularly in a program that interfaces directly with the operating system. For example, a program may have to make a call on the operating system for the allocation of some memory space. The amount of space requested normally depends not only on the number of objects that will reside there but also on their *sizes*. Through use of the **sizeof** operator, such a program may be made machine independent. We will see some examples later.

The **sizeof** operator may be applied in two ways. First, the expression

sizeof*(type-name)*

has a value equal to the number of bytes or characters allocated to the named data type. For example,

sizeof (float)

has a value equal to the number of bytes that your C compiler has allocated to single-precision floating quantities. The various keywords and expressions that may be used for type-names (**int** has already been mentioned) are discussed further in Chapter 3. Second, the expression

sizeof *expression*

where *expression* normally consists of the name of some object in the program, has a value equal to the number of bytes or characters allocated to that object. For example, if **str_name** is the name of a structure, then

sizeof str_name

has a value equal to the number of characters allocated to the named structure.

Notice that the **sizeof** operation is executed at compile time, not at run time.

2.18 Operator Precedence Table

The table below summarizes the precedence and associativity rules for all of C's operators. Each operator class associates *left-to-right* unless it is specifically marked "R-L" in the left-hand margin. All operators on the same line in the table have the *same* precedence. Those having the highest precedence are at the top, and the precedence level decreases as one moves down the table.

	Class	Operators
	Primary	() [] -> .
R-L	*Unary*	++ -- ! ~ - * & (type) sizeof
	Arithmetic	* / %
		+ -
	Bitwise1	>> <<
	Relational1	<= < >= >
		== !=
	Bitwise2	&
		^
		|
	Relational2	&&
		||
R-L	*Conditional*	?:
R-L	*Assignment*	= += -= *= /= %= <<= >>= &= ^= |=
	Comma	,

The information in this table is not as difficult to remember as it may appear to be. First, the associativity rules are relatively easy to recall. All but three classes associate left to right. Since you will rarely come across two conditional operators contending for application simultaneously, it is safe merely to remember that only the *unary* and the *assignment* operators associate right to left.

Second, remembering the basic ordering of the *primary, unary, arithmetic, relational,* and *assignment* operator classes will cover most of the important situations that you will encounter. As discussed in Section 2.9, the "&&" and "||" relationals are given a low precedence to permit parenthesis-free *compound* relational expressions. The only operators whose precedence positions you may have difficulty remembering are the bitwise logical operators: >>, <<, &, ^, and |. A simple rule to follow is merely to explicitly parenthesize all expressions involving them.

2.19 White Space Characters

The space, tab, and newline characters are collectively known as "white space" characters. They are important because they permit us to make expressions and programs more *readable*, but they are generally *ignored* by the compiler—except under very special conditions (none of which we have yet encountered) when they are used to separate otherwise adjacent names, keywords, and constants.

To illustrate: while it is recommended that you surround every binary operator with a pair of spaces (one on each side), just to make the expression in which it appears more readable (i.e., **a + b** is preferred over **a+b**), such spaces will be totally ignored by the compiler.

In C, the special character sequence /* introduces the beginning of a *comment*. All subsequent characters in the program are *ignored* (i.e., considered as white space—convenient for the programmer but irrelevant to the compiler) until the end of the comment is signaled by the occurrence of a matching */ sequence.

Although white space characters in expressions are generally ignored, there are certain sequences in which they may not appear, and there are other sequences in which white space characters are desirable, if not mandatory. Specifically, in the same way that a space may not appear inside an identifier or between the digits of a numeric constant, a space may not appear between the two characters of an escape sequence, like "\n", or between the two characters of a double-character operator, like " ++ ". ("?:" is, of course, an expected exception.) In virtually every case, the two characters that comprise a double-character operator are themselves single-character operators. The presence of a space causes the compiler to interpret the single-character components separately.

Notice, however, that *all* characters inside a string constant (excluding the \ escape character, but *including* all white space characters) are taken literally.

One desirable position for a space (or, possibly, for the beginning of a redundant parenthesis pair) arises in the situation in which the operator "/" is immediately followed by the operator "*" (e.g., in a construct such as **var/*ptr**).While the intended operation is the division of one operand by the value pointed to by another, the "/*" combination will be detected as the start of a *comment*, in which case *all* subsequent source code, until a matching "*/" is finally encountered, will be ignored! An intervening space will defeat detection of this phantom comment, but will still leave the resulting expression unchanged.

C is defined such that comments may *not* be nested. That is, one comment may not be included inside of another comment. An important consequence of this restriction is that, in general, a portion of a program may *not* be "commented out" (i.e., preceded by the insertion of a /* and followed by the insertion of a companion */). A code section may be commented out *only* if it contains *no* comments itself.

Problems

(Reminder: a solution to each problem is provided in the Solutions section in the back of this book.)

2.1 Give the decimal equivalents of the following integer constants: 0377, 030746, 0xFF, 0x4BD6.

2.2 Give the octal and hexadecimal equivalents of the following integer constants: 12, 214, 672, 1999.

2.3 Give an expression for the product of 3.14159 and 4.56E-2.

2.4 Using the ASCII table in Appendix A, give the \ddd equivalents of the following characters: \t, \b, \r, \f, and \\.

2.5 Using the same table, give the decimal equivalents of the following character constants: 'a', '#', '\t', and 'C'.

2.6 What is the length of the string constant "Happy Birthday!" and how much space does it consume in memory?

2.7 What is stored in memory (in hex form) to represent the string constant "0"?

2.8 Explain why each of the identifiers **3_WAY**, **NET_$**, and **abs val** is illegal.

In each of the following expressions (Problems 2.9 through 2.16), insert explicit parenthesis pairs to show what sequence of operations takes place during its evaluation. Refer to the operator precedence table when necessary and, for simplicity, assume that each identifier represents a positive integer.

2.9 a   +   b   /   -   c

2.10 a   =   b   *   c   /   -   d   %   e

2.11 a   <<   b   +   c

2.12 a   =   b   !=   c

2.13 a   -=   -   b   --   -   --   c

2.14 a | b || c

2.15 ! a   ^   ~   b

2.16 a   &&   b || c

Introduction to Remaining Problems

Each of the problems below assumes the same hypothetical set of available objects and the same set of initial values for these objects. That is, each of the objects described below is assumed to be *globally* known, and each problem should be started assuming the same, fresh set of initial conditions—*not* the values left over from the previous problem.

The name assigned to each object is *not* meant to illustrate good practice in identifier selection. Rather, it was contrived specifically to suggest its object's *type*.

We will assume three character variables **c1**, **c2**, and **c3**; three integer variables **i1**, **i2**, and **i3**; three floating-point variables **f1**, **f2**, and **f3**; three structures **s1**, **s2**, and **s3**; three pointers to characters **pc1**, **pc2**, and **pc3**; three pointers to integers **pi1**, **pi2**, and **pi3**; three pointers to floating-point numbers **pf1**, **pf2**, and **pf3**; and three pointers to structures **ps1**, **ps2**, and **ps3**. Further, we will assume the following arrays, all containing three elements (having, of course, indices 0, 1, and 2): an array of characters **ac**, an array of integers **ai**, an array of floating-point numbers **af**, an array of structures **as**, an array of pointers to characters **apc**, an array of pointers to integers **api**, an array of pointers to floating-point numbers **apf**, and an array of pointers to structures **aps**.

We further assume that *all* of the above-mentioned structures have the *same* composition. Specifically, every structure is assumed to contain four members named **m1**, **m2**, **m3**, and **m4**. **m1** is a character variable; **m2** is an integer variable; **m3** is a floating-point variable; and **m4** is a three-character array.

The tables below specify the assumed initial values of all of the objects described above. In the first table, to derive the name of the object whose value is specified at a given position, the value for n, along its row, should be substituted for the letter n in the identifier that labels its column. For example, the initial value of **f2** is 2.5 and the initial value of **s1.m2** is 40. In the second table, the value of n, along a row, is the index value of all array elements in that row. Thus, the initial value of **af[0]** is 4.0 and the initial value of **as[2].m1** is 'U'.

Tables of Initial Values

n	cn	in	fn	sn m1	sn m2	sn m3	sn m4	pcn	pin	pfn	psn
1	A	10	1.5	G	40	4.5	JKL	&c1	&i1	&f1	&s1
2	B	20	2.5	H	50	5.5	MNO	&c2	&i2	&f2	&s2
3	C	30	3.5	I	60	6.5	PQR	&c3	&i3	&f3	&s3

n	ac	ai	af	as[n] m1	as[n] m2	as[n] m3	as[n] m4	apc	api	apf	aps
0	D	15	4.0	S	70	7.5	VWX	&ac[0]	&ai[0]	&af[0]	&as[0]
1	E	25	5.0	T	80	8.5	XYZ	&ac[1]	&ai[1]	&af[1]	&as[1]
2	F	35	6.0	U	90	9.5	ABC	&ac[2]	&ai[2]	&af[2]	&as[2]

Since these are tables of data values and not program statements, there is no need to clutter them by enclosing the characters in quotes. Notice that each of the character arrays does *not* terminate in the \0 (null) character. While this is not typical, it is convenient for our present purposes. You will find it useful, in solving the problems that follow, to have an ASCII table handy. One is provided in Appendix A. Notice that the unary "&" operator is pronounced as "address of."

In addition to the objects defined above, seven different *functions* are available for your use. Again, each function name is contrived to imply the type of data object *returned* by that function and is not meant to illustrate how identifiers should be selected. Since names beginning with "f" are already used to represent floating variables (in this special artificial system), we will employ instead names beginning with "F" to indicate functions. (You are reminded that this is not common C practice and is therefore not recommended.) Thus, for example, Fi is the name of a function returning an integer, while Fpf is the name of a function returning a pointer to a floating-point variable.

The functions that are available for your use are defined as follows:

Fc   is passed a single character argument. If the argument is an uppercase letter, then **Fc** returns its lowercase equivalent. Otherwise, **Fc** returns the same character, unchanged. (As pointed out earlier, **Fc**'s returned value is actually returned expanded to an integer.)

Fi   is passed a single integer argument and returns an integer that is its *square*.

Ff   is passed a single floating argument and returns its *square root*, provided the argument is positive, or zero, if the argument is negative. (Again, as pointed out earlier, **Ff**'s returned value is actually returned expanded to double-precision form.)

Fpc   is passed a *pair* of character arguments. It searches all of the three-character arrays in the tables above until it finds a match with the *first* argument. (The search takes place in the following order: first **ac**, then the **m4** members of **s1**, **s2**, and **s3**, and, last, the **m4** members of **as[0]**, **as[1]**, and **as[2]**.) If a match is found, the matching character is *replaced* with the value of the *second* argument, and a pointer to that spot is returned. Otherwise, the value *zero* (known *not* to be a value that points to a valid object) is returned.

Fpi   is passed a single integer argument. It finds this argument's nearest value, in the array **ai**, and *replaces* the value found with the argument. It also returns a pointer to this position in the array.

Fpf   is passed a single floating argument. It finds this argument's nearest value, in the array **af**, and *replaces* the value found with the argument. In addition, it returns a pointer to this position in the array.

Fps   is passed a single character argument. It searches all of the **m4** arrays of all of the structures (in the same order as specified for **Fpc** above) and returns a pointer to the *structure* containing the first match, or *zero*, if no match is found.

While some of the functions described above are reasonably realistic (you will see programs for some of them later), those that return pointer values are a bit contrived—partly due to the assumed nature of the data. However, for our problem-solving purposes, all of these functions are entirely adequate.

Like some of the constructs in Problems 2.9–2.16, not all of the expressions below are representative of what you will see in typical C programs. They were fabricated to expose you to some of the operator combinations that are possible. The spaces that are included are there to make the expressions readable. In all cases except *one* (see if you can find it), they may be omitted.

One of the problems below is designed assuming that all objects of the same type (e.g., **i1** through **i3**) are allocated *adjacent* locations in memory. Clearly, this is not an assumption that should normally be made. For two or three other problems, you should assume that the lengths of characters, integers, and floating-point numbers are 1, 2, and 4 bytes, respectively (i.e., that the machine is probably a 16-bit computer).

Some problems *use* a pointer value returned by a function without testing it for zero (when this is a possible returned value). This is also not proper programming practice. Again, it is done strictly for convenience.

For each of the expressions given below, write down the *value* of the expression, in three forms: by assuming that this value is assigned to a *character* variable, to an *integer* variable, and to a *floating* variable. In addition, specify any *side effects* that occur during the expression's evaluation. That is, specify whether any of the values, in the tables given above, change, and, if so, what their new values are.

(Note: Whenever the character value of an expression is not printable, specify your answer using the octal \ddd form.)

2.17 c3

2.18 as[2].m2

2.19 s1.m4[0]

2.20 30 * f3

2.21 i2 * f2

2.22 *pi3

2.23 i1 & i2

2.24 i1 && i2

2.25 !i1   &   i2

2.26 !i1   &&   i2

2.27 i1   ^   i2

2.28 i1 | i2

2.29 i1 || i2

2.30 ~i1   &   017

2.31 ~017   &   i3

2.32 *apf[0]   *   i2

2.33 *api[1]   *   *pf3

2.34 Fc('X')

2.35 Fc(ac[1])

2.36 Fc(c3   +   4)

2.37 Fi(8)

2.38 Fi(i1   +   2)

2.39 Fi(*pi3   +   *api[2])

2.40 Ff(af[0])

2.41 Ff(*apf[1]   *   *pi2)

2.42 Ff(aps[2]->m3   *   i1)

2.43 ai[i1/2   -   3]   *   3

2.44 af[ps3->m2/i3   -   1]   *   *ai

2.45 *(ai   +   (pi3   -   pi1)/2   +   1)

2.46 *(*apc   +   ps1->m2   /   *pi2   -   1)

2.47 ai[*ai/5   -   1]

2.48 *((*aps)->m4)

2.49 *Fpc('A','b')

2.50 *Fpc(c3,Fc('Z'))

2.51 *(Fpc(*pc2,*apc[2])   +   1)

2.52 *Fpi(i1)

2.53 *(Fpi(aps[2]->m2)   -   2)

2.54 *(Fpi(*pi2   +   3)   +   1)

2.55 *Fpf(f3)

2.56 *Fpf((aps[0] + 1)—>m3)

2.57 *(Fpf(*apf[2] - 2) + 2)

2.58 (*Fps(c1)).m2

2.59 Fps('K')—>m2 * 3

2.60 Fps(c3 - 1)—>m4[0]

2.61 Fps(Fc(c2)) == 0

2.62 Fc(as[2].m4[2]——)

2.63 Fi(i1++)

2.64 Fi(as[2].m2 = ++*ai)

2.65 *(af + 1) = Ff(——(*(aps + 2))—>m3 + 0.5)

2.66 i1 >= i2++ && i2 >= i3++

2.67 ++i1 <= i2 ‖ ++i2 <= i3

2.68 *(pi3 = Fpi(++i2) + 1) = 0

2.69 *(pf3 = Fpf(——ps2—>m3) + 1) = 75.5

2.70 (*aps = Fps(c1))—>m3

2.71 *(ai + (&i3 - pi1))

2.72 (*aps + (&s3 - ps1))—>m2

2.73 Fi(i1++) % *ai

2.74 (*aps + 2)—>m2 % ——i2

2.75 -5 == i1 - *ai

2.76 f1 != *af

2.77 Fpc(Fc(c2),c3) != 0

2.78 Fps(Fc(c1) + 2) == 0

2.79 *(pc1 = Fpc('Q',Fc(c1)))

2.80 (*aps = Fps(c1))—>m2

2.81 !(c2 >= c1 ‖ c2 >= c3)

2.82 !(i3 % (i1 + i2))

2.83 i1 << ps3—>m2/i3

2.84 *ai >> 2

2.85 Fpc(Fc(c1++),'$')   != 0 ? i1++ : i2++

2.86 Fps(c1) == 0 ? *pi1++ : *(*api)++

2.87 f1 ? f2 : f3

2.88 f1 += f2

2.89 *ai %= i1

2.90 (i1 -= i2) <= 0

2.91 (pi1 = ai,i1 = *pi1++,i2 = *pi1++,
i3 = *pi1)

2.92 i1 = (*ai)++

2.93 ai[(int)f2]

2.94 Ff((float)i3)

2.95 sizeof(float) > sizeof(int)

2.96 sizeof(s2.m4) * i3

2.97 sizeof(*ps1)

2.98 !~i1 == 0

2.99 **api***api

2.100 &i1&&&i2

CHAPTER 3   PROGRAM STRUCTURE

3.1 The External Components of a C Program

A C program, like a program in any other language, is *hierarchical* in nature. It consists of a sequence of objects, each of which may be composed, in turn, of a succession of inner elements. The outermost objects are called the *external* components of the program. They are the ones that are visible from its exterior.

The only external elements possible in a C program are *function definitions* and *external data declarations*. Typically, virtually all of them are function definitions. In other words, a C program is best thought of as a collection of functions.

A function is a packaged computation. A "good" function is one that is relatively autonomous. It is normally short and simple. Its interface is regular and its computation is easy to describe.

Every function definition names a function, specifies the entry arguments that the function expects, and details the computation that the function performs. This computation often includes an expression for the value *returned* by the function to its caller. Functions may be defined *only* at the external level. That is, one function definition may not include another function definition.

A function name is the only identifier that may be referenced *before* it is defined or declared. That is, a function may be called before its definition appears in a program.

A *run* of a C program consists of the execution of just *one* of its functions. Of course, in a typical, well-structured program, function calls are *nested*. That is, each function itself makes calls on one or more other functions while it executes. Thus, the function that is entered at the beginning of a run does not usually remain in control during the entire computation. Rather, it makes calls on other functions, which in turn also make calls, and so on. A program run ends when the function that was originally entered itself returns.

All of the functions in a C program have the same standing. While the programmer is free to choose arbitrary names for all functions, the special function, which is to be entered when the program run first begins, is marked with a special name, namely, the function name **main**. That is, every C program must have one function named **main**. In all *other* respects, this function is entirely ordinary. Its definition must adhere to the same rules that apply to all function definitions. It is unusual only because the operating system transfers control to the **main** function to *start* a program running, and receives control *back* when the function named **main** finally returns.

At run time, a function normally receives its input arguments positioned, in order, on a *stack*. The compiler is responsible for converting every function call into code that evaluates the expression for each argument and pushes the value derived onto the stack, at the instant just preceding entry to the function. The value returned by the function is normally passed back to the calling routine via the same stack.

Typically, a function performs its computation employing *private* registers, which are not accessible to the other functions. That is, virtually all of the variables named *inside* a function's definition are *local* to that function. They are not visible outside the function. (They are normally allocated temporary storage, on the same stack that is used for the passing of arguments.) Such an arrangement simplifies the *interface* that a function presents to its caller. The function merely receives a set of input values, performs some operation based on these values, and (usually) returns an output value to the caller.

A portable function is one that may be employed, preferably with *no* change, in many different programs. Thus, in addition to the properties described earlier, a "good" function is one that is portable. It is portable when it does not implicitly assume the existence of one or more "global" variables, whose names are known *outside* the function as well. In other words, a function that is "wired into" one or more specific global variable names is rarely transportable from one program to another.

All of the objects whose names are referenced within a function must be *declared* before they are used. (Exception: as explained earlier, another function may be referenced before it is defined or declared.) A declaration, whose specific format is given later, informs the compiler of the *type* of every object named in it. Thus, for example, a function definition must begin by declaring the type of every *argument* that the function expects. Similarly, any other local variables employed by the function during its computation must also be declared before they are used. At run time, all such variables are normally "created" (i.e., temporary storage for them is allocated on a stack) each time the function is entered. When the function returns, all of them disappear (i.e., their temporary registers are deallocated). All of these local variables are called "automatic" variables because stack storage for them implicitly appears and disappears as their functions are entered and exited.

Occasionally, however, it is useful to define one or more *global* data objects, whose names are known to *all* functions in a program. For example, it may be desirable to make a common data array directly accessible to every function by the same universal name.

An object is made global if its declaration appears *outside* of all functions— i.e., at the *external* level. Once declared in this manner, its name and type are automatically known to all subsequent functions— without the necessity for any further internal declarations.

The assembly language programmer is used to operating in an environment in which *all* names are global. Such a situation may appear to have some advantages. For example, the passing of arguments to subroutines is apparently simplified because *all* subroutines have direct access to *all* variables. However, making most of the variables in a program global has some distinct disadvantages. First, it is possible that a subroutine may inadvertently modify a variable in an unexpected manner merely because it has *access* to it. Second, subroutines developed under such conditions are rarely transportable from one program to another, because they are written assuming a specific set of globally available names.

In summary, the external objects of a C program are either functions or global variables. All of the variables that are referenced within a function, except for global variables, are local and private to that function alone. This property materially alleviates a problem, familiar to most assembly language programmers, in which the natural name for a variable, within a given subroutine, may not be used because that name is already in use in another subroutine. In C, two identical local variable names, employed in *different* functions, are considered as distinct. Notice that, since a function name is itself an external name, it is automatically a global name.

3.2 C's Basic Data Types

Fundamentally, C permits only two elementary data types: integers and floating-point numbers. Each of these types, however, has two or more *length* variations, and each variation is identified with a different *keyword*.

A keyword is a *reserved* identifier—a sequence of characters that has a special meaning to C. It may not be used for any other purpose. We have already explained the meaning of one C keyword, namely, the keyword **sizeof**.

Virtually all of the C keywords (**sizeof** happens to be an exception) may be subdivided into three categories: those that identify data types, those that identify storage classes, and those that deal with program control flow. We discuss some of the members of the first category here. Others will be introduced in due course. (A list of all of the C keywords that are currently employed appears in Appendix B.)

The keywords that identify the different members of the class of *integers* are **int**, **char**, **short**, **long**, and **unsigned**. As pointed out earlier, the lengths that are assigned to data objects (e.g., those identified by the keywords above) vary from machine to machine. Each C compiler is free to choose lengths that are convenient for it and that best match the characteristics of the processor for which it is generating code.

int identifies a signed integer. Its length is that that is most natural for the object processor. For example, a C compiler for a 16-bit machine would probably choose 16 bits as the length of an **int**, in which case the range of possible **int** values would probably run from -32768 to + 32767. The compiler, however, is free to choose any other length for this data object.

char identifies a character data element. It is the shortest addressable data object—typically, 8 bits (i.e., 1 byte) in length. A **char** is the shortest member of the integer class. (Recall that **char**s are automatically expanded into **int**s during expression evaluation, and that this process involves either sign extension or zero padding. Conversely, conversion of an **int** into a **char** is accomplished by truncation—the discarding of higher-order bits.)

short identifies a signed integer that may be shorter than an **int**. For example, if the host machine's word length is 32 bits, an **int** may be 32 bits long, while a **short** may be 16 bits long. On the other hand, the length of a **short** may be the *same* as that of an **int** on, say, a 16-bit machine. (The compiler is constrained only to make a **short** *no longer* than an **int**.)

long identifies a signed integer that may be longer than an **int**. For example, if the host machine's word length is 16 bits, an **int** may be 16 bits long, while a **long** may be 32 bits long. On the other hand, the length of a **long** may be the same as that of an **int** on, say, a 36-bit machine. (The compiler is constrained only to make a **long** *no shorter* than an **int**.)

unsigned identifies an **int** that has no sign bit. It is always assumed to be positive. Thus, for example, the range of values for an **unsigned**, on a 16-bit processor, is normally from 0 to 65535.

Each of the keywords **short**, **long**, and **unsigned** may be optionally followed by the keyword **int** (e.g., **long int**) without changing its meaning. Common C practice is to omit the implied **int**. Notice that conversions from

short to **int** and from **int** to **long** normally involve sign extension, while conversions in the other direction occur by truncation of high-order bits.

Some compilers permit additional **unsigned** data types—by allowing the adjective **unsigned** to precede any of the keywords **char**, **short**, or **long** (each of which identifies a *signed* quantity). Thus, the keyword combinations **unsigned char**, **unsigned short**, and **unsigned long** may be accepted by your compiler. In each case, use of the prefix **unsigned** effectively doubles the permissible range of positive values, while eliminating all possible negative values. For example, if a **char** is 8 bits long, normally having a numeric value between -128 and 127, an **unsigned char** would accommodate values between 0 and 255.

The keywords that identify the various members of the class of *floating-point numbers* are **float** and **double**. Again, the natural length for a **float** is hardware dependent. For example, it may be 32 bits, either on a 16-bit machine or on a 32-bit system. The range of **float** values is also machine dependent. For instance, if a 32-bit **float** is divided into an 8-bit signed exponent field and a 24-bit signed fraction field, then its approximate magnitude range will be between 1E-37 and 1E38.

double identifies a double-precision floating-point number. Typically, its length is twice that of a **float**. (The keyword combination **long float**, which is rarely used, is a synonym for the keyword **double**.) Recall that all floating-point arithmetic in C is executed in double precision.

3.3 Declarations in C

A declaration in C names one or more identifiers and designates how each one of them should be *interpreted*. That is, a C declaration specifies the *type of object* that each of its identifiers identifies.

A declaration may also contain information specifying how storage for its objects should be allocated and initialized. If a declaration causes storage to be allocated to the objects named in it, then it is also called a *definition*. We begin by ignoring initialization and storage allocation issues.

A declaration contains a *keyword* (or, possibly, a combination of keywords) identifying a specific object *type* (e.g., any of those defined in the previous section) and one or more *expressions*, each of which contains a new identifier being declared. Each expression in the declaration is designed to give the compiler an *example* of a construction whose evaluation will yield an object of the named type. For example, the declaration

```
int count;
```

states that whenever the construct **count** is encountered in an expression, its evaluation will yield an object of type **int**. In other words, **count** has been declared to be a *variable* of type **int**. Notice that every declaration ends in a semicolon.

Similarly, the declaration

$$\text{char symbol, *position;}$$

states that whenever either of the constructs **symbol** or ***position** is evaluated, the result will be an object of type **char**. In other words, **symbol** has been declared to be a *variable* of type **char**, while **position** has been declared to be a *pointer* to a **char**. Notice that, when more than one identifier is being declared, the sample expressions are separated by commas.

Similarly, the declaration

$$\text{double sqrt();}$$

declares **sqrt** to be the name of a *function* that returns a value of type **double**, while the declaration

$$\text{float data[];}$$

declares **data** to be the name of an array of **float**s.

These last two declarations do not *define* the named objects. That is, they do not cause the compiler to allocate storage for them. They merely provide sufficient information to enable the compiler to properly interpret expressions containing the declared identifiers. (Function and array *definitions*, for which storage *is* allocated, are introduced later in this chapter.)

In a similar manner, names that identify many other *derived* object types may be declared. For example, the declaration

$$\text{long **pptr;}$$

declares **pptr** to be a pointer *to a pointer* to long integers, while the declaration

$$\text{char *message[];}$$

declares **message** to be the name of an array *of pointers* to characters. (As you will recall, the "[]" operator has the higher precedence.) Similarly, the declaration

$$\text{unsigned *map();}$$

declares **map** to be the name of a function that returns *a pointer* to an unsigned integer. [Again, as you will recall, the "()" operator has the higher precedence.]

Notice that the declaration

$$\text{short } (*\text{pfunct}) \text{ () ;}$$

(which is relatively rarely used) declares **pfunct** to be a *pointer to a function* that returns a short integer value. The parentheses are included because the "*" operator has the lowest precedence in the expression. Thus, evaluation of the expression ***pfunct** yields an object that is a function, and applying the final "()" operator *calls* that function. Without the parentheses, the declaration would declare **pfunct** to be a function returning a pointer to a **short**.

In summary, a declaration specifies a data type and one or more sample expressions whose evaluation *yields* that data type. Each expression in the declaration effectively explains the interpretation to be given to a new identifier. It permits us (and the compiler) to specify the type of object that that identifier identifies.

Problems at the end of this chapter will help you practice interpreting and constructing declarations.

Now that the concept of a declaration has been introduced, we are in a position to consider when a declaration is a definition and when it is not.

If the sole purpose of a declaration is to provide information that enables the compiler to properly interpret expressions, then it is not a definition. If it is also employed to allocate (either temporary or permanent) *storage* for the objects named in it, then it is a definition as well. How does the compiler tell the difference?

First, if a declaration is preceded by the keyword **extern**, it is automatically *ruled out* as a definition. The keyword **extern** specifically states that the objects named in the declaration are defined *elsewhere*. Details concerning the possible meanings of "elsewhere" and the points in a program where **extern** declarations normally appear are provided in Section 3.5.

Second, assuming that the keyword **extern** is *not* employed, any variable or pointer declaration is *also* a definition. The appropriate amount of (temporary or permanent) storage, depending on the object's type, will be allocated by the compiler. The discussion in Section 3.5 also explains how the compiler decides whether to allocate permanent or temporary storage and where that storage normally resides.

Third, again assuming that the keyword **extern** is missing, an array declaration is also a definition only if sufficient information is provided in it to fully define the amount of storage that is required for the array. This information may be supplied in either of two ways. First, each pair of square brackets, indicating one dimension of the array (discussed further later), may contain a *constant expression* specifying the *number of array elements* in that dimension. For example, the declaration

$$\texttt{float table[100];}$$

defines a one-dimensional array, named **table**, of 100 **float**s. Alternatively, the declaration may contain *initialization* information that *implies* how large the array should be. Initializers are also discussed later in this chapter. (Variable and pointer definitions may also contain optional initializers.)

Function definitions are described in the next section. The discussion there clarifies the difference between a function definition and a function declaration. Similarly, structure declarations are treated later in this chapter.

3.4 Function Definitions and Compound Statements

In order to properly evaluate an expression, C must be aware of the *type* of every operand contained in it. This is the reason why objects must be *declared* before they are used. In particular, whenever a function call appears as an operand in an expression, the type of value that that function *returns* must be known. Yet, it was pointed out earlier that a function call may appear in a program before that function is defined or declared. This statement must now be qualified. It is true only if the function returns an **int** (or if it returns no value at all). If the function returns any *other* type of value, a declaration, as described in the previous section, must precede its use. (A *definition* of a function—whose structure is explained below—serves as a global declaration of its type, for all subsequent calls to it.) Thus, a previous declaration of some form is *not* required only for a function that either returns an **int** or returns *no* value.

Since, by default, every function that returns a value is assumed to return an **int**, unless it is declared differently, in the absence of previous declarations, the first call to a function is an *implicit declaration* of it as being one that returns an **int**.

A function *definition* consists of a header declaration, a (possibly null) set of argument declarations, and a body.

The header declaration has all of the attributes of a nondefining function declaration, as described in the previous section, with two exceptions. First, the normal terminating semicolon is *omitted*. Second, the pair of parentheses, which indicate that the declaration is a *function* declaration, enclose a possibly empty *argument list*—a sequence of argument *names*, separated by commas. These names are called the *formal parameters* of the function. For example,

$$\texttt{factorial(i)}$$

is the header declaration for a function named **factorial** that takes one argument named **i**, while

power (base, exponent)

is the header declaration for a function named **power** that takes two arguments, named **base** and **exponent**, respectively.

If the type of value returned by a function is an **int**, the keyword **int** in the header declaration may be omitted. As explained earlier, it is *implicit*. Thus, the type of value returned by each of the functions **factorial** and **power**, above, is an **int**, by default. Similarly, the type keyword may also be omitted for all functions that return *no* value. On the other hand, for example,

double sqrt (x)

is the header declaration for a function named **sqrt** that takes one argument, named **x**, and returns a value of type **double**. In other words, if the type returned is other than **int**, it must be explicitly specified.

The argument declarations, which follow the header declaration, specify the types of all of the arguments expected by the function. These declarations conform to the rules described in the previous section. Thus, by the time the compiler reaches the *body* of the function's definition, it has been informed not only of the local name, and type, of every function argument, but also of the function's name and the type of value, if any, that it returns.

For example,

factorial (i)
int i;

and

power (base, exponent)
int base, exponent;

and

double sqrt (x)
double x;

are sample header *and* argument declarations for the three function definition examples introduced above.

The body of a function definition is a sequence of zero or more C *statements*, *all enclosed in a pair of braces*: "{" and "}". This construction is known as a *compound statement* or *block*. This body details the computation that the function performs and specifies the value, if any, that the function returns.

After the opening brace of a block, one or more declarations of other local variables that are referenced inside the block may appear. (These issues are discussed further later.)

At this point, the only C statement that we have defined is *an expression followed by a semicolon*—whose execution consists of the *evaluation* of the expression. Other C statement types will be described presently. For our present purposes, it will be adequate to represent an arbitrary compound statement, or block, with either of the following notations: { ... } or

```
{
 .
 .
 .
}
```

In either case, the dot triplet serves to represent an arbitrary sequence of statements.

A compound statement (or block) is syntactically equivalent to a *single* statement. That is, it may appear in any position where a simple statement may appear. In particular, a compound statement may itself contain other compound statements. Note, however, that while every simple statement ends in a semicolon, there is no need for a semicolon after the closing brace of a block.

Having laid down the ground rules for function definitions, let us consider some examples. The most trivial function definition is

$$\textbf{no\_op}\,()\;\{\;\}$$

which takes no arguments, does nothing, and returns no value. Yet it conforms to all of the rules for function definitions outlined above. [**no_op**() is the header declaration; there are no arguments to declare; and { } is an *empty* block.] A C statement of the form

$$\textbf{no\_op}\,()\;;$$

would execute by *calling* this dummy subroutine, in which case it too would do nothing. (Notice that the essential difference between a C statement containing a single function call and an elementary header declaration is merely the presence or absence of the terminating semicolon.) Incidentally, a simpler way to represent a statement that does nothing is with an *isolated semicolon*. It is called a *null statement*. Uses for it will be described presently.

A less trivial example of a function definition is

```
/* return first prime number above input value */
prime (num)
int num;
{
.
.
.
}
```

A leading comment, which summarizes the purpose of the function, is recommended. Since a type keyword is missing from the header declaration, the function is assumed to return an **int** (or no value at all). The single argument that is specified in the header is declared immediately after the header, and the function's body follows that declaration. Notice that calls to **prime**, which are typically of the form **prime (name)**, where **name** is the caller's name for the passed argument, need *not* be preceded by any preliminary declarations—no matter *where* they appear in the program—because **prime** returns an **int**.

We continue with our three earlier examples in a similar manner, deriving

```
/* return the factorial of the input value */
factorial (i)
int i;
{
.
.
.
}
```

and

```
/* return base raised to the power given */
power (base, exponent)
int base, exponent;
{
.
.
.
}
```

and

```
/* return square root of input argument */
double sqrt(x)
double x;
{
.
.
.
}
```

Notice that while calls of the form **factorial(n)** and **power(m, y)**, where **n**, **m**, and **y** are the caller's names for the required arguments, need not be preceded by any preliminary declarations, because these functions both return **int**s, calls to the function **sqrt** must be preceded by the declaration

double sqrt();

if the function **sqrt** has not yet been defined in the program.

Whenever any function is called, it is entered at the opening brace of its body. It returns to its caller either by executing a **return** statement (discussed later) or by "falling through" to the closing brace of its body. As we will see later, a **return** statement may or may not specify a value to be returned. Clearly, if the function returns by falling through to its closing brace, it returns no value.

It was pointed out earlier that, if a function call appears as an operand in an expression, then that function must return a valid value. On the other hand, when this is not the case (because the expression consists *only* of a call), the function may or may not return a value. The statement's terminating semicolon acts like a comma operator, causing any value remaining on the expression evaluation stack to be discarded—no matter *what* expression preceded the semicolon.

Let us consider a more complex example of a function definition:

```
/* return ptr to first matching string in message */
char *match(message, string)
char message[], *string;
{
.
.
.
}
```

The header declaration names the function as **match** and declares that it expects two arguments, whose local names are **message** and **string**, respectively. The header also states that the function's returned value will be cast into the form of a *pointer to characters* before the return is executed.

The second line of the definition (which could have been written in two separate lines) declares that the first argument must be the name of an array of characters (i.e., a pointer to its first element). It also states that this array is *defined* (i.e., allocated storage) elsewhere in the program—probably in the caller's code section. This line also declares that the second argument must be a pointer to characters.

Notice that, in this case, calls to **match**, which are typically of the form **match(array, pointer)**, where **array** and **pointer** are samples of the caller's names for the passed arguments, should normally be preceded by an appropriate declaration, of the form

```
char *match();
```

to specify the type of value that **match** returns (since it is other than an **int**). Such a declaration overrides the compiler's default assumption and permits it to generate the proper code for the evaluation of expressions containing calls on **match**. If the declaration were omitted, the compiler would generate correct code only if the *definition* of **match** *preceded* the call (since external names are global).

From our study of Chapter 2, it should be clear that, since function arguments are expressions whose values are passed via a stack, a function generally has no direct access to the variables whose values it is passed. Rather, it is passed *copies* of these values. For example, the function **abs**, which returns the absolute value of an argument **x**, does not change **x** in storage. It merely returns its result via the same stack by which it received the *value* of **x** in the first place.

The value of a variable in storage is normally changed by a proper *assignment* operation. To permit a function to directly alter a (nonglobal) variable's value in storage, that function must be passed a *pointer* to the variable in question.

Since execution of a function call automatically applies C's implicit expression evaluation conversion rules to every function argument, a typical C compiler will treat as a **double** any formal parameter declared as a **float**, and it will treat as an **int** any formal parameter declared either as a **char** or as a **short**. Maintaining consistency, it will similarly treat any function declared as *returning* a **float** as if it were one declared as returning a **double**, and it will treat any function declared as returning either a **char** or a **short** as if it were one declared as returning an **int**.

3.5 Storage Classes and Scope

A C object is considered to be in existence or "alive" while storage for it is allocated. Registers may be assigned to an object either on a permanent basis or on a temporary basis. Permanent storage is allocated by the compiler at compile time. The registers that are so assigned have only one purpose. They are never reassigned for another purpose. On the other hand, the registers employed for temporary storage (typically, on a stack) have changing assignments as the program runs.

The "lifetime" of an object is that portion of time during which it exists in storage. Temporary objects may remain in existence over a wide range of times. Some may have very short lifetimes. Others may have very long lifetimes. A *permanent* object, on the other hand, endures for as long as the program runs.

The fact that an object exists in storage (as described above) does not necessarily mean that it is *accessible*. The registers that are assigned to it may have been made temporarily "invisible" to the program by the compiler. An object's name is considered to be "defined" or "known" at a given point in a program if its assigned registers are accessible or addressable at that point. The *scope* of a name is that part of a program over which it is defined and known (i.e., that part of the program over which its assigned registers are available for use). We consider here the rules by which the C compiler makes names "visible" and "invisible."

To treat the issue of scope properly, we must take into account that a C program may reside on more than one source file. C is designed to permit each source file to be compiled separately. Specific rules exist to define the conditions under which a name in one source file may be made known (so that it may be referenced) in another source file. These rules are included in our discussion below.

Broadly speaking (subject to various qualifications to be explained as we proceed), an *external* object in a C program, as defined in Section 3.1, is allocated *permanent* storage and is made *globally* visible, while an *internal* object (i.e., one defined *inside* a function definition) is assigned *temporary* storage and is known only *within the block* in which it is defined.

More specifically, a *function* name is automatically known throughout all of the source files that comprise a program. (Recall, however, that if the *type* that a function returns is other than **int**, it must be declared properly before it is called.) On the other hand, any *other* external object's name is automatically known only from the point where that object is defined to the *end of the source file* in which its definition appears. The name is made known in a *different* source file (or in the same file—*before* the definition) with a declaration preceded by the keyword **extern**. That is, the keyword **extern**, in front of a declaration, specifies that the object being declared is defined, as an external object, in *another* source file (or, possibly, elsewhere in the *same* file). For example, the declaration

extern double value;

states that the variable of type **double** named **value**, which is expected to be referenced locally, is actually defined as an external object in another part of the program.

Typically, the definition of an external data object appears at the beginning of one source file (making it globally known within that file), and an **extern** declaration of the same object appears at the beginning of any other source file in which it must also be globally visible. (The compiler ensures that there is only *one* external definition that is referenced by all **extern** declarations of the same name.) Many other variations are possible, however. To appreciate them, we must first discuss the scope of *internal* names, beginning from the lowest inside level.

The scope of an *internal* identifier lasts from the point at which it is declared to the closing brace of the block in which its declaration appears. That is, an internal identifier is visible only *within its own block* (and in any inner blocks that that block encloses). Further, if a name, declared at the beginning of a block, *duplicates* a name known outside of that block, then the new declaration *supersedes* the old one, for the duration of the block. (The outside declaration still remains in effect externally.)

The scope of a function *argument* name—i.e., a formal parameter declared in a function definition just before the block that specifies the action that the function performs—extends throughout the body of the function definition. Notice that the name employed for an argument, in a function *definition*, is regarded as distinct and separate from any name appearing in an expression for that argument in a *call* of the function—even when the two names are identical. Thus, for example, if the construct **fcn_name(arg)** happens to be used not only in **fcn_name**'s *header declaration*, but also in a *call* of **fcn_name**, the two occurrences of the name **arg** would be regarded as identifying two *different* objects.

As pointed out earlier, a temporary, local variable (i.e., one declared inside a block or inside a function definition) is called an "automatic" variable, because it automatically appears and disappears as the program runs. C includes the keyword **auto** in its repertoire to describe such a variable. However, since *all* objects declared internally are, *by default*, automatic, the keyword **auto** is implicit. Since use of **auto** at the external level is not permitted, this keyword is virtually never used.

Notice that an automatic variable *loses its value* whenever it disappears.

When it reappears, the registers allocated to it contain arbitrary values (i.e., garbage), in which case the variable may need to be reinitialized. (The issue of initialization is covered later in this chapter.)

Thus far, we have discussed permanent, external, globally known objects, and temporary, internal, locally known objects. Consider one variation on each of these themes. First, consider *restricting* the scope of a permanent, external object to a limited portion of a program. Second, consider allocating *permanent* storage to an internal, locally known object. In each case, we derive an element that is allocated permanent storage and yet whose scope is limited to a localized region of the program. Such an element is called a *static* element. It is permanent in storage, but its scope is restricted and cannot be extended. Notice that a static object may be either external or internal.

An object is made static, as described above, if its definition is preceded by the keyword **static**. The appearance of this keyword has two possible effects. If it is applied to an *external* definition, the scope of the defined name is restricted only to the remainder of the source file in which that definition appears. Specifically, static *functions* may not be called from other source files and static external variables may not be referenced via **extern** declarations in other source files. If the keyword **static** is applied to an *internal* definition, then *permanent* storage is allocated to the object defined, in which case it *retains its value* even when it becomes (temporarily) inaccessible.

As implied above, use of the keyword **static** has two important applications. First, it is used to *conceal* an external identifier, defined in one source file, so that it cannot be (intentionally or accidentally) referenced in another source file. In particular, a **static** function cannot be called from another file, and the appearance of a **static** variable's name, in another file, is interpreted as a reference to an entirely *different* object. Second, the keyword **static** is used to permit an internal variable to *retain* its value, even when it becomes invisible. For example, a variable that is private and local to a function can retain its value, from call to call, if its definition is preceded by the keyword **static**.

Problems at the end of this chapter will test your comprehension of the external, automatic and static storage classes.

A final storage class, which demonstrates why C is sometimes called a universal or machine-independent *assembly* language, is the **register** storage class. The declaration of any *automatic* variable (including a function argument) may be preceded by the keyword **register**. This keyword merely informs the compiler that the object being declared will have a high degree of activity. It requests that, if possible, the compiler should assign the object to a *processor* register, rather than to a memory register. Thus, C provides the programmer with a mechanism to specify *which* variables will be heavily used. If these variables are indeed assigned to machine registers, the execution time of the program could be materially reduced.

Whether or not the C compiler follows the programmer's recommendation depends on several issues. First, some C compilers ignore the **register** keyword altogether. Since it can only affect a program's execution time, it may be treated as the equivalent of the keyword **auto**, without changing any other aspect of a program's behavior. Second, the effect of the **register** keyword is clearly machine dependent. A compiler for a machine having a large number of processor registers is much more likely to follow the programmer's suggestion than is one for a simpler processor. Third, when several **register** declarations exist, the variables named in the *earlier* declarations are the ones that are more likely to be found residing in processor registers.

The **register** keyword may not be applied to all declarations. As might be expected, only *scalar* objects (i.e., simple variables and pointers) may be placed in machine registers. Further, the realities of the processor may further restrict the variable types that may be assigned to registers to simple integers and characters—with floating and long types ruled out. In addition, once you have decided to request that an object be assigned to a processor register, you *lose* the ability to address it indirectly via a pointer. For example, if the declaration

register int var_name;

appears in a program, then that program is not permitted to also use the construct **&var_ name**.

3.6 Initialization

The definition of a data object may contain information specifying how the storage that is allocated to that object should be initialized. In the *absence* of such explicit initialization information, C automatically initializes all *permanent* data areas (for external and **static** variables) to *zero*. Similarly, in the absence of explicit initialization information, C leaves all *temporary* data areas (for internal, local variables) alone, in which case they begin containing arbitrary values (i.e., garbage).

All permanent data areas (including those for **static** local variables) are initialized *once*—at *compile* time. For this reason, if explicit initialization values are supplied by the programmer, they must be in the form of *constant* expressions (whose values may be determined at compile time). Expressions whose values are addresses that are known at compile time are also permissible.

The initialization expression for an *automatic* variable, on the other hand, may be arbitrary, since it is evaluated at *run* time (at the point where the temporary storage that it initializes is allocated). In fact, the definition of an automatic variable that contains initialization information, is entirely equivalent to one that does not—*followed by* an assignment statement, assigning the specified initialization value to the specified variable. Notice that such an automatic variable is *re*initialized each time its block is reentered.

Before discussing permissible initialization constructs, we begin with a few preliminary observations.

First, we use the term "initializer" to name that added portion of a definition that contains the optional, explicit initialization information. Various permissible formats for initializers are considered below.

Second, while a *permanent array*'s definition may include an initializer (whose structure will be explained), such initialization information is *not* permitted in the declaration of an *automatic* array. Of course, *all* data objects (in particular, automatic arrays) may be assigned arbitrary values as the result of the execution of statements that *follow* their definitions.

Third, the initializer of an array does not only supply initial data values. The *count* of the number of items in it may be used to specify the *size* of the array. This issue is discussed further later.

Finally, notice that, by its very nature, the declaration of the formal parameter of a function may *not* include an initializer. Whenever the function is called, the initial value of the parameter is always the value that is *passed* in the call.

We proceed by considering the permissible formats for initializers.

A *scalar* object (i.e., a variable or a pointer) is initialized by following its name, in its declaration, with an equals sign followed by the expression whose value is to be assigned to it. Thus, for example,

$$\text{int a = b*c;}$$

declares an integer variable **a** and initializes it to the product of (already defined) variables **b** and **c**. In this example, **a** is assumed to be a *temporary, local* variable, because the value of its initialization expression is presumably not known at compile time. Similarly,

$$\text{static float *f\_ptr = \&number;}$$

declares **f_ptr** to be a pointer to **float**s and initializes it with the address of a variable named **number**. In this example, the keyword **static** indicates that the storage to be allocated to **f_ptr** is *permanent*, in which case it is assumed that **number** has already been defined, so that **&number** can be computed at compile time.

If a declaration defines two or more identifiers, whose sample expressions are separated by commas, each of these identifiers may be optionally followed by its own initializer. Thus,

$$\texttt{char letter = 'A', digit = '0';}$$

declares and initializes two character variables. However, as a matter of style, many programmers prefer keeping the components of such a multiple declaration on separate lines.

To summarize: within a block, the definition

$$\texttt{int i = 5;}$$

means that temporary variable **i** is *re*initialized to the value 5 each time the block is entered, while the definition

$$\texttt{static int i = 5;}$$

means that permanent variable **i** is initialized only once, at *compile* time, before the program run even begins.

The initializer for an *aggregate* (i.e., an array or a structure) consists of an equals sign followed by a sequence of appropriate expressions, *separated by commas and enclosed in braces.* As pointed out earlier, such an initializer may be applied only to the definition of a *permanent* aggregate, in which case each of the expressions in the brace-enclosed list is evaluated at *compile* time. Thus, for example, the definition

$$\texttt{int priority[5] = \{6, 5, 4, 3, 2\};}$$

defines an integer array of five elements named **priority** and initializes its components, in increasing subscript order, to the values shown (in which case **priority[0]** gets the value 6).

Several variations on this theme are possible. First, the size of the array (in the square brackets) could have been omitted, in which case the compiler would have computed the array size by *counting* the number of expressions in the initializer. Second, the array size, specified in the square brackets, could have been *larger* than the number of initializer expressions, in which case all of the array elements whose initial values remained unspecified (beginning with the sixth) would have been initialized to zero, by default. Thus, the closing brace may terminate the list of initial values *early*, before all of them have been given. (It is an error to provide too many initial values.)

A brace-enclosed initializer list may *itself* contain one or more brace-enclosed sublists, each of which specifies initial values for an *inner* aggregate. To explain how such an initializer is interpreted, let us first consider how a two-dimensional array in C is declared and constructed.

Since the "[]" operator associates left to right, the construct

name [i] [j]

is *first* interpreted as a reference to element **i** in the array named **name**. This element is then *itself* interpreted as an array, whose element **j** is then accessed. Thus, C treats a two-dimensional array as an array of arrays—specifically, as an array of *rows*, each of which contains as many elements as there are *columns* in the matrix. This scheme was chosen because memory is best envisioned as a *horizontal* sequence of cells. The array is configured in memory *row by row*, starting at a base address that is the value of the pointer naming the array. The left index (**i** above) selects one of the rows, and the right index (**j** above) then selects one of the column elements in this row.

Notice that, in this example, the object

*name

is a *one-dimensional array*.

A two-dimensional array may be defined to C in various ways. To begin with, both dimensions may be given in the declaration, as in

char matrix[20] [30];

which declares an array of 20 rows, each containing 30 characters. Since an initializer is not provided, the array **matrix** might be either a permanent object, initialized to all-zeroes by default, or an automatic (temporary) object, with undefined initial contents.

If an array is permanent, its initializer normally consists of a brace-enclosed list of brace-enclosed lists. For example, the definition

int score[2] [3] = { { 1, 2, 3 }, { 4, 5, 6 } };

fully initializes the declared array. Notice that the individual initialization values are supplied in the order in which they will appear in memory.

The same definition could also have been written as

**int score[2] [3] = {
        { 1, 2, 3 },
        { 4, 5, 6 }
    };**

which is a preferable format for the initializer of a typical two-dimensional array.

In each of the two examples given above, the array dimensions (inside the square brackets) could have been omitted, since *all* of the initial values were fully specified in the initializer. Effectively, the appearance of each inner left brace signals the beginning of a new set of initial values for the next inner aggregate. Thus, the compiler is able to count the number elements in the outer list, as well as the number of elements in each inner list.

Alternatively, when the list of values provided in the initializer starts with the first element and does not skip any elements, the inner braces may be omitted, if desired. Thus, the declarations above could also have been written as

$$\texttt{int score[2][3]} = \{ \texttt{1, 2, 3, 4, 5, 6} \};$$

The compiler merely places the values given into storage, in the order in which they are supplied. After all of these initial values have been consumed, zeroes are provided for those array elements (if any) that still remain uninitialized.

Since the right brace can signal *early termination* of an initializer list, many "partial" initializations are possible. For example, the definition

$$\texttt{static short num[3][3]} = \{ \{4\}, \{3, 2\}, \{1\} \};$$

specifies values only for **num[0][0]**, **num[1][0]**, **num[1][1]**, and **num[2][0]**. (They are 4, 3, 2, and 1, respectively.) Those array elements whose values are omitted from the initializer are set to zero by default.

As a special case, when a *character* array is to be initialized, a *string constant* may be employed—instead of the usual brace-enclosed, comma-separated list of initializers. That is, the two definitions

$$\texttt{char message[]} = \{\texttt{'s','t','r','i','n','g','\textbackslash 0'}\};$$

and

$$\texttt{char message[]} = \texttt{"string"};$$

are entirely equivalent. The latter form is preferred not only because it is shorter, but also because it is clearer.

We should emphasize that a string constant is not normally processed in this way. Usually (as pointed out in Section 2.1), the appearance of a string constant inside an expression is treated as follows: the characters inside the double quotes are placed in some arbitrary area in memory, with a '\0'appended, and the occurrence of the string, in the expression, is replaced by a *pointer* to this area. Thus, for example, if **char_ptr** is declared as

```
char *char_ptr;
```

that is, as a pointer to characters, then the statement

```
char_ptr = "arbitrary message";
```

assigns to **char_ptr** a pointer to the area where the string is stored, *no matter where that may be*.

In a similar manner, it is quite common to initialize an *array* of pointers to characters with pointers to different messages. For example, the definition

```
static char *errmsg[] = {
        "incorrect number of arguments",
        "cannot open file",
        .
        .
        .
        "file capacity exceeded"
        };
```

points each of the elements of array **errmsg** at its corresponding message, no matter where that message happens to be allocated storage. Notice that, in this case, the compiler determines the array size by counting the initializers.

Returning now to the special initialization case

```
char message[] = "string";
```

the compiler, upon recognizing that a *character array* is being defined, does not choose any arbitrary memory area in which to store the string. Instead, it directs the string to the location in storage that has been allocated to this array.

3.7 Structure Declarations

Since an array is a collection of identical objects, we describe its internal composition by specifying their common type and their number. The process is relatively straightforward. On the other hand, the internal composition of a structure, which is also an aggregate of objects, is not as easy to describe, as there is an infinite variety of ways in which the types of its internal components may be intermixed. It is for this reason that the most important step, in defining a structure to C, is declaring its internal composition.

The internal composition of a structure is specified with a *sequence of declarations enclosed in braces*. For example, using the inventory illustration of Section 2.8, either of the constructs

```
{ int id;  char mfgr [50];  short size;  }
```

or

```
{
int id;
char mfgr [50];
short size;
}
```

describes, in detail, one possible internal composition of a structure. (The latter form is preferred because it is more easily read and modified.) Each of these constructs not only orders the members of the structure and specifies a data type for each member (i.e., an integer, followed by a 50-character array, followed by a short integer), but also *names* each member (as **id**, **mfgr**, and **size**, respectively).

Each of these declaration sequences is called a "structure declaration list" or a "parts specification." In general, it is an arbitrary sequence of declarations of *any* data objects—including arrays and other structures. (A structure may not contain an instance of itself, but it may contain a *pointer* to another instance of itself. For our present purposes, however, we will ignore the issue of "self-referential" structures.) In our discussion below, to represent an arbitrary structure declaration list, we will use the notation { **parts** } when we find it convenient.

Since a structure's parts specification may be quite complicated, C provides a mechanism whereby it can be *named*. Once this has been done, the identifier that names a specific structure composition can be used as a shorthand for its parts specification. Such a name is called a structure "tag" or, better, a *template name*. You should bear in mind that such an identifier names a specific structure *composition* or shape. It does *not* name a specific instance of that structure in storage.

A structure template name is defined with a declaration of the form

```
struct name { parts };
```

which connects the identifier **name** with the parts specification given. The keyword **struct** is employed in all structure declarations and definitions. Here, it is used in a declaration that associates a name with a specific structure template.

For example, the declaration

```
struct label {
    int id;
    char mfgr[50];
    short size;
};
```

names the data organization given in the parts specification as **label**. Once this has been done, any subsequent use of the construct

struct label

specifies a *new data type* (i.e., *a structure of a given composition*), in which case it may be used in any context in which any other type keyword, such as **int**, may be used. For example, the subsequent declaration

struct label item;

defines a structure in storage named **item**, which has a specific internal organization. Similarly, the declaration

struct label inventory[500];

defines an array of such structures named **inventory**.

This discussion reconfirms the fact that C requires that the *type* of every *derived* object be fully spelled out, down to one of C's *fundamental* object types, before that derived object's name may be used in an expression.

The fundamental data types (**char**s, **int**s, **float**s, and so on) were described in Section 3.2. As we have seen in several places, all other (derived) types must be "anchored" to one of these basic data types. For example, it is not sufficient for you to say that a certain identifier names a pointer, or a function, or an array, or a structure. C effectively asks: "pointer *to what?*," or "function *returning what?*," or "array *of what?*," or "structure *containing what?*" These hypothetical queries continue until the compiler encounters one of the fundamental data types.

Thus, it is your responsibility to make proper declarations of the objects that your program uses. In particular, a structure is not fully defined until every aspect of its internal composition has been spelled out. This is the reason why the construct **struct template_name** (once **template_name** has been defined) is considered a *type* (like **char**).

Returning to structure declarations, it is possible to combine the declaration of a structure template name with a definition of one or more instances of that structure in storage. This is done by following the declaration for the template with a list of names to be given to separate instances of that structure in storage. For example, the declaration

```
struct label {
    int id;
    char mfgr[50];
    short size;
} item, inventory[500];
```

not only links the name **label** to the parts specification given, but also defines one instance of this structure in storage, named **item**, and another 500 instances of it in storage, collectively known by the array name **inventory**. The identifier **label** is also made available for use in subsequent structure definitions.

Occasionally, if the structure template name is not needed (because it is clear that subsequent structure definitions will not use it), it may be omitted, in which case only one structure declaration of a given type is employed to define one or more instances of that structure in storage. For example, the declaration

```
struct { int id; char mfgr[50]; short size; } item;
```

defines one structure named **item** in storage. Its specific internal organization is *not* recorded for subsequent use.

Note that every structure declaration should include either a template name or one or more storage names, *or both*. A declaration containing *only* a parts specification has no immediately useful purpose.

Observe also that a structure member name may *duplicate* another variable's name without causing an error message from the compiler. The two names are distinct, because they are distinguishable by context. That is, a member name in an expression is always preceded by either the "." operator or the "->" operator.

An external or **static** (i.e., a *permanent*) structure is initialized in the conventional manner—namely, by following its storage name, in its definition, with an equals sign followed by a list of initializers enclosed in braces. (As pointed out earlier, the declaration of an *automatic* structure may not contain an initializer.) Like the initializer for an array (discussed earlier), the format for a structure's initializer has several possible variations.

First, if all of its members are scalars, a list of initial value expressions enclosed in braces is proper. For example, the declaration

```
struct time_of_day {
      short hour;
      short minute;
      short second;
} startup = { 8, 30, 0 };
```

not only defines the structure template **time_of_day** as indicated, but also defines one instance of this structure in storage, named **startup**, and initializes its members with the integer values 8, 30, and 0, respectively.

Second, it is frequently the case that at least one of a structure's members is itself an aggregate. Under these conditions, the inner initializer for that aggregate is itself enclosed in inner braces. Thus, for example, the definition

```
struct appointment
   {
   short week;
   short day;
   struct time_of_day time;
   } meeting = { 2, 4, { 8, 30, 0} };
```

defines a structure composition named **appointment**, as consisting of three members, named **week**, **day**, and **time**, respectively, and defines one instance of that structure in storage, named **meeting**. The members of this structure are initialized with the values indicated.

Since all that was said earlier about array initializers applies also to structure initializers, many other initializer formats are clearly possible. For example, the initializer for an *array* of structures, which is a common data object, has a format similar to that for a two-dimensional array, except that each inner initializer is a structure initializer. Similarly, *several* of the members of a structure may themselves be arrays or structures, in which case the system's initializer would contain several inner brace-enclosed lists, generally having different formats.

Many of the other variations cited earlier for array initializers apply also to structure initializers. For instance, inner braces may be omitted if all of the values in the initializer list are present. Conversely, initial values for certain inner elements may be omitted (e.g., by terminating an inner list prematurely, with a closing brace), in which case they are given zero values, by default.

Problems at the end of this chapter include exercises in initializer construction and interpretation.

3.8 Type-names

In Section 2.17, during the discussion of casts and the **sizeof** operator, the subject of *type-names* was introduced. A general definition of a type-name was postponed, pending completion of the discussion on C declarations. We are now in a better position to define a type-name.

A type-name is essentially a declaration—with its identifier *omitted*. That is, it contains all of the information specifying an object *type*, but it does not name a specific *instance* of that type. For example,

```
float
float *
float * [5]
float * ()
```

respectively name the following types:
   floating-point number
   pointer to a floating-point number
   array of five pointers to **float**s
   function returning a pointer to a **float**

Given this more general definition of a type-name, we are in a position to better understand the conditions under which the constructs

(type-name) expression

and

sizeof (type-name)

are used.

The first form is employed when it is desired to reinterpret (possibly via a data conversion) the value of an expression—from another point of view. For example, if **ptr_expr** is an arbitrary pointer expression, then the cast

(int (*) [3]) ptr_expr

casts **ptr_expr** into the type "pointer to an array of three integers." (The parentheses around the "*" operator are necessary to distinguish the type from an "array of three pointers to integers.") Notice that a cast of a pointer in no way changes the *value* of the pointer. It merely causes the compiler to treat this value from a new point of view. For example, if such a value were *incremented*, the scaling of the increment would, in general, be affected.

Similarly, the second form permits the compile-time computation of the size (in bytes) of any *derived* data type. For example,

sizeof (struct label)

where **label** is a structure template name, is automatically replaced (at compile time) by the size (in bytes) of such a structure, no matter how complex its composition.

We will encounter specific uses of these constructions later.

Problems

Problems 3.1 through 3.12 involve those variables and functions that were employed in Problems 2.17 through 2.100. These objects were described in detail in the "Introduction to Remaining Problems" section at the end of Chapter 2. Recall the tables of initial values that were provided there. Recall also that, for convenience, all variables were assumed to be *global* in nature and that all character arrays did *not* terminate in the '\0' character, as is normally the case. You are now in a position to declare and initialize these variables and functions.

3.1 Declare and initialize variables **c1, c2, c3, i1, i2, i3, f1, f2,** and **f3**.

3.2 Declare and initialize structures **s1, s2,** and **s3**. Start with a declaration of their *template*, naming it **mixed**. (Recall that a character string initializer of the form "ABC" should *not* appear in your solution because, for simplicity, terminating null characters were not employed in Problems 2.17–2.100.)

3.3 Declare and initialize pointers **pc1, pc2, pc3, pi1, pi2, pi3, pf1, pf2, pf3, ps1, ps2,** and **ps3**.

3.4 Declare and initialize arrays **ac, ai, af,** and **as**. Try a variation on each structure initializer in which the pair of braces surrounding its internal character array initializer is omitted.

3.5 Declare and initialize arrays **apc, api, apf,** and **aps**.

3.6–3.12 Define functions **Fc, Fi, Ff, Fpc, Fpi, Fpf,** and **Fps**. In each case, provide a comment describing the function's operation. Name the function's formal parameter **z** (or **z** and **y**, when two are employed) and represent the *body* of the function using the notation:

```
{
    .
    .
    .
}
```

While you might leave it up to the compiler to make certain implicit type conversions (as described earlier in this chapter), it is recommended that, in the interest of clarity, you explicitly specify the *actual* data types that will be passed or returned.

3.13 Write as much as you can of the detailed structure of a program having one global integer variable **i** and two functions **fcn1** and **fcn2**, each of which accepts no arguments and returns either an integer value or no value at all. The program executes by first calling **fcn1** and by then calling **fcn2**. (Use the {. . .} notation to represent the body of each function.)

3.14 Modify your answer to Problem 3.13 to give **fcn1** a local integer variable **j** and **fcn2** a local integer variable **k**.

3.15 How should your answer to Problem 3.14 be modified if each of the functions **fcn1** and **fcn2** is designed to return not an integer but a pointer to characters instead?

3.16 The **printf** library function will be explained in detail later in this book. Accepting on faith, for the moment, that the C statement

$$\textbf{printf ("\%d\textbackslash n", j) ;}$$

prints the value of **j** (in decimal form) and then starts a new line, what does the following program print?

```
main(){
    int j = 1;
    {
        int j = 2;
        {
            int j = 3;
            printf("%d\n",j);
        }
        printf("%d\n",j);
    }
    printf("%d\n",j);
}
```

3.17 A program consists of the contents of the three source files given below. For each line in the program, specify the names of all of the variables that are *visible* at that point.

```
file 1:
   int a;
   static float b;
   main(){
        short c;
        .
        .
        .
   }
   funct(d)
        int d;
        {
        short e;
        .
        .
        }
```

```
file 2:
   subr(f)
        float f;
        {
        extern float b;
        .
        .
        }
```

```
file 3:
   float b;
   {
   int g;
        .
        .
        .
   }
```

3.18 Assuming that the processor for which your C compiler generates code contains several internal registers, including a Program Counter (PC) and a Stack Pointer (SP), and that it executes conventional CALL and RETURN instructions, compose and describe in detail a protocol for your machine's *stack contents* during the time period when the expression

$$\texttt{funct\_name(arg1, arg2, arg3)}$$

is being evaluated. Briefly explain any special assumptions that you make.

3.19 Construct a matrix having its columns labeled with the following five storage classes for variables: **automatic**, **external**, **static external**, **static internal**, and **register**. Label the rows of the matrix with the following seven properties:

1. Retains its value while program leaves its block
2. Visible to all subsequent functions in its source file
3. Available to other source files
4. Zero default value when not initialized
5. Initialized once, at compile time
6. Aggregate declarations may include initializers
7. May be stored in processor registers

At each matrix intersection, place an "X" if a variable having the storage class labeling its column has the property labeling its row.

3.20 Give three examples of declarations that are not definitions.

3.21 Given the declaration

$$\text{char string[]} = \text{""};$$

to what does **string** point?

3.22 Declare **lptr** as a pointer to long integers, **a_ptrs** as an array of pointers, each pointing to a *pointer* to a **float**, and **pch** as a character pointer initialized to point to the character string "xxyy".

3.23 Combine in one statement a declaration of an array of ten **floats** named **vector** and a pointer to a **float**, named **fptr** initialized to point to the beginning of the just-declared **vector** array.

3.24 Given the declaration

$$\text{int *abc(), (*def)[], (*ghi[])();}$$

write a phrase describing the type of object named by each of the identifiers **abc**, **def**, and **ghi**.

3.25 What is the difference, if any, between the following two external declarations?

$$\text{int matrix[3][3]} = \{\{1\}, \{2,3\}, \{4\}\};$$

$$\text{int matrix[3][3]} = \{1, 0, 0, 2, 3, 0, 4, 0, 0\};$$

3.26 Write the declaration of a structure template, named **node**, having the following composition: a five- character array named **name**, an integer named **degree**, a floating-point number named **weight**, and a pointer, named **next**, to another similar structure.

Write the definition of one such structure in storage, named **firstnode**, and initialize its respective members with the values: "root", 2, 3.7E4 and with a pointer to another similar structure in storage named **othernode**.

3.27 Making the same assumptions as described in Problem 3.16, for each call on the following function, what is printed?

```
funct(){
  static int j;
  j++;
  printf("%d\n",j);
}
```

3.28 Write the declaration of an integer named **length** that is initialized to the length of a previously defined character array named **a_chars**.

3.29 A function **calloc** is designed to be passed two parameters: **n**, the number of objects in a set of identical objects, and **l**, the length of one of these objects. It returns a character pointer to the origin of sufficient memory space to house all of these objects. Write a statement that calls **calloc** in order to point an integer pointer **ip** at the base of an area of **n** integers. Precede this statement with any necessary declarations.

3.30 Given the declaration

```
struct {
  char *word;
  int count;
  float number;
} name;
```

and assuming that your C compiler generates code for a typical 16-bit microprocessor, estimate the value of the expression

sizeof (name)

State any assumptions that you make in deriving this value.

3.31 Given the global declaration

```
char array[] = "123456789", *ptr = "123456789";
```

what are the values of the following expressions: **sizeof ptr**, **sizeof "123456789"**, **sizeof *ptr**, **sizeof array**, and **sizeof *array**?

CHAPTER 4 THE C PREPROCESSOR

4.1 Introduction

A typical C compilation begins with a preliminary step during which a program within the compiler, known as the *preprocessor*, makes a pass over the entire set of source files. During this pass, the preprocessor *modifies* the source program's text, at appropriate points, to make it ready for compilation. These modifications principally consist of source text *insertions*. We will study here the rules by which the preprocessor operates.

A typical assembly language program consists of statements and assembler *directives*. The directives (e.g., the EQUates and the INCLUDEs) advise the assembler. They control how the assembly process will take place. In a similar manner, the C preprocessor obeys certain directives. It recognizes a directive using a very simple rule: Any source line that begins with a **#** character must be a preprocessor directive— also called a "control" line. The purpose of this line is *not* to communicate with the compiler directly, but to communicate instead with the preprocessor.

The rules that the C preprocessor obeys are virtually *independent* of the C language. That is, the same preprocessor could have been employed to execute the same preliminary pass over a program written in some *other* language. It is important to recognize, at the outset, that the preprocessor has little, if any, understanding of C.

The C preprocessor has three basic functions: text replacement, source file inclusion, and control over conditional compilation. We will study these in order in the following three sections.

4.2 Text Replacement

The repertoire of command words that are recognized by the C preprocessor (those that may follow the leading **#** in a control line) is quite small. The most common command word is the verb **define**. A control line of the form

#define *identifier arbitrary-text*

instructs the preprocessor to replace all subsequent occurrences of the named identifier with the arbitrary text that is specified in the control line. The effect of such a control line lasts from the point at which it appears until the end of the source file in which it was encountered. For example, the control line

#define BLOCK_SIZE 512

will cause all subsequent occurrences of the identifier **BLOCK_SIZE** to be replaced by the integer constant **512**. Notice that it is common C practice to employ *uppercase* letters in the identifier named in a **#define** directive—so that it will be easily distinguished from those identifiers assigned to other C objects. Similarly, the control lines

#define AND &&

and

#define OR ||

might be employed to permit more readable relational expressions.

Notice that a typical **#define** control line does *not* end in a semicolon. This is true of *all* preprocessor directives. Were a semicolon to appear at the end of a **#define** control line, it would be taken to be part of the verbatim replacement string, in which case it might later be detected by the compiler as an error at the point of replacement.

Observe also that the first example given above is the most common means by which a specific numeric constant normally appears in a program. A good programmer usually represents each numeric value with an appropriate special *symbol*, like **BLOCK_SIZE** above. This practice not only makes the program more readable, but also makes it more *maintainable*. If any numeric value later requires modification, the program needs to be changed in only *one* place. Most programmers have been made aware (sometimes painfully) of the fact that even the most "unchangeable" numeric value has a way of later requiring some modification. In this regard, notice that a control line of the form

$$\texttt{\#define PI 3.1415926}$$

is quite convenient, even though its numeric value is a known universal constant. (It *too* might require later revision—e.g., if more significant digits have to be added to the fractional part of the constant to improve the accuracy of results calculated by the program.)

Every **#define** directive is also called a *macro*, following terminology long used by assembly language programmers. The macro facility of an assembler permits a packet of assembly language statements to be given a special name. Once this has been done, any later appearance of this name is replaced, *in-line*, by the sequence of instructions (i.e., the *text*) that it represents. Thus, for example

$$\texttt{\#define NAME } st1; \ st2; \ st3; \ st4;$$

could be employed to represent a sequence of four arbitrary statements (named, for convenience, *st1* through *st4* above) with the single identifier **NAME**.

In summary, the simple macro facility described here is employed, first, for convenience—to permit each occurrence of a complex expression to be represented by a simple global symbol; second, for readability—to permit a cryptic or cumbersome construction to be represented by a more descriptive name; and third, for maintainability—to permit all occurrences of a specific value to be globally changed by a change in only one place, i.e., in the macro definition itself. For example, if the construct `printf("%d\n",j);` (recall its use in Problems 3.16 and 3.27) appeared sufficiently often in a program, then a macro definition of the form

$$\texttt{\#define PRINTJ printf("\%d\textbackslash n",j);}$$

might be convenient and might also provide for more readable code. Similarly, if a program made frequent reference to a file named `"document.txt"`, then a macro definition of the form

$$\texttt{\#define FILE\_NAME "document.txt"}$$

would permit easy modification of the program when the referenced file was later renamed.

Several other observations regarding the use of simple macros are appropriate at this point. First, there are certain contexts in which the appearance of a macro name will *not* be replaced by the text in the definition. Specifically, if the name is found inside a string or character constant or inside a longer identifier, then it will not be replaced. Thus, the definition

$$\textbf{\#define XYZ abcde}$$

will *not* cause the occurrence of **XYZ** either in **"UVW XYZ PQ"** or in **OBJ_XYZ** to be replaced.

Second, once a replacement has been made, the preprocessor scans the *replacement* text to see if it contains any replaceable portions. For example, given the two definitions

$$\textbf{\#define D   a + B}$$
$$\textbf{\#define B   c}$$

then the later construct

$$\textbf{x = D;}$$

will be replaced by

$$\textbf{x = a + c;}$$

Notice that a circular definition like

$$\textbf{\#define A   B}$$

followed by

$$\textbf{\#define B   A}$$

either may be detected by the preprocessor as an error or may cause the preprocessor to enter an infinite text substitution loop when the first replaceable **A** or **B** is later encountered.

Third, it is common for a macro definition to be followed by a comment explaining the significance of the parameter being defined. For example,

```
#define MAX_LEN 14 /* Maximum file name length */
```

While the comment could be considered as part of the replacement text (since the compiler will subsequently ignore it), the preprocessor is normally designed to recognize the comment and to omit it from the replacement string.

Fourth, if the text replacement string of a macro definition is sufficiently lengthy, it may be continued on the next line by terminating the previous line with a \ character. (The trailing \ and the following newline character, in the source file at that point, are both ignored by the preprocessor.)

Fifth, a macro definition may be *superseded* by a *new* definition for the same identifier. The latest definition is always the one currently in force.

Finally, another preprocessor command, having the form

#undef *identifier*

is designed to cause the preprocessor to "forget" the macro definition associated with the named identifier. (Typically, if the definition being forgotten is a replacement for a *previous* definition, then the previous definition is restored.)

All of the examples discussed above involve simple text replacement, in which the appearance of a macro's name (which is also known as a macro *call* or a macro "reference") is replaced by the text in that macro's definition. The macro call does not *modify* the text that is employed in the replacement process. The text in the macro definition is copied *verbatim*.

Macros *having arguments* are also processed by the C preprocessor. They provide a mechanism by which the replacement text depends on the way in which the macro is called.

A macro is recognized as one that has arguments if its name, in its definition, is *immediately followed* by a left parenthesis, followed by a list of one or more argument names, separated by commas and terminated in a right parenthesis. There must be no space between the macro name and the succeeding left parenthesis that begins the argument list. If a space is present, the argument list will be instead interpreted as part of the replacement text string to be copied verbatim. Thus, the definition of a macro that employs arguments has the form

#define *identifier(arg_name,...,arg_name) arbitrary-text*

The arbitrary text field in such a definition normally includes at least one occurrence of each argument name. A *call* of such a macro has the form

identifier(arg-replacement-text,...,arg-replacement-text)

In this case, during the text replacement process (which is also called macro "expansion"), the arbitrary text field in the definition first replaces the call. Then each occurrence of an argument name in this text field is in turn replaced by its corresponding *arg-replacement-text* field in the call. For example, given the macro definition

#define MAX(a,b) ((a) > (b) ? (a) : (b))

a macro call having the form

MAX *(expr1, expr2)* ;

will be converted, *in-line*, by the C preprocessor into

((expr1) > (expr2) ? (expr1) : (expr2)) ;

where *expr1* and *expr2* represent arbitrary expressions.

The use of explicit parenthesis pairs in macro definitions (as demonstrated in the above example) is very important. Without them, it is not guaranteed that arguments that are arbitrary expressions will be evaluated *before* their values are used in the evaluation of the entire macro expansion. For example, if all of the parentheses in the definition of **MAX**, above, were *omitted*, the macro call

MAX(k & 1, m | n)

would expand into

k & 1 > m | n ? k & 1 : m | n

in which case the expression to the left of the **?** would not be evaluated properly.

We are now in a position to appreciate why the sample expression given in Section 1.3 included parentheses around all occurrences of the identifier **p**. This expression happened to be extracted as the text replacement portion of the macro definition of a function known as **getc** (which will be discussed further later). To present the entire macro definition, the expression given in Section 1.3 should be preceded by the text

#define getc(p)

in which case we see that **p** is a macro argument, which may take on any form in a *call* to **getc**.

The discussion above implies an important new application of a macro— particularly since arguments may be employed in macro calls. While we began by explaining that a **#define** control line is a convenient means to define symbolic constants and to represent often-used constructs that might be lengthy or complicated, we now find that a macro may be used *as an alternative to a function*. For example, rather than have a *function* named **MAX**, which takes two arguments and returns the value of the larger, we can employ instead a macro to accomplish the same result. Notice that we cannot distinguish between macro and function implementations by looking at the *call*. Both calls have the same format. The implementation differences are significant, however, and we are led naturally to a discussion of the trade-offs between macros and subroutines—a topic that is well known to assembly language programmers.

The trade-off that is most often discussed compares the memory consumed by repeated insertions of in-line code, using the macro approach, with the execution speed gained by avoiding the complex CALL and RETURN protocols that are normally associated with function usage. (Recall a discussion of the latter issue in Problem 3.18.) Generally, if the macro implementation is sufficiently simple (as it is in the **MAX** case, above), it is the preferred alternative, because there is a certain base amount of code normally generated even to link to a function that *does nothing*. Thus, the assembly language programmer prefers the macro implementation for very short code sections, or to attain the fastest execution speed, or when the number of calls made is limited. Conversely, the function implementation is preferred when the operation called for becomes complicated (requiring a significant amount of memory space), or when the number of calls made becomes significant. This issue is not quite so simple in C, however, for the following reasons:

Since macro expansions involve only text substitutions (in which any portion of a substituted string may itself be replaced), they are generally much more prone to errors. For example, the types of the arguments that are employed in a macro definition are never checked for consistency. While there are occasions when this may be considered an advantage, because it yields a "type-independent" function (e.g., the **MAX** macro, above, works properly for a pair of **int**s as well as for a pair of **float**s), the possibility of erroneous calls is usually increased. Care must be taken to ensure that macro definitions are properly specified. Specifically, as pointed out earlier, it is important to properly parenthesize all macro arguments as well as the entire macro bodies that enclose them. It is also important to avoid macro bodies that contain obscure or inconsistent side effects and, particularly, to avoid macro *calls* that involve side effects. While some of these precautions apply equally to functions, they are especially important in dealing with macros.

In program development, it is generally advisable to avoid macro implementations of functions initially, and then to introduce them later, during program refinement, to achieve their speed advantages.

When we discuss the functions that are available from the standard I/O library, we will specifically identify those "functions" that are in fact implemented via macros.

Having been introduced to the topic of macros, we are in a better position to appreciate the statement, made in Section 2.19, that, while white space characters are generally ignored, there are a few places where they are mandatory and others where they are forbidden. Specifically, in a macro definition having arguments, no white space may appear between the name of the macro and the (character that begins its argument list. Conversely, if the macro has no arguments, some white space *must* separate the macro name from the beginning of its substitution text field.

4.3 Source File Inclusion and File Search Paths

The second most common command word in the C preprocessor repertoire is the verb **include**. A directive having either of the following forms:

#include *"filename"*

or

#include <*filename*>

directs the preprocessor to insert into the source text stream, at this point, the contents of the named source file. The inserted text is treated as if it were an integral part of the file that called for it.

Each possible format for a **#include** control line specifies a different means by which the preprocessor should *search for* the named file. The most common interpretations for these formats will be given later in this discussion.

The **#include** directive facilitates the partitioning of a program (particularly a sizable one) into logical subdivisions, each residing in a separate file. For example, a typical C program begins with a set of **#define** directives and global data declarations. A preferred practice, particularly for a large program, is to place all such directives and **extern** data declarations in one or more *separate* files. Then, any source file that *uses* this common set of statements can begin with one or two appropriate **#include** control lines. Such a practice ensures that all source files that depend on a common set of ground rules will be properly anchored, even when the ground rules change. Notice, of course, that whenever any one of the common **#include** files is modified, every program that relies on it must be recompiled.

A necessary practice in a typical C programming environment is to terminate every C source file name with a ".c" extension (e.g., **prog_name.c**). However, if the source file is a so-called "header" file (i.e., one designed to be **#include**d in other source files, as explained above), then it is normally given a ".h" extension. (Recall the allusion to the file named **stdio.h** in Section 1.3.)

#includes may be *nested*. That is, an included file may itself contain **#include** statements. Typically, the preprocessor limits the nesting depth to some reasonable level (like four, for example).

Source files containing common macros and functions are often named in **#include** directives. One can make a strong case for a separate source file containing universal macros, since every macro definition must be available at compile time. (Recall that each macro call causes an in-line change in the source code being compiled.) Thus, for example, every C programming environment provides a common header file, called **stdio.h**, that contains not only those **#define** directives that are assumed by the "standard I/O library" (explained further later), but also some I/O-oriented macros, like **getc** (mentioned in the previous section). In a similar manner, a typical C environment also provides another header file, named **ctype.h**, that contains a set of universal, character-testing macros. Each one takes a character argument and returns a truth value concerning a specific property of that character. For example, the macro **isdigit** returns *true* if the character argument that it is passed is a digit. Otherwise, it returns *false*. (Similar macros are discussed further in problems at the end of this chapter.)

It is often convenient, during program development, to partition a program into separate source files, each containing the code for one or more functions. It is not usually necessary, however, to **#include** any one of these files in any other, because the compilation process normally permits the user to specify a *sequence* of source files that comprise the program to be compiled. While you might prefer to **#include** all subordinate source files into one "parent" file, for convenience, you must remember that such a practice may have some distinct disadvantages. For example, consider how the scope of a **static** external variable changes if its file is **#include**d in another file.

The case for a separate **#include** file containing the source code for one or more universal functions is less persuasive than is the case for a file containing universal macro definitions (discussed earlier). It is preferable—if the programming environment permits it (as most do)—to *compile* the universal function file and to store its *object* code in an object *library*, which is later searched during the *linking* process. This returns us to the file search question, postponed earlier, which we consider now, while we introduce the related issue of object file linkage.

It is claimed that the "native" C language is very simple because it omits many of the operations (e.g., I/O functions) that are integral parts of other high-level languages. Rather, C assumes a mechanism in which those functions not provided in the native language are made available via a *library* of standard functions. In fact, no C programming environment is considered complete without such a library.

This library not only contains certain source files (like the ".h" files mentioned earlier), but also contains, primarily, the *object* modules for many "uni-

versal" functions (e.g., **printf**, mentioned briefly in Problems 3.16 and 3.27).
Many of these functions are explained further later in this book.

During the compilation of a source file, all references to external names
not defined in that file (i.e., all *unresolved* references) are recorded. Many of
these references are calls to functions residing elsewhere. Some may be functions
defined by the programmer in separately compiled source files. Some may be
standard functions, available from the standard library. Before a run can take
place, all of these references must be resolved by adding, to the object module
just compiled, all of the referenced object modules and by appropriately adjusting
addresses in all of the components of the composite package so that proper
linkage is established between them. This step is accomplished by a *linker*
program. In some environments, the linkage process is an implicit part of the
compile process. In most environments, linkage is a separate step, invoked after
the compilation has completed successfully. How does the linker *find* a referenced
object module?

Typically, in the absence of explicit information supplied by the programmer, the linker first searches for a referenced module by examining those files
previously defined *by the programmer*. If this search fails, the linker proceeds
to search the library. Both of these searches are system dependent. In a large,
multitasking environment (e.g., under the UNIX operating system), the linker
might first search all files in the user's current directory. In a personal computing
environment, on the other hand, the linker might first search all user files residing
on the disk that contains the just-compiled source program.

The library searching sequence is also system dependent. Typically, the
library is divided into several files, possibly on separate disks or in different
directories.

The programmer may provide explicit information to the linker, to control
the file search process. For example, the programmer may ask that the linker
skip the initial search of all user files. Alternatively, the programmer may provide
a specific *name* of the library file to be searched first.

This brings us back to the **#include** examples at the beginning of this
discussion. The path that the *preprocessor* employs to find the named source
file is also system dependent. Typically, if the file name in the directive is
surrounded by *double quotes* (as in the first example), the search begins in the
user's file space. If the file name is surrounded by *angle brackets* (as in the
second example), the user's file space is ignored, and the system library is
searched for the named file.

4.4 Conditional Compilation

Of all of the preprocessor control statements normally encountered in C
programs, the vast majority are either **#define** or **#include** directives.

However, the C preprocessor also recognizes a small group of command words that together provide a *conditional compilation* facility. Such a facility gives the programmer a means to insert in a program *conditions* that determine *whether or not* specific portions of that program will be compiled. If a section of code is *not* compiled, it is *ignored* by the compiler (i.e., it is treated as if it were a sequence of comments). There are three questions that must be answered to explain such a facility: First, how are conditionally compiled code portions identified? That is, how are they delimited or circumscribed? Second, what are the possible conditions that determine whether or not they are compiled? And third, how is such a facility employed in program development?

Every conditionally compiled code portion begins with one of three possible **#if** directives and ends with a **#endif** directive. It may also include an optional **#else** directive, positioned anywhere between the **#if** and the **#endif**.

The **#if** is the directive that specifies the condition to be tested. If that condition is found true (it is tested by the preprocessor at compile time, of course), then the code portion between the **#if** and the succeeding **#endif** (only up to the intervening **#else**, if one exists) is compiled. If the condition is found *not* true, then that code portion is *not* compiled.

If a **#else** directive exists, then the code portion between it and the succeeding **#endif** is compiled only if the specified condition is found *not* true.

The three possible command words in a **#if** directive are **if**, **ifdef**, and **ifndef**. Let us temporarily use the notation **#if_directive** to represent any one of these three possible variations, followed by the condition that is specified as the one to be tested (explained further below). With this notation, we may represent any arbitrary conditionally compiled code portion as follows:

```
#if_directive
    .
    .
    .
"A"CODE
PORTION
    .
    .
    .
#else /* NOTE: This directive is optional. */
    .
    .
    .
"B"CODE
PORTION
    .
    .
    .
#endif
```

Reiterating the rules: If the **#else** is present, and if the condition specified in the **#if_directive** is found true, then the "A" code portion is compiled and the "B" code portion is ignored. If that condition is found false, "B" is compiled, while "A" is ignored. If the **#else** is not present, compilation of the combined "A" and "B" code segment takes place only if the specified condition is found true.

These control directives may be *nested*. That is, a conditionally compiled code section may itself contain internal **#if**, **#else**, and **#endif** directives— all following the rules outlined above. In such a situation, an outer condition must *permit* a code section to be compiled, before any of its inner conditions are even tested.

The three permissible forms for a **#if** directive are

#if *constant-expression*

#ifdef *identifier*

and

#ifndef *identifier*

The last two forms operate by determining whether or not the named identifier is presently defined (i.e., whether or not it has been the subject of a previous **#define** directive that has not been canceled by a subsequent **#undef** directive). If the named identifier *is* defined, then the **#ifdef** condition is considered true, while the **#ifndef** condition is considered false (vice versa, of course, if the named identifier is found *not* defined).

The first of the three forms above causes the specified constant expression to be evaluated. Any nonzero value is interpreted as true, while a zero value is considered as false. (Note the restriction to a *constant* expression, as originally defined at the end of Section 2.3.)

We are left with the question of the conditions under which such a conditional compilation facility might be employed. To explain what is, perhaps, its most common application, let us consider a situation in which a single program is to be designed so that it can be easily *tailored* to two or more possible applications. That is, it is to be designed to have two or more possible versions, or variations, or "personalities." The conditional compilation facility is ideally suited for use in such a situation because it is designed to *choose* specific code sections based on as little as one special parameter (such as a version "descriptor"), specified at the very beginning of the program.

For example, suppose a program is to be designed to communicate with any one of several possible terminal devices. The differences between the behavioral characteristics of these devices may be significant and may affect how the program is designed. While it is possible to **#include** one of several small source files, each having statements tailored to a single terminal device, it is also possible to include *all* of these tailored code sections in a single source file and then to choose only *one* of them by using the conditional compilation facility, controlled—in this case—by a single parameter given at the beginning of the program. Thus, for instance, a single header statement such as

#define VT100 version

will activate all those conditional code sections beginning with the directive

#ifdef VT100

and will deactivate all sections beginning with **#ifdef**'s having other terminal identification codes. Notice that, in this special case, the string "version", in the **#define** header, is not actually used.

The conditional compilation facility also permits a program to include a large number of code sections specifically designed to be employed only during the testing and debugging phase. When a "production" version of the program is to be compiled, the testing portions may be deactivated with a *single* special header control statement. This will have the effect of causing all testing portions of the code to be ignored. (They may be *re*activated later, however, if subsequent modifications to the program require further testing and debugging.)

Notice that such a mechanism is preferable to the alternative—used by some programmers—in which each testing code section is isolated manually, and then "commented out." As you will recall from the discussion in Section 2.19, a portion of code may be "commented out" by the insertion of a leading /* and a trailing */. Recall, however, that this process is not, *in general*, possible in C, because C is defined such that *comments may not be nested*. This means that the only section of code that may be "commented out" is one that does not *itself* contain comments. Observe also that, even if this were not the case, the conditional compilation approach is a much more elegant means to accomplish the same results.

In this regard, we should point out that a common means to cause a section of code to be ignored is to bracket that section with the directives **#if 0** and **#endif**.

Problems

4.1 A program begins with the directive

#define CONSTANT 35;

and with the global declaration

$$int\ x,y;$$

Briefly explain how the compiler would subsequently react to each of the following statements (each is contained within some function's definition):

$$x\ =\ y\ +\ CONSTANT;$$

and $$x\ =\ CONSTANT\ +\ y;$$

4.2 The ASCII character whose reception rings the bell on a terminal has a value of 7 (octal or decimal). It is desired to represent any occurrence of this character in a program with the symbol **BELL**. Show how this should be done.

4.3 It is desired to use the identifier **void** to represent a "dummy type"—namely, the type returned by a function that returns *no* value at all. Such a practice will help the programmer to distinguish between definitions of functions that actually return values and definitions of functions that return no values. Each of the latter would begin with a header declaration of the form

$$void\ function\_name\,(argument\_names)$$

Briefly explain how this objective may be accomplished.

4.4 As pointed out in Section 4.3, the standard C library provides a macro **isdigit**, which receives a single character argument and returns *true* if that argument is a numeric digit. Otherwise, it returns *false*. Write a definition for this macro.

4.5 The standard C library similarly provides a macro **isupper**, which receives a character argument and returns *true* if that character is an uppercase letter. Otherwise, it returns false. Write a definition for this macro.

4.6 Assuming the existence of the macro **isupper** (above), write the definition of another standard C library macro, called **tolower**, that receives a character argument and either returns its *lowercase* equivalent, if the input character is an uppercase letter, or returns the input character value *unchanged*, if it is *not* an uppercase letter.

4.7 Assuming the definition of the macro **MAX**, given in Section 4.2, what are the effects of the call **MAX(p++, q)**, assuming that **p** and **q** are integers having values, *before* the call, of 5 and 3, respectively?

4.8 Some of the standard C library functions (explained further later) return *noninteger* values. Suppose a program consists of a set of separately compiled source modules, each of which may call one or more of a specified subset of these functions. Briefly explain an efficient mechanism to ensure that each of these functions is properly *declared* in every source file that calls it.

4.9 A function in a source module is given the storage class **static** to make it callable only within that module. Is this privacy maintained when the module is **#included** within another source file? Briefly explain why.

4.10 A C compiler is delivered accompanied by a single *source* file, named **basicio.c**, that contains a subset of the standard I/O library of functions. The manual for the compiler directs the user to begin every source program that uses one or more of these functions with the directive

#include "basicio.c"

Briefly explain the disadvantages of this approach. What is a better approach?

4.11 A program is available in two versions. The first is a *portable* version, in which all of the I/O functions that it calls reside in the standard I/O library. The second is a nonportable, but much *faster*, version, in which five of the most critical I/O functions (for simplicity, let us assume that their standard I/O library names are **fcn1** through **fcn5**) have been rewritten to directly access the most-used I/O devices in the fastest way possible. (Assume the new functions have the names **newfcn1** through **newfcn5**.) Explain a mechanism that will permit the source file for this program to be easily converted, in either direction, between version 1 and version 2.

4.12 A program is available in two versions. The first is a "basic" version, which is faster and requires less memory space than the second, which is an "extended" version, in which many of the internal functions have been given added facilities. For example, the basic version of every arithmetic computation does little error checking or data analysis, while its extended version includes a more comprehensive packet of code for these purposes. Thus, the extended version of each function contains additional code sections that may be omitted in the basic version. Explain a mechanism to permit easy conversion from the basic version to the extended version, and vice versa.

4.13 A program begins with the following sequence of statements:

```
#define  REC_LEN        256
#define  NAME_FIELD     30
#define  ADDR_FIELD     50
#define  ID_FIELD       NAME_FIELD + ADDR_FIELD
int data_length = REC_LEN - ID_FIELD;
```

What is the initial value of the variable **data_length**?

CHAPTER 5   FLOW OF CONTROL

5.1 Introduction

It was pointed out in Section 3.2 that, except for one or two exceptions, the keywords of C are broadly divided into three categories: those that identify data types—namely, **int**, **char**, **float**, **double**, **long**, **short**, **unsigned**, and **struct** (all of which we have studied) plus **union** (which we cover in the next chapter); those that identify storage classes—namely, **auto**, **extern**, **static**, and **register** (all of which we have studied) plus **typedef** (which we cover in the next chapter); and those that deal with control flow, which we cover here.

We have already discussed what is perhaps the most fundamental means by which flow of control is altered in a program—namely, through use of the *function call*. However, we have not yet studied how a programmer specifies the value that a function should *return* to its caller.

We have also learned that the most fundamental C statement is an *expression followed by a semicolon*, whose execution consists of the *evaluation* of the expression; that a special case of this is the *null* statement—consisting of an isolated semicolon; and that a *compound statement* or *block*, which is *syntact-*

107

ically equivalent to a single statement, consists of a sequence of zero or more statements all enclosed in a pair of braces { and } (possibly beginning with declarations of local variables).

Each of the other possible C statements is one whose execution may alter the flow of control in a program. These statements employ keywords such as **return, if, else, while, do, for, switch, case, default, break, continue,** and **goto**—many of which are probably already familiar to you. In the succeeding sections, you will be introduced to each of these statements. Once you have completed this study, you will have learned virtually all of the aspects of the "native" C language, and will be able to consider programs of arbitrary complexity—provided that *I/O* mechanisms are temporarily ignored. The I/O issue is covered in Chapter 7, where we study aspects of the standard C library of functions.

5.2 The **return** Statement

A **return** statement consists of the keyword **return**, optionally followed by an expression, and terminated in a semicolon. If the expression is missing, namely, if the statement is merely

$$\textbf{return};$$

then control passes back to the caller with no value returned. (Recall that the brace that closes the body of a function definition is an *implicit* return of this type.) If an expression is present, namely, if the statement has the form

$$\textbf{return } \textit{expression};$$

then the value of the expression is returned to the caller.

A function definition may contain an arbitrary number of **return** statements (including none). Control passes back to the caller when any one of them is executed. If a value is returned by one of them, we would expect all of the others to similarly return appropriate values. However, the compiler does not check that all of the **return** statements inside a function definition are compatible. It is possible—although, clearly, not recommended—that one **return** will return a value while another will not. For that matter, even if only *one* **return** of a value existed, the problem of guaranteeing that there are no conditions under which control will fall through to the function body's closing brace, during execution, is, in general, nontrivial.

It is common for a function body to consist *only* of a **return** statement.

For example, as an alternative to the macro realization described in Chapter 4, we may write

```
double max(a,b)
double a,b;
{
return (a > b ? a : b);
}
```

Notice that the value returned by a function may be automatically converted into another form, *before* the return is actually executed, if the *returned type*, as declared in the header declaration of the function's definition, *disagrees* with the type of the value of the expression in the **return** statement. Such an implicit *cast* is rarely intentional.

5.3 if and if—else Statements

Almost all of the statements that affect the flow of control in a C program have the following common property: what is executed depends on the evaluation of a condition presented in the form of an arbitrary *expression*. In all of these cases except one (the **for** statement is a minor exception), the expression whose evaluation is the decision-making condition is *enclosed in parentheses*. That is, the syntax for the statement includes the construct (*expression*). When the condition is a *true–false* condition, it is considered as true if the expression evaluates to any *nonzero* value, and false only when the expression evaluates to *zero*. The **if** and the **if—else** statements are our first examples.

The **if** statement has the form

if (*expression*) *statement*

You should interpret every occurrence of the syntactic element called "*statement*" as *any* acceptable form for a C statement—including any of those constructs that we already know about (e.g., expressions followed by semicolons, isolated semicolons, compound statements, **return** statements) *plus* any other permissible forms that we will learn about as we proceed in this chapter. In particular, the *statement* above could itself be another **if** statement, or an **if—else** statement, or a brace-enclosed sequence of statements, some of which are themselves **if** statements, and so on.

The **if** statement above executes as follows: If the condition is true, the specified statement is executed. Otherwise, the statement is skipped. For example, the statement

$$if \ (a \ >= \ b) \ n \ += \ CONST;$$

executes as follows: **n** is incremented by the value **CONST** only if **a** is found to be greater than or equal to **b**. (In all of the examples to follow, an uppercase identifier will be taken to represent a value specified in a previous **#define** directive.) Notice that, while the expression that is the condition is usually a relation of some kind, it is not constrained to be of that form. For instance,

$$if \ (*ptr++) \ n++;$$

executes by incrementing **n** only if the object pointed to by **ptr** has a nonzero value. The evaluation of the condition, which is an arbitrary expression, may involve side effects (illustrated above by the advance of the pointer after it is used), function calls, or any other permissible operations. Thus,

$$if \ (get\_record() \ != \ NONE\_LEFT) \ process\_record();$$

executes by calling a function **get_record**, which presumably gets a record (if one is available) and returns a value indicating whether or not one was found. If a record was found, it is processed by the function **process_record**. Otherwise, the record processing step is skipped. This example naturally leads us to consider the **if–else** construct, because it is typical, in such a situation, to specify *two* alternative processing paths—one to take if the specified condition is found true, and the other to take if it is found false.

The **if–else** statement has the form

$$if \ (expression) \ statement1 \ else \ statement2$$

As you might expect, if the value of the expression is found true, *statement1* is executed. Otherwise, *statement2* is executed. For example, in

```
if (get_record() != NONE_LEFT) process_record();
else new_file();
```

the function **new_file** is called when there are no more records currently available.

As the above example illustrates, the **if–else** statement typically appears on two or more lines in a source file, particularly when either *statement1* or *statement2* is a compound statement. Notice that the **else** normally appears underneath the **if** for which it is the alternative. (This issue of programming style—more specifically, commonly employed and recommended *indenting* practices—is discussed later in this chapter, after all of the statements that affect control flow have been introduced.)

Since the **else** portion of an **if** statement is optional, when two or more **if** statements are *nested*— i.e., when the statement that is conditionally executed is itself an **if**, with its own optional **else**—the C compiler has to decide *to which* **if** an isolated **else** belongs. (Remember that indentation in a program is totally ignored by the compiler. White space is available for arbitrary use strictly as a convenience for the programmer.) The compiler uses the rule that an isolated **else** matches the most recent **else**less **if**. For example, in

```
if (!found) if (arg_count != 0) next_arg();
else exists();
```

the indentation implies that the programmer intends to employ the **else** as the alternative for the *first* **if**. The compiler, however, will associate it with the *second* **if**. There are several ways by which such a statement may be clarified. First, *braces* may be used to clearly delineate single or multiple statements. Thus, if braces were placed around the second **if** statement, *excluding* the **else** clause, the **else** would be associated with the *first* **if**. Second, in sufficiently simple cases, a conditional expression may be altered to clarify the programmer's intention. Thus, if the above were written instead as

```
if (!found && arg_count != 0) next_arg() ;
else exists();
```

the **else** would be associated with the **if** for which it was intended.

The above examples are also designed to remind you of two points that were introduced in Chapter 2. First, whenever a variable is used as a Boolean— having one of two possible truth values (zero and nonzero)—it is common to employ it as a lone condition (possibly preceded by the "!" operator). Thus, the first **if** reads as "if not found." Second, whenever a **(var != 0)** condition appears in a statement, it may be replaced by the simpler condition **(var)**, yielding the same results. (Such a step may also result in more compact code, if the compiler is not able to recognize that the **! = 0** portion of a conditional expression is redundant.) Thus, the second **if** condition above may be replaced by the simpler construct **(arg_count)**.

When **if—else** statements are nested, they are frequently configured in the following manner:

> **if** *(expression1) statement1*
> **else if** *(expression2) statement2*
> **else if** *(expression3) statement3*
>
>   .
>   .
>   .
>
> **else** *statement-n*

where any of the statements above may be a *compound* statement. During execution, the expressions are evaluated in order, and the first *true* value causes the corresponding *statement* to be executed, after which control leaves the system, typically by falling through to the statements following it. Notice that the last statement is executed as a *default*—only if *none* of the conditions above it are found true. For example,

```
if (signal > threshold) above();
else if (signal < threshold) below();
else undecided();
```

executes by calling an appropriate function based on the relation between the value of a variable **signal** relative to the value of a reference variable **threshold**.

The multiway decision that is executed by a nested **if–else** configuration (like the ones shown above) occurs so often that most programming languages provide a special statement specifically designed to accommodate the express situation in which all of the designated conditions test various alternative values for the same expression. In C, this statement is called a **switch** statement. It is explained in detail in Section 5.7.

5.4 **while** and **do–while** Statements

Every programming language provides at least one *iterative* statement, to implement what is probably the most fundamental algorithmic process, namely, the program *loop*. A loop is a sequence of one or more operations that continues to repeat until a condition develops that causes the loop to terminate—at which time, control passes to some other program segment. In C, loops are mechanized using **while** and **for** statements. (The **do–while** construct is also employed to implement a specialized form of a loop, as explained further below.)

The **while** statement has the syntax

> **while** *(expression) statement*

in which it is often the case that *statement* is a compound statement. The **while** executes by continuing to repeat its specified statement so long as the value of its conditional *expression* remains true. On each pass, the conditional *expression* is tested first. If it is found true, *statement* is executed once again, after which control returns to the **while** condition for a new test. Control falls through to the code that follows (with the specified statement *not* executed) the very first time that the condition is found *false*. (If the expression evaluates to false on the *first* test, *statement* is not executed at all.)

Notice that a **while** statement is conceptually equivalent to a simple **if** statement (having no **else** alternative) whose specified *statement* portion ends with an implicit, unconditional return of control to the **if**.

For example, the statement

$$\textbf{while} \ \ (\textbf{--level} \ >= \ \textbf{reference}) \ \ \textbf{output(level)};$$

repeatedly calls the function **output** (passing to it the argument **level**) until the value of **level**, which continually decrements, falls below a reference value.

Typically, the body of a **while** statement is a block, in which case the statement often has the form

$$\textbf{while} \ (expression) \ \{$$

.

.

.

$$\}$$

where the positioning of the braces, as shown above (with the closing brace directly under the **while** that it closes), is only one of the recommended means to ensure that the group of statements that constitutes the iterated portion is clearly delineated. This issue is discussed further later in this chapter.

The expression that is the **while** condition may be more complicated. For example, the statement

$$\textbf{while} \ ((\textbf{c} \ = \ \textbf{getchar())} \ \ != \ \textbf{EOF}) \ \ \textbf{putchar(c)};$$

executes by calling a standard library function **getchar** (explained further later), which, in turn, returns the next character value from a file. That value is then assigned to a variable **c**. In addition, it is compared to a special returned value that is possible—symbolically named **EOF** (also explained further later)—that is specifically designed to indicate when the end of the file has been reached. If it has not yet been reached, the returned character value is used as an input argument in a call to the function **putchar** (also part of the standard library), which processes the character (in a manner that is not of immediate concern to us here). This procedure continues, character by character, until the end of file is reached.

Some very simple **while** statements can also be very useful. For example,

$$\text{while } ((c = \text{getchar}()) == \text{' '});$$

returns, in **c**, the first character past an arbitrarily long sequence of spaces, while

$$\text{while } (*\text{char\_ptr}++);$$

positions **char_ptr** past the next null character encountered. Notice that, in both of these cases, the "specified statement" portion of the **while** statement is the *null* statement.

To clarify that this is indeed the case, most programmers prefer placing the isolated semicolon on its own separate line, as in

$$\text{while}(*\text{char\_ptr}++)$$
$$;$$

Occasionally, it may be desirable to define what appears to be an "infinite" loop with the construct

$$\text{while } (1) \textit{statement}$$

with the proviso that the contents of the *statement* portion include at least one *exit* provision, e.g., a **return** statement or a **break** statement (discussed later).

The **do–while** statement has the format

$$\text{do } \textit{statement} \text{ while } (\textit{expression}) ;$$

Notice that it employs two keywords and that a terminating semicolon is explicitly shown because the statement's form ends with the conditional expression. During execution, on each pass, the specified statement is executed *before* the repeat conditional expression is evaluated. If its value is found false, control falls through to the following statement. Otherwise, the statement is reexecuted.

The **do–while** statement is employed sparingly—only in those situations in which at least one pass through the loop is guaranteed. Typically, since programs ought to behave properly in *limit* situations (e.g., in situations in which they are given *no* data on which to operate), the **while** and **for** statements are universally preferred—because each makes the conditional test *before* its body is executed. Occasionally, however, a set of circumstances arises in which the **do–while** is convenient. For example, suppose a program is required to print a prompt message to the user and to receive in return a value, typed in by the user in response to the prompt. The program is to continue processing only if the user's input value is a valid one (say, a value greater than zero). If an invalid input value is received, the program should merely repeat the prompt message and receive a new user value. Under these conditions, code such as

```
do {
    user_query();
} while (var < VALID);
```

might be appropriate. Here, it is assumed that the function **user_query** prints the question and gets the value of global variable **var** from the user. This value must be greater than or equal to the threshold value **VALID** before the program will continue processing. The unnecessary pair of braces is included to ensure that the programmer will not mistake the last line as the *beginning* of a new **while** statement.

5.5 The **for** Statement

The **for** statement is C's most sophisticated iteration statement. It combines the properties of the **while** (namely, the ability to test an arbitrary conditional expression to decide whether or not to reexecute the statement's body) with an *initialization* portion—executed *before* the loop is entered—and with a *loop-ending* portion—executed at the completion of each pass through the loop. Thus, it provides all of the processing characteristics normally required in the most general type of program loop.

Syntactically, the **for** statement has the following structure:

for (*expression1*; *expression2*; *expression3*) *statement*

Each of the expressions may be arbitrarily complex. *expression1* is evaluated (or executed) *before* the loop is entered, while *expression3* is evaluated (or executed) *after each* execution of the statement that comprises the body of the loop. That is, *expression3* is evaluated at the completion of each pass through the loop. Typically, each of the first and third expressions is an assignment, or a function call, or some combination of the two. In a sufficiently complex situation, it may consist of two or more comma-separated subexpressions. (Recall the comma operator, introduced in Chapter 2.)

expression2 is evaluated before each pass through the loop. Typically, it is a relation of some kind. Its function is entirely equivalent to that of the conditional expression in a **while** statement.

Thus, the **for** statement, as described above, is operationally equivalent to the construct

> *expression1* ;
> **while** (*expression2*)
> {
> *statement*
> *expression3*;
> }

Note the alternative form for indenting and pairing braces. This issue is discussed further later in this chapter.

If either *expression1* or *expression3* is omitted, its portion of the execution is similarly omitted. If *expression2* is omitted, it is taken to be *always true*, in which case some alternative exit (e.g., a **break** statement or a **return** statement) must exist within the body of the loop. The semicolons, however, must remain. Thus, a loop of the form

```
for  (;;)
{
    .
    .
    .
}
```

is an entirely possible construction. In fact, some programmers prefer to employ the directive

#define FOREVER for (;;)

for better readability.

Typically, a **for** statement is employed in the following way:

```
for (row  =  0;  row  <  MAX_ROWS;  row++)
    for (col  =  0;  col  <  MAX_COLS;  col++)
        display (row, col);
```

where the body of the *second* **for** is the statement that calls the function **display**, while the *entire* second **for** statement is the body of the *first* **for**.

In this example, the function **display** is passed the coordinates of one matrix element at a time, starting with row0–column0, then row0–column1, and so on.

In a manner similar to that discussed earlier for the **while**, the body of a **for** statement may be nonexistent. For example, the loop

$$\textbf{for (count = 0; getchar () ! = EOF; count++)}$$
$$\textbf{;}$$

exits with **count** having a value equal to the number of characters in the file accessed by **getchar**. Similarly, assuming **ptr** is a character pointer, initially pointing to the beginning of a null-terminated string, the statement

$$\textbf{for (count = 0; *ptr++; ++count)}$$
$$\textbf{;}$$

computes the *length* of that string.

5.6 break, continue, and goto Statements

A **break** statement provides a convenient means to *exit prematurely* from a loop or from a multiway **switch** (explained in the next section) at any arbitrary point. The purpose of a **break**, which is simply written as

break;

is similar to that of a **return**. While the execution of a **return** causes an immediate exit from the function in which it appears, the execution of a **break** causes control to pass to the statement that *immediately follows* the loop (or **switch**) in which the **break** appears.

When the loop that contains the **break** is inside of *another* loop, the exit applies only to the *inner* loop. Control passes to the next statement in the *enclosing* loop. Similarly, if a **switch** statement (described in the next section) is embedded inside a loop or inside another **switch**, a **break** out of it causes control to pass to the statement immediately following it, in which case control remains *inside* the *enclosing* loop or **switch**.

Notice that the phrase "immediately following statement" should be carefully interpreted in the case when what immediately follows the loop (or **switch**) that contains the **break** is the closing brace of *another* (outer) loop or switch. For example, execution of the **break** in

```
{
    .
    .
    .
            {
                .
                .
            break;
                .
                .
            }
}
```

causes control to exit from the inner block, in which case it reaches the closing brace of the *outer* block. In other words, a **break** causes a branch to a point *just beyond* the brace that closes the block in which that **break** appears.

While the **break** statement is employed as an unconventional exit from a **while**, **do–while**, or **for** loop, we will see momentarily that it is used as a relatively conventional exit from a multiway **switch**. In a loop, the **break** is usually employed in the following manner:

```
while (expression) {
    .
    .
    if (condition) break;
    .
    .
}
```

where the occurrence of the specified *condition*, during the loop's computation, causes an early exit from the loop. For example,

```
while (x >= 0) {
    .
    .
    if (x == NUM) break;
    .
    .
}
```

defines a loop that continues to process so long as the value of **x** remains positive.

However, the special value of NUM for **x** causes an exception—an immediate exit from the loop.

Notice that, if the **break** test occurs at the *beginning or end* of a loop, it is likely that a reexpression of the general looping condition can eliminate the **break** entirely. For example, if the statement containing the **break** above were positioned as the *first* loop statement, a preferable means to write the loop would have been

```
while (x >= 0 && x != NUM) {
     .
     .
     .
}
```

Generally, **break**s in loops are used to handle special exceptions. If you find yourself using too many **break**s in a loop, it is likely that there is a way to reexpress that loop's looping condition to eliminate some or all of them.

You are reminded that, while a **break** in a loop is associated with an exception that should cause a premature exit, we will soon see that a **break** inside a **switch** statement is the *rule*, rather than the exception.

The **continue** statement is permissible only inside of a loop. Its execution causes the remaining portion of the loop to be *skipped*. However, control *remains* within the loop. Specifically, in a **while** or in a **do–while** loop, control immediately passes to the step that reevaluates the looping test condition, while in a **for** loop, control passes to the "loop-ending" step, specified as *expression3* in Section 5.5. A **continue** statement may not be used inside of a **switch** (unless that **switch** is itself part of a loop, in which case execution of the **continue** causes control to pass to the end of the enclosing loop).

As a typical use of a **continue** statement, consider the following loop:

```
while (c >= ' ') {
     .
     .
     if (c == EXCEPTION) {
          count++;
          continue;
     }
     .
     .
}
```

Control remains within the **while** loop so long as the value of **c** (a character variable) remains printable. However, if the value of **c** during any pass has a special **EXCEPTION** value, a count is incremented and the remaining portion of the processing in the loop is skipped. **c** might be a value read from a keyboard. The number of occurrences of the special exception value are counted, and these exceptions are not processed in the normal manner.

Notice that, while the execution of a **break** in a loop causes control to pass to a point just *beyond* that loop's closing brace, the execution of a **continue** causes control to pass to a point just *inside* the same closing brace.

C also provides a **goto** statement—to be employed only in those rare situations in which all of the other conventional transfers of control prove inconvenient. Since all of the transfer mechanisms normally needed by a programmer are provided in C, the **goto** statement is almost never used. Occasionally, however, it is useful.

The *target* of a **goto** is a *label*. A label is an identifier immediately followed by a colon. This follows a practice employed in most assembly languages. Thus, the statement

```
goto location;
```

executes by directly transferring control to the statement that begins with the label

```
location:
```

To demonstrate what is, perhaps, the most common example showing the applicability of the **goto**, consider a situation in which part of the processing in a specific function is code to be executed only in the event of the detection of an error condition. Suppose, further, that an error condition is detected within a deeply nested loop. Rather than include, within that loop, and within all of its enclosing loops, appropriate means to "unravel" it in the event of an error, it is often much simpler merely to employ a *direct branch* to the exception code. For example, the **goto** in

```
          .
          .
while (a >= 0)
{
              .
              .
    while (b >= 0)
    {
                  .
                  .
        a += b;
        if (a > LIMIT) goto overflow;
                  .
                  .
    }
              .
              .
}
          .
          .
overflow: code to recover from overflow
```

immediately exits from the inner loop to the label **overflow**, where the error response code resides.

Any statement may be preceded by a label, which serves only as the possible target of a **goto**. The scope of a label is the entire function in which it resides.

In practice, a **break** is rarely used (except as employed in **switch** statements, explained in the next section), a **continue** is used even less, and a **goto** is almost never used.

5.7 The switch Statement

It was pointed out in Section 5.2 that a sequence of nested **if–else** statements of the form

```
          if (expression1) statement1
          else if (expression2) statement2
          else if (expression3) statement3
                          .
                          .
                          .
          else statement-n
```

is frequently employed as a means to realize a multiway decision or branch— in which only *one* of a set of alternative statements is selected and executed— based on conditions existing at the instant when the branch is reached. Typically, all of the conditional *expression*s in such a construct are similar in structure. In fact, they may all be virtually *identical*. For example, they may all have the common form

if (*common_expression* **==** **value**) ...

so that each conditional relation's evaluation requires, first, an evaluation of the same *common_expression*, and second, a comparison of the value derived with a unique **value**, also specified in the conditional relation.

Since such a situation arises frequently, most programming languages provide a special statement, usually called a "case" statement, specifically designed to accommodate it. During execution of this statement, the common expression is evaluated *only once*, after which the value derived is compared with a set of alternative constant values (or "cases"). When a match is found, the statement associated with the matching value is executed. In C, such a statement is called a **switch** statement.

A **switch** statement may have the following form:

```
switch  (expression)
{
case  constant-expression1  :  statement1
case  constant-expression2  :  statement2
             .

             .

             .

case  constant-expression-n  :  statement-n
default  :  statement-n + 1
}
```

That is, a **switch** statement consists of the keyword **switch**, followed by an arbitrary expression enclosed in parentheses, followed by a *block*. The block (like any other block) contains a sequence of zero or more statements. A typical statement in the block is preceded by the keyword **case**, followed by an arbitrary *constant expression* (i.e., one evaluated at *compile* time), followed by a *colon*. There may be, at most, one prefix containing the keyword **default**, followed by a colon.

Unlike the conventional "case" statement, alluded to above, C's **switch** statement has several special properties. First, not all of its internal statements need be preceded by prefixes ending in colons. (Thus, the example shown above is only one possible form.) Other special properties will be pointed out as we proceed.

The **switch** statement executes by evaluating the parenthesized expression and by comparing the value derived (which must be integral) to all of the constant values (also integral) that follow **case** keywords. If a match is found, a transfer of control (i.e., a branch) is made to the matching statement, after which execution continues, *in-line*, through *all* of the statements that follow it. This is another unique property of C's **switch** statement: There is *no implicit exit* after execution of the matching statement. That is, each construct of the form

case *constant-expression* :

is actually treated *as if it were a label* to which the equivalent of a **goto** may be made. Since there is no implicit exit from the block, an explicit **break** statement must be present to force an exit—wherever one is desired. If no **break** exists (as the example above illustrates), execution proceeds through *all* statements following the matching one.

If *no* match is found, the statement labeled with the keyword **default** is taken. This statement may be positioned at any arbitrary point—not necessarily the last—so that, again, control proceeds through all of the statements following it until either a **break** or the end of the block is encountered. If no match is found and no **default** label exists, *no* statement in the block is executed.

. It is important to recognize that C's **switch** statement behaves in a distinctly different manner from the conventional "case" statement. Specifically, *not all* of its internal statements need be labeled, and an exit from the structure is *not* implicit. It must be explicitly indicated with the **break** statement. Thus, a more conventional form for the **switch** statement is as follows:

```
switch  (expression)
{
case  constant1  :   statement1
                     break;
case  constant2  :   statement2
                     break;


                .

                .

                .

default  :           statement-n
                     break;
}
```

The **break** after the *last* case, which happens to be the **default** in this example, is good programming practice. It ensures proper behavior when additional **case**s are added to the bottom of the list later.

Any single statement in a C program may have more than one label. For example, in

```
err_exit:
restore: statement
```

the labels **err_exit:** and **restore:** both apply to the same statement. Similarly, a statement inside a **switch** may also have multiple **case** labels. This permits the same statement to be chosen by *more than one* matching **case** value.

Let us consider two specific examples of the variations discussed above. First, the statement

```
switch (op_char)
{
case'+' :  c = a + b;
            break;
case'-' :  c = a - b;
            break;
case'*' :  c = a * b;
            break;
case'/' :  c = a / b;
            break;
default :  printf("Bad operator character");
            break;
}
```

illustrates the most conventional **switch**. It executes by branching to one of five points based on the value of the character variable **op_char**. For each expected value, an appropriate statement is executed, after which control exits from the **switch** block—as the result of the execution of a **break** statement. For any unexpected value, an error message is printed.

Notice that an arbitrary number of statements may be positioned between any **case**-labeled statement and its subsequent **break** exit. Execution will continue, *in-line*, until either a **break** or the closing brace of the **switch** block is encountered. (There are, of course, other possible exits, including **return**s and **continue**s.)

Second, the statement

```
switch (user_input)
{
case RESTART:
case PLOT:        clear_screen();
case SHOW:
case CALCULATE:  scroll_screen();
case MESSAGE:    clear_line();
default:         do_operation(user_input);
}
```

illustrates a hypothetical **switch** statement that takes advantage of its "fall through" properties. Variable **user_input** is assumed to have an integer value, selected by the operator in response to a prompt from the program. The symbolic constants **RESTART** through **MESSAGE** represent some of the possible values that the user may select. Let us assume that function **clear_screen** erases the entire user terminal screen, that **scroll_screen** shifts the information on that screen upward until its lower half is blank, and that **clear_line** clears only the bottom line of the screen. All user inputs are ultimately processed by the function **do_operation**, which is passed the user's input value as an argument. However, two of the user inputs require a clear screen before that operation is executed. Two others require a clear lower half screen, and one requires a clear bottom line. Notice that execution of **clear_screen**, followed by **scroll_screen**, followed by **clear_line** still results in a blank screen, while execution of **scroll_screen**, followed by **clear_line** still results in a blank lower half screen.

5.8 Indentation Practices

Having covered essentially all of the permissible C statements and, particularly, the issues of loops and nesting, we are in a better position to appreciate the importance of proper documentation technique—specifically, the use of a consistent *indentation* style that clarifies the internal logic of a program.

All of the alternative styles to be discussed here have already been introduced in previous code examples. It is worthwhile, however, to take the time to summarize all of them in one place.

Indentation is employed to graphically indicate that a certain body of code belongs to, or is subordinate to, a "heading" code line—defined as the first code line above the indented portion that has *less* indentation. Since almost all such bodies of code are brace-enclosed blocks, at a minimum, indentation should clearly indicate to which *opening* brace each *closing* brace belongs. The compiler, of course, ignores the specific position on a page at which a brace occurs. It merely "nests in" every time it encounters a left brace and "nests out" every time it encounters a right brace.

There are a few trade-offs to consider when selecting a specific indentation style. First, the *size* of each indent affects the amount of nesting that is possible before some deeply nested portion of a program reaches the right margin of the display screen (or the printed page). Normally, indents are implemented with horizontal tab ('\t ') characters—whose width on a display (or page) is typically eight spaces. Such a practice is particularly convenient because a single key stroke causes a clearly visible indent. It is also especially applicable in systems that permit wide listings (having a sufficiently large number of characters per line). While the constraint of a narrow display or page may dictate some use of *spaces* in place of tabs, we will henceforth ignore this issue—assuming that the *amount* of each indent is sufficiently large to make it clearly discernible.

The number of indentation styles that are actively in use is not very large. Most prevalent is the practice of allocating, to each left or right brace, its own *separate* line. Further, the position of a right brace is usually *directly under* its matching left brace.

Assuming that one employs this documentation technique, there are still a few possible choices. They involve, first, whether or not the pair of braces is indented with respect to the heading line to which it is subordinate, and second, whether or not the code that comprises the enclosed block is indented with respect to its surrounding braces. The two most common choices are

```
heading line
{
   internal
   code
   lines
}
```

and

```
heading line
   {
   internal
   code
   lines
   }
```

The "heading line" is either the first line of a function definition or the leading portion (i.e., the part preceding the brace-enclosed *statement*) of any decision or looping construct—as explained in this chapter. The second choice shown above has the advantage of permitting the leading portion of the heading line to stand out. It is particularly useful when the heading line begins with a function name. The first choice above has the advantage of highlighting the opening and closing braces of the subordinate block.

The only other choices that are possible are used less frequently. In the first case given above, if the internal code were written *without* indentation, the result would contain *no* indentation at all. In the second case given above, if the internal code portion were *also* indented, with respect to the braces, the result would contain what many would regard as *too much* indentation.

Notice that, in the second case above, if the heading line is the header declaration of the definition of a function that receives formal parameters, the *declarations* of these parameters, which appear *before* the opening brace, may or may not be indented. Both arrangements are in use. You should select one and use it consistently.

Let us consider a specific example of the above alternatives. The nested loop construct

```
for  (pass  =  1;  pass  <=  PASSES;  pass++)
   {
   .

   .

   for  (j  =  0;  j  <  LENGTH;  j++)
      {
      .

      .

      if  (flag[j])
         {
         .

         .

         .
         }
      }
   }
```

makes **PASSES** passes over a loop that contains an inner loop that makes **LENGTH** passes over a sequence of statements that includes a block that is conditionally executed based on the value of a Boolean called `flag[j]`. This indentation technique follows the second example given earlier. Notice that it is convenient even when the *statement* that follows a conditional expression is *not* a brace-enclosed block, as in

```
for (i = 0; i < MAX_SIZE; i++)
    arbitrary single statement
```

which is preferable to

```
for (i = 0; i < MAX_SIZE; i++)
arbitrary single statement
```

An alternative form, for the same code section, using the first indentation technique explained earlier, is

```
for (pass = 1; pass <= PASSES; pass++)
{
    .
    .
    .
    for (j = 0; j < LENGTH; j++)
    {
        .
        .
        if (flag[j])
        {
            .
            .
            .
        }
    }
}
```

In either case, notice that the matching of opening and closing braces is easily discernible, and that the nesting within the system is clearly evident. Similarly, the choice between

```
fcn_name()
{
    .
    .
    .
}
```

and

```
fcn_name ()
   {
      .

      .

      .
   }
```

is a matter of style. One should choose one style and use it consistently.

An alternative bracketing and indenting technique that is frequently employed is one in which the opening brace of a block is *not* given a separate line. Rather, it is placed at the *end* of its "header" line. Its matching closing brace is then placed directly under the *beginning* of this header line. Using this approach, our original example would appear as

```
heading line {
   internal
   code
   lines
}
```

and the specific nested loop example given above would be written as

```
for (pass = 1; pass <= PASSES; pass++) {
   .

   .

   for (j = 0; j < LENGTH; j++) {
      .

      .

      if (flag[j]) {
         .

         .

         .
      }
   }
}
```

A function definition, using this notation, would appear as

```
fcn_name () {
   .

   .

   .
}
```

which has the disadvantage of *not* being conducive to the inclusion of formal parameter declarations.

Whichever of the above indentation techniques you choose (or even if you create your own), it is most important that you be *consistent* in its use. Such a practice will make your programs much more readable.

Problems

5.1 Knowing that the most common C statement is an expression followed by a semicolon, and that an expression consists of operands and operators, what do you expect are the most likely *operators* in such statements?

Introduction to Remaining Problems

Having studied all of the C statements that affect the flow of control in a program, you are now in a position to write some realistic C programs. All but one of the next 24 problems ask you to design an elementary function—typically, one having fairly wide utility. These 24 subprograms, when collected together, comprise a set of six elementary applications, each of which may be separately tested. Although more general versions of many of the functions that you will write are already available in the standard C library (discussed in Chapter 7), they are excellent vehicles to employ to introduce the practice of C programming.

It is assumed that you have at your disposal a system to create, edit, compile, and run C programs. The problems below are designed to be solved in order. Specifically, it is assumed that each of your problem solutions will be appended to the same, already-existing C source file (created empty), which will be periodically recompiled and tested. The application currently under test will be the current **main** function. After it has been debugged and is operating properly, it will be given a *new name* (e.g., **counter**), after which a few more functions will be added to the source file—culminating in the addition of a *new* **main** function—defining the *next* application. After all six applications have been successfully tested and renamed, a final **main** function will be designed as a general user interface—to permit the user to selectively activate and run any of the available applications.

The solutions given in the Solutions section, in the back of this book, were extracted, verbatim, from the author's test file. (Problem numbers were the only additions to it.) It is assumed that you will examine a specific solution, in detail, only after you have written and *successfully debugged* the application that uses it. Thus, each solution is provided only for *comparison* purposes. Clearly, since every programming problem has an infinite number of solutions, it is very likely that your solution will not duplicate the one given in this book. You should remember that your primary purpose is to derive a *working* program. Your secondary purpose—albeit, one that is still very important—is to write concise, efficient, and readable code. It is in this area that the solutions provided will be of some help. They purport to demonstrate good documentation technique and efficient coding practice. Such claims are, of course, open to dispute. Thus, it is quite possible that one or more of your solutions will be "better" (in some sense) than the one(s) provided.

To minimize the amount of time necessary for you to develop working solutions, some of the function specifications were intentionally simplified. In particular, insufficient attention was paid to many of the (usually, rare) *exception* conditions that can arise. For example, the calculator solution does not include any checks that its results are within valid bounds. It also assumes only *integer* operands. Similarly, the word sorter unrealistically restricts the way in which white space may separate input words. Thus, the working solutions that are developed may not be fully "robust" and "ready for market." However, for our present purposes, they are more than adequate.

Finally, since we have not yet discussed any of the detailed properties of the functions available from the standard C library, we must minimize the number of system functions that need to be assumed at this point. Specifically, we will assume the availability of only two functions (actually coded as macros), named **getchar** and **putchar**, and one symbolic constant, named **NULL**—all defined in the standard header file, named **stdio.h**, that was alluded to earlier (in Sections 1.3 and 4.3). **getchar**() (no arguments) returns the next keyboard input character. Normally, keyboard characters are stored, by the system, in a memory buffer—until the RETURN or ENTER key is hit. **getchar** actually returns the next character from that buffer. (It is assumed that every keyboard input character is automatically displayed on the terminal screen.) **putchar(x)** prints the argument **x** as a character. It also returns this value. **NULL** is a symbolic constant whose value is zero. Typically, it is used as a returned pointer value, when an exception condition is detected and a valid pointer value cannot be returned.

5.2 Begin your program with a set of header statements and global data declarations that it will require. In addition to **#include**ing the **stdio.h** file, you will find it convenient to **#define** the following symbolic constants: **YES** and **NO** (true and false equivalents), and **MAX_LINE**, **MAX_WORDS**, and **MAX_STACK**, which are, respectively, the maximum number of input characters expected in an input line, the maximum number of words expected in an input line, and the allocated size of an integer stack, named **stack**. Give these constants the values 100, 25, and 20, respectively. Also declare **stack** as a global data object and, in addition, declare a global pointer to it, named **stack_ptr**, initialized to point to its bottom element.

5.3 Define a function **get_string** that reads a RETURN-terminated string of characters from the keyboard and stores it in memory, beginning at the point specified by the function's single input argument. It also replaces the string's terminating newline character with a null character. [Note that the function (as defined here) returns no valid value—for simplicity. It could have been further defined as one returning the *length* of the string just read. Its library equivalent, known as **gets** (discussed in Chapter 7), returns the value of its pointer argument—which subsequent code will find useful. Nevertheless, we will retain this simplest definition.]

5.4 Define a function **put_string** that outputs the null-terminated string beginning at the point specified by the function's single input argument. It also appends a newline character to the output line. (Notice that you may write an elementary **main** testing function that exercises **get_string** and **put_string**, to ensure that they are operating properly.)

5.5 Define a function **str_len** that is given a pointer to a null-terminated character string and returns the length of that string.

5.6 Define a function **reverse** that is given a pointer to a null-terminated character string and reverses the contents of that string, in place. It returns no valid value.

5.7 Define, as a first application, a **main** function that begins by prompting the user with the message: "Reverses all input strings:". It then proceeds to read arbitrary input character lines, printing each one back in reverse order. The program terminates when it receives a *null* line, namely, a single RETURN. (This function should call all of the others previously defined.) When you have it working to your satisfaction, rename it as **reverser**.

5.8 Define a function **int_to_digits** that receives two input arguments—the first, an integer, and the second, a pointer to characters. It converts the integer value into an equivalent null-terminated string of digit characters, beginning at the point specified by the pointer. If the integer is negative, a minus sign should begin the string. The function returns no value. (Note: You may find it convenient to use the function **reverse**, defined earlier.)

5.9 You will find it convenient to include in your program, at this point, your solutions to Problems 4.4 through 4.6—namely, the three macro definitions **isdigit**, **isupper**, and **tolower**. (Alternatively, you may **#include** in your program the header file **ctype.h**, which is normally available in a typical C programming environment.) Now define, as a second application, a **main** function that begins by prompting the user with the message: "Counts digits and vowels in input strings and outputs the difference between them:". It then proceeds to read arbitrary input lines. After each input string, it outputs the difference between the number of digits in it and the number of vowels (upper- or lowercase) in it. It terminates on the input of a null line (a single RETURN). Again, make use of as many of the previously defined functions as possible. When you have this function working to your satisfaction, rename it as **counter**.

5.10 Define a function **digits_to_int** that receives a pointer to a sequence of digits and returns an integer whose value is its equivalent. For simplicity, assume that all input strings are *positive*. The function should return on the first nondigit encountered.

5.11 Define a function **power** that receives two (assumed positive) integer arguments. It returns a value that is the first number raised to the second's power.

5.12 Define a function **push** that receives an integer argument and pushes it onto the global stack, introduced in Problem 5.2. **push** also returns the pushed value. Let us assume that **stack_ptr** points to the first *available* stack cell. If the stack is full, **push** merely ignores the call. (Normally, an error procedure should be entered under these conditions.)

5.13 Define a function **pop** that discards the top stack entry and returns its (integer) value. If the stack is empty, **pop** merely returns zero. (Clearly, this is not good practice, but adequate for our present purposes.)

5.14 Define, as a third application, a **main** function that begins by prompting the user with the message: "Enter integers, or any of the binary operators +, -, *, /, %, # (power) :". It then proceeds to read arbitrary input lines. Any line beginning with a digit is assumed to contain a single positive integer. Otherwise, the line should normally contain a single operator character. Other inputs [except the single RETURN (null) line—which causes program termination] are ignored. After each input, the contents of the stack are printed vertically (top above bottom)—shifted to the right by a space or two to make the program's output distinguishable from the program's input.

The program should operate as a stack-oriented integer calculator. Every integer input is pushed onto the stack. Every operator input causes that operation to be executed— using the top two stack entries as operands. The result of the operation *replaces* the operands that were used. When you have this function working to your satisfaction, rename it as **calculator**.

5.15 Define a function **border** that receives three input arguments—the first, a character, the second, a positive length (an integer), and the third, a truth value. It prints a horizontal line, of the specified length, containing only the specified character. The third argument specifies whether or not the line should terminate with a newline. This function returns no valid value.

5.16 Define a function **scan** that receives two input arguments—the first, a pointer into a stream of characters in memory, and the second, a positive integer displacement from that point. The function returns a pointer to the *rightmost space* character (i.e., ' ') within the specified range. At least one space is assumed to exist within the range (which is an oversimplification that is sufficient for our purposes), unless the range includes the string's null terminator.

5.17 Define, as a fourth application, a **main** function that begins by prompting the user with the message: "Enter a column width, then strings. Will print text within column specified:". It then proceeds to read a single integer, followed by any number of arbitrary text lines. After each text line, it reprints that line in a column of the specified width. To highlight the column, each text reprint begins and ends with a horizontal border, of the specified column width, containing a special highlight character, like '*' or '-'. The printed text is *not* right-justified. That is, spaces are *not* inserted to produce an even right margin. The text is, of course, left-justified. It is assumed that no single word is wider than the specified margin. (Clearly, many simplifications are included here. The more interesting problems of right-justification and, even more complicated, *hyphenation* are beyond our present scope.) When you have this function working to your satisfaction, rename it as **printer**.

5.18 Define a function **swap** that is passed two character pointers and swaps the characters at which they point. It returns no valid value.

5.19 Define a function **str_cmp** that is passed two pointers to separate null-terminated character strings. It compares them, character by character, and returns the *difference* (first-second) between their first *nonmatching* character values. When a null is encountered in either string, a return of *zero* (indicating a match) occurs. Thus, one can find out whether the first string is "greater than" or "less than" (in the ASCII sense), or equal to, the second string.

5.20 Define a function **index** that is passed two pointers to separate null-terminated character strings. It returns a pointer to the *leftmost* occurrence of the first string (normally the shorter of the two) in the second. If no match is found, it returns NULL. (The solution given in the back of this book employs the **swap** and **str_cmp** functions. It is not necessarily the fastest realization, but it is interesting.)

5.21 Define, as a fifth application, a **main** function that begins by prompting the user with the message: "Finds first match. Enter one long string, then many short strings:". It then proceeds to read one arbitrary "long" string, followed by any number of shorter test strings. It responds to each test string by reprinting the long string, with the leftmost occurrence of the test string in it replaced by a "highlight" string—consisting of a sequence of the same special character (like '*'). If no match is found, it prints instead the message: "Match not found". The program terminates on the entry of a null test string. When you have this function working to your satisfaction, rename it as **finder**.

5.22 Define a function **exchange** that is passed two.pointers *to pointers* to characters. It exchanges the pointers at which the argument pointers point. It returns no valid value.

5.23 Define a function **sort** that is passed two arguments—the first, a pointer to an *array* of pointers to character strings, and the second, a positive integer representing the *number* of such strings (hence, pointers in the array) that are to be processed. (Clearly, this number must be less than the size of the array.) The **sort** function reorders the pointers *in the array* so that the strings at which they point are sorted into ASCII lexicographic order. One means of accomplishing this is to find the "smallest" string (in the ASCII lexicographic sense) and then to exchange its pointer with the one in position *zero*. This process can then be repeated using the *remainder* of the array, beginning at position *one*. The process continues until only the pointer to the "largest" string remains.

5.24 Define, as a sixth application, a **main** function that begins by prompting the user with the message: "Enter sequences of words to be sorted:". The user responds by entering lines containing arbitrary word sequences. For simplicity, let us assume no leading or trailing blanks and that words are separated by *single* spaces. (This is an undue restriction in a realistic situation, but it is convenient for our present purposes.) For each line entered, the program responds by reprinting, in a column, the same set of words that were just entered. However, they are now positioned in ASCII lexicographic order. The program terminates on entry of a null line. When you have this function working to your satisfaction, rename it as **sorter**.

5.25 Define a final **main** function that ties the six applications above together. It begins by prompting the user with a "menu" that reads:

```
Select one of the following functions:
1: reverser   2: counter   3: calculator
4: printer    5: finder    6: sorter
A NULL input string causes an EXIT
from the current function.
```

After the user enters the selected digit (invalid inputs cause a repeat of the prompt above), the selected function is entered. When it exits, the menu is repeated. Finally, the entry of a single RETURN (a null string), in response to the above prompt, causes the entire program to exit to the operating system.

CHAPTER 6   ADVANCED TOPICS

6.1 Unions

Given a means to define structure templates, to name and allocate storage space for structures, and to access the members of structures, all of the facilities necessary for the definition and access of *unions* are in place. The reason for this is that a union is nothing more than a structure all of whose members are *superimposed* in storage. That is, while the *offset* from the structure's origin, of each successive member of a structure, increases monotonically (i.e., the first member has zero offset; the second member begins at an appropriate point just beyond where the first member ends; and so on), the offset of every union member is *the same*, namely, *zero*.

Thus, a union is a structure all of whose members *share* the same storage. The amount of storage allocated to a union is that sufficient to hold its *largest* member. At any given instant, *only one* member of the union may actually reside in that storage. The way in which a union's storage is accessed depends, then, on the *member name* that is employed *during* the access. It is the programmer's responsibility to keep track of *which* member currently resides in a union.

A union is identified to C through use of the keyword **union** *in place of* the keyword **struct**. Virtually all other means for declaring and accessing unions are *identical* to those for structures. For example, the declaration

```
union dual
{
int value;
int *ptr;
}
element[SIZE];
```

declares an array named **element** of **SIZE** cells, each of which may hold either an integer (if it is accessed through use of the member name **value**, as in **uptr->value**) or a *pointer* to an integer (if it is accessed through use of the member name **ptr**, as in **element[i].ptr**). It is the programmer's responsibility to ensure that a cell is not accessed using the member name **value**, for example, while it is *actually* holding a pointer.

Incidentally, the template name **dual**—also defined in the above declaration—is, of course, available for use in subsequent union declarations.

While unions and structures are declared and accessed in identical manners, there is one additional difference between them. As might be expected, a union may not be initialized.

Unions are employed in programs only in relatively special circumstances. There are occasions, for example, when a union may be employed to significantly reduce the amount of storage space occupied by a program. Consider, for example, a program that accesses either of two large data arrays (of different sizes and containing elements of different types). If it is true that these accesses are mutually exclusive (i.e., there is never a time when *both* arrays need to be available to the program simultaneously), it may be convenient to permit the arrays to share storage by declaring a union of both of them.

A union is also employed as an important convenience for the programmer. For example, it is often useful to name a single cell to hold a *type-independent* value (say, one returned by any of several functions or one returned by a macro whose arguments may have different types). Using a union permits the same name to identify several different objects. For example, Problem 5.18 (the **swap** function) and Problem 5.22 (the **exchange** function) both asked for essentially the same operation. Two separate functions were required only because the *types* of the elements to be exchanged were different. Consider instead a *single* **swap** macro and an associated global union named **tmp**. Specifically, let **tmp** be defined as follows:

```
union {
    char c;
    int i;
    float f;
    double d;
    char *pc;
    int *pi;
    float *pf;
    double *pd;
        .
        .
        .
} tmp;
```

(You may notice a resemblance to the identifiers that were employed in the set of expression evaluation problems at the end of Chapter 2.) Only some of the possible object types that may be exchanged are included. The "..." notation indicates that more can be added. Given this global definition, the macro

```
#define swap(a,b,c)  (tmp.a = *(b), *(b) = *(c), \
                       *(c) = tmp.a)
```

(recall that a backslash may be employed to continue a long macro definition) permits the following call to be employed, *independent* of the type of the objects being exchanged:

```
swap(t,p1,p2);
```

In this example, **t** represents any one of the **tmp** member names—chosen to designate the *type* of the objects being exchanged, and **p1** and **p2** are *pointers* to such objects.

Similarly, in the symbol table of a compiler or an assembler, an identifier must be associated with a constant value that may be either an address or any one of several other data types. Yet, it is convenient to employ only *one* cell to hold the value associated with a given symbol. Again, a table configured as an array of unions yields the required data structure.

The first example given in this section represents a similar situation. Here, the array **element** contains a set of cells, each of which may contain either an integer or a *pointer* to an integer. Such a data structure may be useful as a *stack* realization in which each cell has the option either of holding a variable directly or of indirectly pointing to that variable.

Finally, since it is the programmer's responsibility to keep track of the contents of a union, when the nature of a program is such that this is not directly predictable from the source code, it may be necessary to define a variable whose only purpose is to define the current type stored in that union. A problem at the end of this chapter treats this issue further.

6.2 Fields

A structure is a set of objects—generally of differing lengths—that are assigned adjacent positions in storage. Normally, the *smallest* permissible length for one of these objects is that of a **char**. Occasionally, however, it is useful to lay out, contiguously in storage, objects having arbitrary *bit* lengths—e.g., a sequence of *flag* bits in adjacent positions within a single word. Such objects are called *fields*. C employs its structure declaration and access mechanism not only to permit definition and reference to unions, but also to permit definition and reference to fields.

A field is identified to C if its declaration, within a structure declaration list, terminates in a *colon* followed by a *constant expression*. For example, the declaration

```
struct {
    unsigned op : 3;
    unsigned mode : 4;
    unsigned reg : 4;
    } instr;
```

defines a field of 3 bits, named **op**, followed by a field of 4 bits, named **mode**, followed by a field of 4 bits named **reg**—all contained within a structure named **instr**. These fields are normally assembled in storage left-to-right within the "holding" object, which is virtually always an *unsigned integer*. A field is not permitted to straddle the boundary of the holding object. If it does, a *new* holding object (i.e., another unsigned integer) is assembled, adjacent to the previous one, and that field is given the leftmost position within it. In the example above, only one unsigned integer is required as long as its length is greater than or equal to 11 bits. (In practice, of course, an **unsigned**'s length is probably never shorter than 16 bits.)

Once a field is defined in the manner illustrated above, it may be referenced in the same fashion as that used to reference any conventional structure member. Thus, for example, the expression

instr.mode

refers only to the 4-bit **mode** field within the single unsigned integer named **instr**.

As you might expect, field *templates* may be named for use in subsequent declarations. (The template name happens to be missing from the example given above.) However, as you might also expect, fields do have some special properties. First, a field's name may be *omitted* from its declaration, in which case it cannot, of course, be referenced. Such a procedure is employed to define an *unused* field of bits—e.g., to force the proper alignment of those fields that are in use. Second, the special field width of *zero* is employed to force allocation of a *new* holding object—for those fields that are declared next. Third, since a field is positioned arbitrarily inside of an addressable object, the unary "&" operator may not be applied to it, so there are no *pointers* to fields. Fourth, you should be aware that C does not restrict the sense in which a sequence of fields is assembled within a word. While virtually all current compilers utilize a left-to-right rule, at least one implementation is known to exist that employs a right-to-left rule.

As the cost of storage continues to decrease, the use of bit fields within programs will probably also decrease, particularly since fields are not totally machine-independent objects. However, there are still applications in which the use of fields is quite important—e.g., those that employ large tables whose entries may be compressed into fields to save storage space, and those in which the amount of memory that is available for use is limited.

6.3 Structure Linkage

A structure is C's most versatile data element. It is employed in any application in which two or more data objects (generally of different types) must be "packaged together" for convenience in processing. A structure is sometimes called a "record," in which case each of its members is interpreted as one of the *fields* of that record. A structure is also sometimes called a "control block" or an "attribute node," in which case each of its members is a status variable or an attribute value.

It has already been pointed out that a structure member may itself be an array or another structure. Certainly a character array is a very common record field—or structure member. The discussion in Section 3.7 included an illustration of a structure, packaged to contain all of the attributes of an appointment, one of whose members was another structure containing time-of-day information. It was also pointed out that an *array* of structures is an extremely valuable data object, since it is the most common memory image of a data *file*.

Thus, while we know how to configure a set of structures, all of the same composition, into a linear sequence called an *array*, we do not yet know how to *nest* structures of the same composition or how to develop more complex linkages between them. Such linkages are fundamentally important because they permit us to build more complicated data structures—like trees, lists, or hierarchical data bases—out of the atomic records and data nodes that we call structures.

A member of a structure may *not* be another instance of the same structure. That is, if a structure is declared as

```
struct template {
        .
        .
        member
        declarations
        .
        .
} struc_name;
```

then one of the member declarations may *not* be of the form

```
struct template name;
```

Thus, one means by which a hierarchy is built—in which a composite object may itself contain other instances of the same object, each of which may, in turn, contain still other instances of the same object, and so on—is *not* available to the C programmer. However, a structure *may* contain a member that is a *pointer* to another structure of the same composition. That is, using the same example above, one of the member declarations above *may* be of the form

```
struct template *name;
```

The availability of such a facility (i.e., the possibility of *self-referential* structures, in which one structure may *point to* one or more instances of itself elsewhere in storage) makes it possible for one data node or record to be *linked to* one or more other similar nodes or records. This linkage mechanism makes it possible for us to build more complex data structures like trees and linked lists. Typically, the linkage pointer either points to another valid instance of the same structure, elsewhere in storage, or has a NULL (zero) value—if it is not being used in the normal manner (because, for instance, it is the *last* member of a list). Consider, for example, a set of basic building blocks declared as

```
struct block {
        int count;
        char name[NAME_SIZE];
        struct block *next;
} first_block, second_block, ..., last_block;
```

and a structure pointer declared as

struct block *top;

If **top** were initialized to point to one of the blocks as the "top" one in the list, then the statement

top—>next = &nth_block;

would link that block to the one named **nth_block**. Having done this, the statement

top—>next—>count++;

would increment the count value in **nth_block**. Similarly, the statement

first_block.next—>name[0] = 'A';

sets the first character, in the character array of the block that is *linked to* **first_block**, to the value 'A'. (It is assumed here that **first_block.next** has a valid non-NULL pointer value.)

A problem at the end of this chapter relates to self-referential structure declarations and initialization.

6.4 Pointers to Functions

Consider the design of an interpreter that periodically fetches a new "op code", from a program undergoing interpretation, and then executes a multiway branch to the function that corresponds to that op code. Typically, such an interpreter is implemented using a large **switch** statement of the form

```
switch (op_code)
{
case 0: funct0(); break;
case 1: funct1(); break;
    .
    .
    .
case n: functn(); break;
}
```

During execution, the **op_code** value is sequentially compared to each of the possible **case** values. When a match is found, a call to the corresponding function is made. After that function returns, the subsequent **break** causes an exit.

Consider, instead, an array of pointers to the same functions, which would be declared as

$$\texttt{int (*funct[NUM\_FCNS]) ();}$$

The parentheses and brackets are necessary to properly define the object being declared. Remember that we test that a declaration is a proper one by making a trial expression evaluation, given the identifier being declared to start with. The operators are applied, in the above example, in the following order: first "[]", then "*", and finally "()"—meaning that **funct** must be an *array*, of *pointers*, to *functions*, that return **int**s. Once this array is properly initialized, a statement of the form

$$\texttt{(*funct[op\_code]) ();}$$

will execute the equivalent of the large **switch** statement given earlier. An interpreter based on this second realization should be much faster than one based on the first.

A pointer to a function is not only useful in an array. It has, perhaps, its greatest utility as a parameter passed during a function call. Consider the design of a function **funct** that, during its execution, in turn makes a call on a function named **operation**. Imagine a situation in which the function executed by **operation** *depends* on the way in which **funct** itself was called. For example, **funct** may be designed to process two or more different types of data, and the operation executed by **operation** may vary with the data type. One solution to this problem is to permit the *caller* of **funct** to specify not only the type of data to be processed, but also the specific function that **funct** should use *in place of* **operation**.

As a second example, consider a function that is to be designed to scan a large data block in a specific (possibly complex) manner. It is further to be designed so that the operation that it executes, whenever it reaches a new data item during its scan, should be controllable by the caller. Again, we have a situation in which the caller of a function needs the option of specifying *which* function, the function that it calls should *in turn* call, at a specific point in its computation.

The following example illustrates how the "host" function is normally defined:

```
funct(arg, operation)
int arg, (*operation)();
  {
  .
  .
  while (expression)
        if ( (*operation)(arg) ) return;
  .
  .
  }
```

Notice the declaration of **operation** as a pointer to a function returning an integer. Several simplifying assumptions have been made here. First, the sample function above returns no valid value. Second, we assume that there is only one key statement that uses the dummy **operation** function. Third, we assume that any function employed *in place of* **operation** expects one input argument and returns a *truth* value. Given the definition above, the call

$$funct(value1, op1);$$

would cause **op1** to be called at any point where **operation** appeared within **funct**. Similarly, the call

$$funct(value2, op2);$$

would substitute **op2** for every occurrence of **operation** in **funct**. A problem at the end of this chapter treats this issue further.

6.5 Recursion

A C function may call *itself*—either directly (i.e., the function's body includes the call) or indirectly (i.e., the call exists in the body of *another* function that is called *by* it). In either case, the process is called *recursive*. We concentrate here on examples of direct recursion.

Whenever a recursive call is made, the values of all local variables employed at the "calling level" of the function are preserved in the stack area for that level, and a fresh set of registers for local variables is established, in a *new* stack area, for the "called level." As you would expect, copies of calling level variables may be passed on to the called level as arguments. Similarly, values ultimately returned from the called level can find their way back into calling level expression evaluations.

Perhaps the most common example of the use of recursion is the factorial function, which may be written as

```
factorial(n)
int n;
    {
    return ((n <= 1) ? 1 : n * (factorial(n-1)));
    }
```

The computation continues to "nest in," **n-1** times, until the deepest level returns a value (which happens to be 1) to its caller. This returning process then continues to "spiral" out (the next level out returns 2, the next 6, and so on) until the outermost level is reached, after which the function returns the proper result to its original caller.

As another example of a recursive function, consider an alternative realization of the **int_to_digits** function—that converts an input integer into an equivalent string of ASCII digits. (One implementation was given as the solution to Problem 5.8.) For simplicity, we will assume only positive integers and also the existence of a global character pointer, named **ptr**, positioned at the point where the digit string is to be stored. With these simplifying assumptions, the function

```
int_to_digits(num)
int num;
    {
    if (num >= 10) int_to_digits(num / 10);
    *ptr++ = num % 10 + '0';
    }
```

illustrates the heart of the process. At any level, given a positive integer **num**, the function passes on to the next inner level all of the digits of **num** (if there are any) except for the least significant one. Thus, the next inner level is responsible for placing all of *these* digits into storage and for advancing **ptr** past them. When this inner function returns, all of the digits of **num**, except the least significant one, will have been placed, in sequence, in memory. The second statement in the body of the function then deposits the least significant digit of its value of **num** and advances **ptr** past it.

Thus, for example, if the original argument has a value 345, the first function called passes the value 34 to the next inner level and remembers its argument value of 345. The next inner level passes on the value 3 and remembers its argument value of 34. The third inner level, given an argument less than 10, places it in storage (advancing **ptr** past it) and returns. The middle level then deposits the 4 and returns, and the outer level then deposits the 5 and returns.

Notice that there are as many different **num**s as there are levels of nesting, and that there are as many levels of nesting as there are digits in the string version of the original **num** argument.

We have ignored, in the version above, the placement of the null terminator character. This was done to strip away all of the ancillary issues, leaving only the essential characteristics of the recursive process.

While recursive procedures are generally slower and consume more memory space than alternative realizations, they do offer the advantage of compactness and elegance of code. They are usually easier to understand and may be easier to prove correct.

6.6 Multidimensional Arrays

We have already discussed (in Section 3.6) that a two-dimensional array is defined to C literally as an array of arrays, and that it is configured in storage as a contiguous sequence of rows—as many as are specified by the first, or leftmost, dimension in the definition. These rows are laid out side by side, and each of them contains as many elements as are specified by the second dimension in the definition. Thus, the reference

$$\textbf{name[i][j]}$$

selects the **j**th element (i.e., the **j**th "column") in the **i**th row. Notice that C converts this reference into a *pointer* by first adding, to the address origin of the array (the value of **name**), an appropriate number of multiples of the row width (the row width is the total number of "column"s), before indexing into the selected row to find the addressed element. That is, the reference above is actually converted into an equivalent access address using the formula

$$\textbf{access\_address = origin + (i * row\_size) + j}$$

or, in other words, **name[i][j]** is actually evaluated by converting it into its equivalent pointer version, which is

$$\textbf{*(*(name + i) + j)}$$

To explain this a bit further, recall (from Section 2.6) that the two expressions **name[i]** and ***(name + i)** are equivalent expressions, i.e., that the

name of an array is a pointer to its first element and that any increment of this
pointer is *scaled* by the *size* of the elements in that array. Further, recall (from
Section 3.6) that, from this, we can conclude that the name of a two-dimensional
array is treated by C as a *pointer to one-dimensional arrays*, namely, those rows
that comprise it. This means that

$$\textbf{name} \ + \ \textbf{i}$$

is the address of the **i**th row (counting from zero) in the two-dimensional array
named **name**, and

$$\textbf{*(name} \ + \ \textbf{i)}$$

is that row. That is, it names a one-dimensional array. Or, equivalently, it is a
pointer to the first element of that array. Therefore,

$$\textbf{*(name} \ + \ \textbf{i)} \ + \ \textbf{j}$$

must be the address of element **j** in the row that is referenced, and

$$\textbf{*(*(name} \ + \ \textbf{i)} \ + \ \textbf{j)}$$

must be that element. Thus, the compiler treats the name of a two-dimensional
array as a pointer to an entire *row*.

There are at least two conclusions that we can draw from this. First, in
practice, it is preferable to address the elements of a multidimensional array *via
pointers*, rather than to employ indices in brackets—because the indexed expressions are always converted into their pointer equivalents anyway. For example,
the sequence

```
for (i = 0; i < IMAX; i++)
    for (j = 0; j < JMAX; j++)
        if (name[i][j] == val) ...
```

is far slower than its pointer equivalent of

```
for (i = 0, row_ptr = name; i < IMAX; i++, row_ptr++)
    for (j = 0, ptr = *row_ptr; j < JMAX; j++, ptr++)
        if (*ptr == val) ...
```

(Note: A problem at the end of this chapter considers proper *declarations* of **row_ptr** and **ptr**.)

Second, when a two-dimensional array declaration (as opposed to a definition) is made—e.g., of an array argument that is passed to a function—sufficient information must be provided to allow all permissible uses of that array name in expressions. Nondefining array declarations were first introduced in Section 3.3. It was pointed out there that, in the one-dimensional case, a declaration such as

$$\textbf{char array[];}$$

carries sufficient information to permit constructs like **array[i]** to be freely employed in subsequent expressions. However, a declaration like

$$\textbf{float array[][];}$$

does *not* provide sufficient information for **array[i][j]** to appear in an expression, because the compiler has not been informed of the *row size* in that array. Thus, any (nondefining) declaration of a multidimensional array *must include all of its dimensions except the lowest*. In other words, a declaration like

$$\textbf{float array[][ROW\_SIZE];}$$

is adequate, since expressions like **array[i][j]** are now resolvable into equivalent code. (It is, of course, permissible to provide *all* of the array's dimensions in the declaration, if this is desired.)

Similarly, as you might expect, a three-dimensional array is literally treated as an array of two-dimensional arrays (and so on), so that the reference

$$\textbf{name[2][3][4]}$$

selects the fifth element in the fourth row of the third two-dimensional array. Such a higher-dimensional data array is relatively rare in C because the typical program that needs it is usually coded instead using a pointer array as the vehicle by which the data in a collection of separate arrays are referenced.

However, if a higher-dimensional data array is employed, the same rules specified above apply to it. In particular, a nondefining declaration of such an object may leave, at most, only the *first* pair of brackets empty.

6.7 `typedef`

While the number of atomic data types in C (`char`s, `int`s, `float`s, and so on) is quite small, the number of *derived* types is conceptually infinite. That is, in a declaration that specifies the *type* of an identifier, with few restrictions, we are free to make arbitrary combinations of phrases like "array of," "pointer to," "function returning," "structure containing," and so on, in virtually any order. Of course, many of the types that are possible to define are virtually useless. For example, the declaration

$$\texttt{struct block *(*(*name)[])();}$$

declares **name** to identify an object that is a pointer to an array of pointers to functions returning pointers to structures of composition **block** (assuming that the specific details of **block**'s arbitrary internal structure have already been spelled out). It is not clear whether such an object has any possible computational value.

Since the number of potential types is so large, C is equipped with a mechanism to associate a *single name* with an arbitrarily complex object type. This is done by preceding a sample declaration of that type with the keyword **typedef**. The identifier that is employed in this sample declaration is then defined to C as a *shorthand* for the type declared in the **typedef** declaration. For example, assuming that the detailed composition of the structure template named `control_block` has already been established, the declaration

$$\texttt{struct control\_block *block\_ptr;}$$

declares `block_ptr` to be a single pointer to structures of that composition. On the other hand, the declaration

$$\texttt{typedef struct control\_block *BLOCK\_PTR;}$$

declares **BLOCK_PTR** to be a *shorthand for this type*, so that subsequent uses of **BLOCK_PTR** in declarations of the form

$$\texttt{BLOCK\_PTR x, y, z;}$$

can easily declare other instances of the same type. In this example, the objects **x**, **y**, and **z** have all been declared to be pointers to structures of composition `control_block`.

The keyword **typedef**, appearing *before* a declaration as it does, exhibits a similarity in its *positional use* to a storage class keyword, like **static** or **extern**. However, its actual purpose, as the explanation above indicates, is quite different.

Notice that it is common practice, as it is for **#define**d symbols, to employ uppercase characters in **typedef**-defined identifiers. It is also evident that **#define** and **typedef** have some distinct similarities. That is, in simple situations, either mechanism can be employed to define a convenient alternative symbol for a type. For example, using the example first introduced in Problem 4.3, the two lines

$$\textbf{\#define VOID int}$$

and   **typedef int VOID;**

both define the identifier **VOID** as being a synonym for the type **int** (presumably to be employed to identify those functions that return no values). Similarly,

$$\textbf{\#define COUNTER int}$$

and   **typedef int COUNTER;**

are two alternative means to permit subsequent use of the identifier **COUNTER** as a synonym for the type **int**. Either one will permit a later declaration like

$$\textbf{COUNTER i, j, k, count;}$$

to more clearly identify all those variables that are to be used as general-purpose counters.

Notice, however, that these parallels between **#define** and **typedef** break down for types having only slightly more complexity. For example, the declaration

$$\textbf{typedef char *CHAR\_PTR;}$$

makes subsequent declarations like

$$\textbf{CHAR\_PTR string, message, words[MAX\_WORDS];}$$

possible. Here, **string** and **message** are declared as pointers to characters, while **words** is declared as an array of such pointers. Such a declaration of multiple objects cannot be duplicated using only text substitution. Similarly, the objective accomplished by the declaration

$$\textbf{typedef char *(*MESSAGES)[];}$$

which defines **MESSAGES** to be a synonym for the type "pointer to an array of strings (pointers to characters)," cannot be duplicated by mere text substitution.

As the examples above demonstrate, the identifier that is being declared as a type synonym in a **typedef** declaration does not appear directly after the keyword **typedef**. Rather it appears in the position where the identifier in the sample expression would normally appear. Notice also that **typedef**'s only purpose is to introduce synonyms for types that can already be defined in other ways. It is *not* used to *def*ine any new *type*s.

6.8 Command Line Arguments

As pointed out in Section 3.1, the **main** function in a C program is entirely ordinary. It is special *only* in that it is the "highest-level" function. That is, it is the one that receives control when a program run first begins. Yet, all of the **main** functions that we have considered so far have implied another special property that they all appear to possess. Since they have all had the structure

```
main()
{
    .
    .
    .
}
```

we are led to conclude, erroneously, that a **main** function cannot itself receive input arguments. On the contrary, a **main** function *can* accept input arguments. However, they are delivered to it in a special way. To understand how they are delivered, we must consider how a typical C program is actually invoked.

As pointed out in Section 4.3, in a typical C programming environment, every C source file name has a ".c" extension (e.g., **prog_name.c**). After a source program has been properly compiled and linked, the object file that is created by this process is available for loading and running. The name of this file is, in general, specified by the user during the compilation/linkage phase. A "default" file name is normally employed in the event that the user forgoes the option of naming the executable file. In the UNIX environment, this default file name is **a.out**. In other environments, the default name is typically the same as that of the source file, but with an extension of ".exe" (for executable) substituted for the ".c" extension in the source file name.

In a typical situation, an object file is invoked (i.e., loaded into memory by the operating system and run) in response to a *command* typed by the user at the terminal. In most environments, this command is merely the *name* of the file containing the selected program. (Your experience in writing and running the sequence of programs at the end of the previous chapter should corroborate the procedures described here.) The line on which the object file's name is typed, typically in response to a prompt (like "%" or "A>") from the operating system, is called a *command line*.

Many operating system functions are invoked using this procedure. For example, if the user types the command **dir**, a program having that name is loaded and run. The function executed by this program is to display on the terminal the current contents of the user's *dir*ectory. Similarly, entering the command **time** invokes a program whose only function is to print on the terminal the current time. (We are assuming, for simplicity, that these operating system functions are not already resident in memory.)

In many situations, it is convenient to specify on the command line not only the command—i.e., the name of the program to be run—but also certain parameters that will affect the nature of that run. For example, the command **copy**, asking that a file be copied, naturally requires more information from the user (e.g., the name of the file, the name to be given to its copy, and so on). Similarly, a command like **delete** or **erase**, asking that a specific file be removed from the directory, naturally requires that the name of that file be specified.

All of the character strings that are specified on a command line *after* the initial command (the name of the program to be invoked) are called *command line arguments*. Clearly, the information provided by these arguments must be made available to the running program. How is this done?

The command line is normally stored by the operating system in a character line buffer in memory. The contents of this buffer are analyzed and responded to only after a RETURN or ENTER key is hit—indicating termination of the command line. Normally, if the first name on the command line is not the name of an available executable file (usually because a typing error has occurred), the operating system returns the error message: "Command not found," or its equivalent. If the file is found, the selected program is loaded (from disk) and run.

There are numerous alternative means by which the remainder of the command line may be "passed on" to the running program by the operating system. In some environments, a call by the program to the operating system receives, in return, the address of the first character of the remainder of the command line buffer. If there are numerous string arguments, it is up to the program to separate them before analyzing their contents.

In a standard C environment, the operating system provides the running program with more information than this. Specifically, the program is passed both the *number* of command line arguments (each one an arbitrary character string, separated from the others by white space) and a separate *pointer* to each one of them. The program is still responsible for analyzing the specific *meaning* of each argument string, but it does not have to *separate* them. In addition, just looking at the *number* of arguments will frequently indicate whether or not the command line has been properly formatted. (As you would expect, one of the most common command line arguments is merely the *name* of a file.)

Thus, a **main** function that expects command line arguments should specify *two* formal parameters—first, an *integer*, which will receive their count, and second, a pointer to an *array of pointers to characters*, which will hold the pointers to the individual arguments. By convention, the first argument is called **argc** (*arg*ument *c*ount) and the second is called **argv** (*arg*ument *v*ector). (Note, however, that, in the same way that you are free to choose arbitrary names for *all* function arguments, you are not constrained to use these argument names.)

By convention, each of the argument strings is automatically null-terminated. Further, by convention, the **argc** count that is passed to **main** *includes* the *first* string—namely, the name of the program—in which case the pointer in position zero in the **argv** array points to it. Most programs ignore this first argument, since it is implicit.

With this introduction, we can now write a "template" for a **main** function that expects command line arguments. It looks like this:

```
main(argc, argv)
int argc;
char *argv[];
    {
        .
        .
        .
    }
```

Notice that, like all array arguments, only a pointer to the **argv** array is passed. The size of this array is unknown to **main**. It is allocated by the operating system and is presumed sufficiently large to hold all of the argument pointers. (A typical maximum number of arguments is 32.) As you might expect, the pointers in the **argv** array appear in the same order as the strings on the command line at which they point.

We are now in a position to write a program that uses command line arguments. Perhaps the simplest is one that merely proves that we indeed *have access* to these arguments in the manner that has been indicated. Therefore, let us ignore their *meaning* and merely show their accessibility by printing them back to the terminal. The program below is designed to do just that—by "echoing" each argument string encountered in the command line on a separate output line. The program makes use of the **put_string** function that was the subject of Problem 5.4, so the file **stdio.h** must be **#include**d. (In the next chapter, we will see that the library equivalent of **put_string** is a function called **puts**.) The program looks like this:

```
#include <stdio.h>
main(argc, argv)
int argc;
char *argv[];
      {
      int i;
      for (i = 0; i < argc; i++)
            put_string(argv[i]);
      }
```

As written, this program first prints the command (the name of the program). By modifying the initial value of **i**, in the **for** loop, this behavior may be changed.

After we have had a chance to study some of the functions that are available from the standard library—particularly those that relate to *file* access—we will return to command line arguments. Some problems at the end of this chapter give you some practice in writing programs that involve them.

Problems

6.1 A union named **arg** contains either an integer named **i**, a floating-point variable named **f**, or a five-character array named **string**. Its use in a program is sufficiently complex that it is necessary to maintain *another* variable, called **type**, whose value is checked, before every access to **arg**, to ensure that the prospective access is proper. Devise and declare a data arrangement that links **arg** and **type** and briefly explain how it would be used. Choose one that is *extendable* to a similar situation in which there are *many* **arg**s and corresponding **type**s.

6.2 Briefly explain the essential differences between how an *array of unions* would be used in a program and how a *union of arrays* would be employed.

6.3 Assuming that a mechanism to define and access fields were *not* available in C, suppose you still wanted to use an unsigned integer, named **flags**, to hold a set of flag bits for an application. For example, suppose that each bit specified whether or not a specific property of an *identifier* existed. Specifically, let bit 0 be the STATIC bit, bit 1 the EXTERNAL bit, and bit 2 the KEYWORD bit. Write a statement whose execution sets both the STATIC and the EXTERNAL bits. Write another statement that resets these same two bits. Now, assuming the normal field declaration mechanism of C, write a declaration of the above unsigned integer in which the individual flag bits are named **is_static**, **is_external**, and **is_keyword**, respectively. Ignore their specific bit positions. Now write a single statement that sets both the static and external bits, and write another statement that resets them both.

6.4 A program is designed to simultaneously access several related files. Associated with each file in storage, we wish to define a file access control block containing key information about that file—including linkages to up to three *other* accessible files that are in some way "related" to it. Specifically, the control block should contain the file's name, a pointer to its buffer in storage, a count of the number of records currently residing in that buffer, a pointer to the current character in the buffer that is about to be processed, and three possible pointers to other "related" file control blocks. Declare a structure template, called **control_block**, for such a control block. Then declare an array of **MAX_BLOCKS** such control blocks, and initialize only the first three, using appropriate symbolic constant values that are assumed **#defined** elsewhere. In particular, initialize one of the links in each of the first three blocks so that they are linked together in a *chain*—with the third block linked back to the first.

6.5 The solution to Problem 5.23 (the **sort** function) is to be modified to permit the *caller* to specify the routine that is to be called to determine whether one string is greater than, less than, or equal to another. Such an enhancement would permit sorts on many other criteria other than the standard ASCII character table. For example, strings could be sorted by initial *numeric* value, assuming an initial floating-point numeric string of characters (containing an arbitrarily positioned decimal point and possible scientific notation). What specific changes are needed to the sort program to realize this enhancement?

6.6 Write the definition of a recursive function, called **sum**, that is given a positive integer argument **num**, and returns the sum of all positive integers up to and including **num**.

6.7 In the pointer version of the nested **for** loop in Section 6.6, assuming that (for example) the array **name** is defined as

$$\text{char name[ROWS] [COLUMNS] ;}$$

how must pointers **row_ptr** and **ptr** be defined in order for the code to compile and run successfully? Write specific declarations.

6.8 Write a sequence of **typedef** declarations that declare the following identifiers to be synonyms for the following types:

Name	Type that it is a synonym for
FCH	Function returning a character
PFCH	Pointer to a function returning a character
APFCH	Array of pointers to functions returning characters
PAPFCH	Pointer to an array of pointers to functions returning characters

Introduction to Remaining Problems

Each of the following problems is a modification of one of those given at the end of the previous chapter. In writing a solution to it, you may assume that all of those functions that were developed as solutions to the problems at the end of Chapter 5 are available for your use. In addition, you may assume that the **stdio.h** file has already been **#included**. Further, if you need it, you may employ a call to the standard library function called **printf**, passing to it a single character pointer argument, to get the *same result* as that from a call to **put_string**, but with the *final newline omitted*. (**printf** is much more sophisticated than this suggested use implies. Its detailed capabilities will be described later.) Each of the following programs receives *all* of its inputs *from the command line*. Therefore, *prompt* messages to the user are *not* necessary.

6.9 Define a **main** function that is a modification of the **printer** function of Problem 5.17. The first argument on the command line is the margin width. The rest of the arguments on the command line comprise the arbitrary text that should be reprinted in a left-justified column of the specified width.

6.10 Define a **main** function that is a modification of the **finder** function of Problem 5.21. The first argument on the command line is the short match test string. The other arguments on the command line are arbitrary words. The program prints back each of these words, on a *separate* line, with the first occurrence of the match string in it replaced by a string of highlight characters. If no match is found in the word, it is merely printed back verbatim.

6.11 Define a **main** function that is a modification of the **sorter** function of Problem 5.24. All of the arguments on the command line (*including* the name of the program) are printed back to the terminal, in a column, properly sorted.

CHAPTER 7   THE STANDARD LIBRARY

7.1 Introduction

Although the facilities provided by the functions that comprise the library in one C programming environment do not necessarily match those available from the functions in another library, there is general agreement regarding a basic set of routines that may be expected to be available in almost *any* "self-respecting" C system. We will cover many of these functions here. They are sufficiently universal that their names are normally considered as reserved words. That is, they are not employed to identify objects other than those in the standard library.

The number of such functions that have been named in this book so far has been intentionally minimal—so that sufficient groundwork could be laid to permit each function to receive a comprehensive explanation before it is used.

Most of the functions to be discussed implement I/O operations—since I/O functions are not mechanized in the native C language. Specifically, we will begin by explaining how *files* are defined and the means by which files are accessed. In particular, we will emphasize the fact that all I/O *devices* (e.g., keyboards and displays) are considered as the *equivalents* of files.

Several of the functions that are normally considered as necessary components in a comprehensive C library are ignored, either because they require little special explanation (e.g., we omit all mention of mathematical functions, like **sqrt** and **sin**, and of the related standard header file **math.h**), or because they are beyond our present scope (e.g., we omit all discussion of concurrent processes, "pipes," interrupt signals, and consequently, the standard header file **signal.h**).

Appendixes D and E contain capsule summaries of all of the functions that will be discussed in this chapter. It is expected that, once you have completed studying the details to be presented here, you will find the information provided there sufficient to refresh your memory concerning the properties of any single function.

We proceed with a discussion of files and of the difference between low-level and conventional-level I/O.

7.2 File Access Control Blocks

A *file* consists of a sequence of bytes or characters. From the point of view of many of the functions in the standard I/O library, a file has *no other* logical partitioning—except that, if it is a conventional *text* file, it is normally divided into *lines*, each terminating in a newline ('**\n**') character.

Since a file is either the source or the destination of a byte stream, any I/O device may be considered as the logical equivalent of a file. For example, a keyboard—which is the source of a character sequence—may be regarded as the equivalent of a read-only "file." Similarly, a display or a printer—which is the destination of a byte sequence—may be regarded as the equivalent of a write-only "file."

The I/O interface that a C program sees treats *all* components—disk files, other input and output devices, even other *programs*—as if they were files. Typically, a program simultaneously communicates with *several* files as it runs.

The operating system—i.e., the supervisor program, with which a few of the functions in the C library directly interface—is responsible for properly handling requests to create, read, and write files. It maintains one or more *directories* containing, at least, the names and the locations of all of the accessible files. One of its fundamental responsibilities is to keep track of the *extent* of each file on the storage medium. When an attempt is made to read a file past its last character, the operating system must properly signal the caller that the end of the file has been reached. For example, as we will see momentarily, a low-level **read** call returns the number of bytes that were actually read, so that a return of *zero* indicates that the *end* of the file must have been reached.

The C library follows the generally accepted convention that, before a file (or device) can be accessed by a program, it must be "opened." Of course, if the file does not yet exist, the program must have a means available to it by which that file may be created. The fact that a file is open indicates that it is accessible for appropriate access. Once access is no longer required, that file is "closed" by the program.

Normally, data is read from or written to files in *blocks* of a fixed size— one that is convenient for the storage medium. Thus, the *physical* partitioning of a file has little to do with its *logical* partitioning. An active block is stored in an area of memory called a *buffer*. A program normally accesses the data in a file via that file's memory buffer. Periodically, when the buffer is either full (on writing) or empty (on reading), a new data transfer between the buffer and the storage medium takes place.

A C program may elect to employ "low-level" I/O functions, which interface more or less directly with the operating system. Such a program must keep track of many details of the buffering process. For example, it must request allocation and deallocation of buffers. It must remember the location and the size of each buffer, and the position of the character in it that is currently being processed. By keeping a count of the number of characters not yet processed, it is able to ascertain the extent to which the buffer is "full" or "empty."

On the other hand, a program may be relieved of many of these concerns by calling "conventional-level" I/O functions (which, *in turn,* call the low-level routines). Using the higher-level I/O calls permits the program to treat the file as a stream of bytes, no matter *where* these bytes actually reside. Thus, the conventional-level I/O routines make the reading and the writing of data buffers *transparent* to the program.

To support all *conventional-level* I/O functions, special data structures, which may be called *file access control blocks*, are defined. Each one holds key information about an active file. Although the conventional-level I/O programmer need not be aware of the detailed contents of each control block, for completeness, we cover it here.

The **stdio.h** header file, which must be **#include**d in any program that employs conventional-level I/O calls, contains the declaration:

```
struct  _iobuf{
  char *_ptr;  /* current character position */
  int _cnt;    /* number of bytes remaining */
  char *_base; /* base address of the buffer */
  char _flag;  /* access control flags */
  char _file;  /* file number or descriptor */
};
```

and either of the definitions:

```
#define FILE struct _iobuf
```

or

```
typedef struct _iobuf FILE;
```

This means that the symbol **FILE** has been defined as a *shorthand* for a new data type, namely, a structure of the composition given above. This structure, or file access control block, contains the kind of information that needs to be maintained at the low level, in order to properly control the access to, and the filling and the emptying of, a file's memory buffer. (You may recall that some of the structure member names given above first appeared in the example in Section 1.3. The use of the byte called **_file** will be explained further in the next section.)

An *array* of such structures—as many as there may be files that are open simultaneously—is also declared in **stdio.h**. As will be explained further later, at the conventional level, the opening process *assigns* one of these blocks to the opened file, while the closing process deassigns the same block.

When a program treats a file as a stream of characters, there has to be a mechanism to signal to the program that the *end* of that file has been reached. It is often convenient to employ a *special character value* for this purpose. However, if *all possible* byte values are to be accommodated, how can this be done? Fortunately, since characters (or bytes) are actually passed in C as **int**s, a special **int** value can be assigned to signify the end of a file—without restricting the set of possible data values that can arise. Typically, a character value (8 bits long—having 256 possible values) is passed with zeroes in all of the upper **int** bit positions. The convention that has been adopted, in virtually all such C systems, is to employ an **int** value of **-1** (all binary 1's, in two's-complement form) as the end-of-file indicator. This value is given to the symbolic constant **EOF** by a **#define** directive in the **stdio.h** header file.

Notice that, since a keyboard may act as a read-only file, a means must exist to permit *it* to also signify the "end-of-file" condition. Typically, a special control character, like **ctrl-D**, is used for this purpose.

In summary, any program that expects to use any form of conventional-level I/O should contain the directive

```
#include <stdio.h>
```

which, among other things, gives a value to the **EOF** symbol and defines another symbol, named **FILE**, as representing a file access control block. This block is employed in the servicing of all conventional-level I/O calls.

7.3 I/O Initiation, Termination, and Redirection

Before a file may be accessed, it must be *opened*. This is accomplished either with a call to the conventional-level function **fopen** or with a call to the low-level function **open**.

The above statement immediately brings up several notational issues that should be cleared up before we proceed any further.

First, we will henceforth dispense with the terms "conventional-level" and "standard-level." Since most C programs employ library functions at this level— primarily because their use ensures portability and less dependence on the detailed characteristics of the operating system—this level will be *implied* unless explicitly stated otherwise (through use of the adjective "low-level," for example).

Second, the use of the names **fopen** and **open**, above, illustrates that many C library functions come in pairs or in triplets whose names differ only slightly. As might be expected, their operational descriptions also differ only slightly. Typically, the most general function in a set is the one whose name begins with an **f** (as in **fopen**). The other(s) in the set provide specialized or restricted variations on the general theme. For example, we will soon see that the function **fprintf** provides a formatted print (explained fully later) to *any* file or device. The function **printf** supplies the same function, but with the output implicitly directed to the standard output device (normally, the terminal), while the function **sprintf** supplies the same function, but with the output implicitly directed to a string destination in memory.

Third, you should bear in mind as we proceed that the interface provided by each function in the C library is a good example of one that should be provided by *any* well-designed function. Specifically, you will find that its operation is normally describable in a few sentences and that it usually returns a value that clearly indicates whether or not the requested operation was successfully executed. (Appendixes D and E contain capsule summaries of all of the functions described in this chapter.)

Fourth, as we proceed, we will occasionally need to introduce a new *abbreviation*—either for a function argument type or for a returned value type. Each abbreviation will then serve as a shorthand for that type throughout the remainder of this chapter. It should be understood that any such name is employed strictly for uniformity in notation, and that any other name that you find more convenient may be substituted for it. For example, we will use all of the notations **n**, **i**, and **b** to represent *integers*. Specifically, **n** will usually represent a count, **i** will stand for any integer, and **b** (for "Boolean") will be an integer that has one of *only two* possible values (either representing *true* and *false* or representing the possible values returned by a function to indicate either *success* or *failure*).

We now return to the calls **fopen** and **open**. The **fopen** call has the format

$$\mathbf{fopen(s, "m")}$$

where **s** is an abbreviation for a pointer to a null-terminated character *string*, and **m** represents a mode-of-access character. (Note: Each of the library function explanations to follow will begin in this manner—namely, with the abbreviated format of the *call*, as shown above. This format is the one employed in any capsule summary of the function that appears in Appendixes D and E. After an explanation of what is executed by the function and what value is returned by it, an example of how the call would appear in a typical statement will be given when necessary.)

The string specified by the first argument is the *name* of the file to be opened. The **m** character may have either of the values **r** (for *read* access), **w** (for *write* access), or **a** (for *append* access). (Note that the second argument is also a character string. However, its value is normally specified directly in the call, rather than indirectly via a pointer.) If the file does not yet exist, it is automatically created (in response to the write and append requests only). When an existing file is opened for *write* access, its previous contents are discarded.

After passing the request on to the operating system (by employing appropriate low-level calls), the **fopen** function activates an available file access control block and returns a *pointer* to it. If any error is detected (e.g., because an attempt was made to open a nonexisting file for reading, or because too many files are already open—so that no file access control block is available), a **NULL** pointer value is returned. The symbol **NULL** is defined as the equivalent of a zero in the **stdio.h** header file. (Recall that a **NULL** may be returned by any pointer-returning function to indicate that an exception condition was detected.)

The value returned by **fopen** is called a **FILE** pointer (i.e., a pointer to a structure having the composition of a file access control block). We will henceforth refer to this pointer by using the abbreviation **fp**.

In practice, the **fopen** call is frequently embedded in a statement having the form

```
if ((fp = fopen(filename_ptr, "w")) == NULL) error code
```

so that, normally, the named file is opened for the type of access specified in the call, and the *error code* portion is *not* executed. Notice that both the pointer **fp** and the function **fopen** must have been previously declared as follows:

```
FILE *fopen();
FILE *fp;
```

Since the typical **stdio.h** file contains declarations for the most common non-integer-returning functions in the standard I/O library (see Appendix E), the *first* of the above declarations is normally implied by the **#include <stdio.h>** directive. The second declaration above is required, however, since **fp** is only a sample name. (There may be *several* files open, each with its own unique **fp** identifier.)

Once a file has been opened in this manner, all subsequent calls referring to it must *identify* it by providing its assigned **fp** value as one of the call arguments. (Some books use the term "stream" as a synonym for an **fp**.) Numerous examples of such calls will be given in the discussions that follow. In particular, the call

fclose(fp)

"unopens" the file identified by **fp**. If necessary, that file's buffer is first "flushed" (written back to the file) before it is closed. The **fclose** function also deassigns the file access control block that was allocated to the deactivated file—making it available for use in subsequent **fopen** responses.

Most **fclose** realizations return a value indicating whether or not the close operation was successful. While it may appear that it should *always* be successful, there are error conditions that can arise. For example, it may be that the buffered data cannot be properly written to the file, or that the specified **fp** value points to an *inactive* file access control block. Thus, testing the value returned from an **fclose** call (by convention, a zero indicates *success*) is good defensive programming.

fclose is *automatically* called, for each open file, whenever a program terminates normally. However, it is good programming practice to *explicitly* close each open file, when it is no longer needed, not only to free its file access control block but also to ensure that its buffer is properly written out. Otherwise, a subsequent abnormal exit could cause some data to be lost.

Since a file is treated as a stream of bytes, all reading from or writing to it takes place sequentially—normally starting at its beginning. The append mode, of course, causes writing to begin at the end of the file.

As part of the process of initiating a program run, the first three file access control blocks in the array of such blocks are *automatically activated* (i.e., their "files" are automatically opened). These blocks are predefined as corresponding (respectively) to the following elements: the "standard input" (normally, the keyboard), the "standard output" (normally, the terminal display), and the "standard error" device (also, normally, the terminal screen). The **stdio.h** header file **#define**s three special symbols: **stdin**, **stdout**, and **stderr**, as having (respectively) the *address* values of the first three file access control blocks. Thus, for example, if an **fp** parameter in any I/O call is specified as

stdout, the operation called for (say, a character write) will be directed to the standard output device.

As we will see momentarily, several file I/O operations have counterparts that reference one of the standard I/O elements. For example, the call

$$\textbf{fputs(s, fp)}$$

(discussed further later) writes string **s** onto the file identified by **fp**, while the call

$$\textbf{puts(s)}$$

is defined as the *equivalent* of **fputs(s, stdout)**. In other words, **puts(s)** writes string **s** to the standard output device.

Thus, those elements that almost always communicate with a program are implicitly activated when a program run begins.

To further demonstrate the equivalence of files and devices, let us consider how the "standard" I/O elements may be *redefined*. As explained in Section 6.8, a command line may contain not only the name of the program to be run but also arguments that are to be passed to it. In most environments that support C, a command line may *also* contain a means to designate that a *file* should be employed as *substitute* for the standard input or the standard output device. Such a process is called "I/O redirection."

If a command line includes the construct

$$\textbf{>filename}$$

then the standard output character stream is redirected to the named file, instead of to the terminal. Similarly, if the command line contains the construct

$$\textbf{<filename}$$

then the standard input character stream is taken from the named file, instead of from the keyboard.

Thus, for example, a command line of the form

$$\textbf{process}$$

would load the named object file and transfer control to it. Any standard input or output would be directed from or to the terminal. On the other hand, the command line

$$\texttt{process <infile >outfile}$$

would run the same program. However, in this case the program would take its input from file **infile** and it would write its output onto file **outfile**. As you might expect, a command line may also redirect only *one* of the character streams. We should point out in addition that most C environments also accept command lines containing the construct

$$\texttt{>>outfile}$$

to cause the output file **outfile** to be opened *for appending only*. Notice that the same rules for opening files (explained earlier) apply to the opening of files in preparation for I/O redirection. For example, the file **infile** must exist. On the other hand, the file **outfile** will be created if it does not already exist.

Calls equivalent to **fopen** and **fclose** exist at the low level, for those programs that need to interface more directly with the operating system. Specifically, the call

$$\texttt{open(s,u)}$$

where **u** will be our abbreviation for an unsigned integer, opens the file named **s** for the access mode specified by **u**. The reason that the second parameter is designated as an **unsigned** is to ensure a positive value. Since low-level calls interface more directly with the operating system, they can be expected to be more system dependent. For example, some systems only permit **u** values of 0, 1, and 2, representing read, write, and read/write access, respectively. Others permit additional **u** values, to allow distinction between accesses to ASCII *text* files and accesses to more general *binary* files.

The **open** function returns a small positive integer, called a *file descriptor* (which we will henceforth abbreviate as **fd**), that identifies the just-opened file. (**open** returns **-1** to indicate an error.) Again, all subsequent calls to access that file, until it is later closed, must use this identifying value as an argument. In particular, the call

$$\texttt{close(fd)}$$

closes the file (returning zero to indicate success and **-1** to indicate an error). After a **close**, the **fd** value specified in the **close** call is available for a new **open**.

Note: The **fd** values of 0, 1, and 2 are specifically associated with the first three file access control blocks (i.e., those whose addresses are **stdin**, **stdout**, and **stderr**, respectively).

It is illegal to try to **open** a nonexisting file. The special low-level call

$$\texttt{creat(s,u)}$$

performs the equivalent of an **open** (for writing) of a nonexisting file. That is, it also returns an **fd** value. In this case, however, the **u** argument may specify an access control code, containing file protection bits. (See your system's manual to determine its meaning.) As explained for **fopen**, if a file is opened for writing, its present contents are discarded. (By the way, the name **creat** is *not* misspelled. It probably was originally coined to get around some system restriction and has come down through the ages in the same form.)

It was pointed out earlier that the implementation of a typical standard I/O function, like **fopen**, itself uses low-level calls. It is interesting to consider what the implementation of **fopen** should look like. First, it should search for a free file access control block. Having found one, it should then attempt to **open** the named file, for the access mode given. If the **open** call returns an error code indicating that the file does not exist, an attempt to create the file should be made, using the **creat** call. The parameters of the just-found file access control block should then be properly *initialized*. This may entail calling an appropriate system routine for allocation of a memory buffer. One of the last steps is to write the **fd** value, returned by either of the **open** or **creat** calls, into the **_file** slot in the file access control block, so that *other* I/O functions will then be able to *reference* the proper file at the low level. Finally, the function should return a pointer to the just-initialized access control block.

7.4 Character and Line I/O

Since a file is a sequence of characters, it stands to reason that virtually all file I/O operations are built up out of single character transfers. The basic calls

$$\texttt{getc(fp)} \quad \textbf{and} \quad \texttt{fgetc(fp)}$$

perform *identical* operations. Each returns (as an **int**) the next character read from the stream **fp**. (If the end of the file has already been reached, each returns **EOF** instead.) **getc** is implemented as a *macro*, while **fgetc** is implemented as a *function*. The usual trade-offs apply. Namely, if the number of calls in a given body of code is large, then the use of **fgetc** will reduce the amount of memory consumed, since each occurrence of **getc** results in an in-line macro expansion. On the other hand, the macro realization is preferred if the fastest possible response is desired, since use of the macro dispenses with the overhead involved in a function call.

In this connection, we should emphasize that, in Appendixes D and E, each function that is normally implemented as a macro is specifically marked as such. It is important that the programmer be aware of which functions are actually implemented as macros, because many macros use the conditional operator (recall the discussion in Section 4.2). Under these conditions, the argument expression(s) that are passed to the macro may be evaluated *more than once*, and this may cause unexpected results if these expressions involve any *side effects*.

The macro expansion for **getc** (which is normally defined in the **stdio.h** header file) was originally introduced in Section 1.3, as an example of a C expression that employs a large number of C operators. The code for this macro was analyzed in detail in Section 2.13, and it was finally recognized as a macro having an *argument* in Section 4.2.

Typically, **getc** (or **fgetc**) appears in a statement in the form

$$\text{while } ((c = \text{getc}(fp)) \mathrel{!=} \text{EOF}) \; \dots$$

where **c** is the abbreviation that we will employ for a character variable. Each time that a new valid character is fetched from the file identified by **fp**, the "..." code portion is reexecuted. Finally, when **EOF** is encountered, an exit from the loop takes place.

In a similar manner, either of the calls

$$\textbf{putc}(c, fp) \quad \textbf{or} \quad \textbf{fputc}(c, fp)$$

writes the character **c** onto the stream identified by **fp**. Again, **putc** is the *macro* implementation, defined in **stdio.h**, while **fputc** is implemented as a *function*. Each of these functions returns the character value that it was given as an argument. Such a return protocol permits convenient statements of the form

$$\textbf{while } (\textbf{fputc}(*\text{ptr}++))$$
$$;$$

to be employed to write out a string of characters up to, but *not including*, the terminating null character. (See the solution to Problem 5.4.) We will soon see other examples to demonstrate that it is often convenient to have a function return one of the arguments that was passed to it, even though that argument is known to the programmer.

The functions **getchar** and **putchar** (both introduced in the Problems section of Chapter 5) are actually implemented as macros. They are also defined in the **stdio.h** file as follows:

```
#define getchar()   getc(stdin)
#define putchar(c)  putc(c,stdout)
```

In other words, normally **getchar** is a **getc** from the terminal, while **putchar** is a **putc** to the terminal. Again, the value returned by **putchar** is the character value that was just written out.

Typically, **getchar** is employed in a statement of the form

```
while ((*ptr++ = getchar()) != '\n')
                 ;
```

to deposit a *line* of characters (in this case, all those up to, but not including, the final newline) into the string of memory locations pointed to by **ptr**.

Similarly, **putchar** might be employed in a statement of the form

```
while ((c = getc(fp)) != EOF) putchar(c);
```

to print the contents of the file identified by **fp** onto the standard output device.

Occasionally, it is useful to "unget" a character that was just read—via a call to **getc** or **getchar**—from a character stream. Here, "unget" implies pushing that character *back* onto the source of characters, so that it will be later *re*fetched on the very *next* **getc** or **getchar**. Such a process is useful, for example, when a string of characters, all having the same property, are to be processed in sequence. The process should stop when the first character *not* having that property is encountered. However, by the time the stop occurs, one character too many has been fetched from the input stream. The C library provides the call

```
ungetc(c,fp)
```

to push the just-read character **c** back onto the stream **fp** (where **fp** should be replaced by **stdin**, if **c** was fetched by a previous **getchar**). Only one push-back is guaranteed, provided something has been previously read from the file. This function also returns its argument **c**.

A *line* is a character sequence terminating in a newline ('\n'). Most conventional text files (e.g., source programs and document files) are composed of variable-length lines. A line is, perhaps, the simplest form of "record" in a C file. Thus, it is helpful to have available functions that read and write lines.

The call

$$\mathbf{fgets(s,n,fp)}$$

reads the next line (up to a maximum of **n** characters in length) from stream **fp** and writes it into memory at location **s**. Typically, **n** is the number of bytes available in the buffer at **s**. **fgets** returns its argument **s**. All characters, up to *and including* the final newline, are stored—with a terminating null ('**\0**') character appended.

The call

$$\mathbf{gets(s)}$$

is almost, *but not exactly* the same as **fgets(s,n,stdin)**. First, there is no limit specified to the length of the line being read. Second, the string that is read is placed in memory with its terminating newline *replaced* by the null character.

Although these differences may be due to historical accident, they may also be due to the ways in which these calls are normally used. Typically, **gets** is employed to read an arbitrary string from the keyboard and to place it in memory in standard null-terminated form. In this case, the purpose of the RETURN or ENTER key, which generates the newline, is merely to *signal* the end of the input string.

On the other hand, when the line comes from a *file*, the newline character signals the end of an elementary variable-length "record." Normally, this character must be retained because the same record may later be *rewritten* to the same or to a new file, in which case its terminating delimiter must remain to separate it from the *next* record. An example will be presented shortly.

Notice that **gets** is the standard library's equivalent of the functions that was called **get_string** in Problem 5.3.

The call

$$\mathbf{fputs(s,fp)}$$

writes the (null-terminated) string beginning at **s** onto the file identified by **fp**. The terminating null character is *not* written out. The function returns a Boolean (**b**) indicating whether or not the operation was executed successfully. (By convention, *zero* indicates success, while **-1**, which is normally **EOF**, indicates an error.)

The companion call

$$\mathbf{puts(s)}$$

is, again, essentially the same as **fputs(s,stdout)**. However, **puts** appends an extra newline to the output string. It also returns an integer indicating whether or not the function was executed successfully.

Notice that **puts** is the standard library's equivalent of the function that was called **put_string** in Problem 5.4.

We have already shown one example to demonstrate that it is often useful for a function to return one of its arguments (when it has nothing more important to return), even though that argument is already "known" to the programmer. Consider another example:

Several of the problems at the end of Chapter 5 were designed to operate by continuing to read input lines from the terminal, until a null (zero-length) line was read. Since **get_string** (not a standard library function) was (for simplicity) *not* defined as returning its pointer argument, the solution statement

$$\text{while (get\_string(line), str\_len(line))}\ldots$$

was employed to execute the "..." portion so long as the length of the string read was not zero. (**str_len** is also *not* a standard library name. We will soon see that its standard library equivalent is named **strlen**.) A more elegant construct, to execute the same operation, given that **gets** returns the pointer to the just-read string, is

$$\text{while (strlen(gets(line)))}\ldots$$

where **line** is the pointer to the string buffer in storage.

Notice that the fact that **fputs** does *not* append a newline to the output string is a consequence of the way in which **fgets** was defined in the first place. The definitions, as they now stand, permit statements of the form

$$\text{while (fgets(line,MAX\_LINE,fp1) != NULL)}$$
$$\text{fputs(line,fp2);}$$

to be employed to copy lines from stream **fp1** onto stream **fp2**.

To demonstrate how higher-level standard I/O functions are composed out of lower-level standard functions, one possible realization of the function **gets** is presented:

```
/*************************** gets ***************************
* Given  a  pointer  to  a  buffer  in  storage,  place  the
* input  string  from  stdin  there  and  return  the
* pointer.
*********************************************************/
char *gets(s)
char *s;
    {
    register char *p; /* moving pointer */
    register int c;   /* character slot */
    p = s;            /* start at buffer beginning */
    while ((c = getchar()) != '\n' && c != EOF)
        *p++ = c;     /* deposit characters until end */
    *p = '\0';        /* append null terminator */
    return ((p == s && c == EOF) ? NULL : s);
    }
```

It is assumed that the **stdio.h** header file has already been **#include**d.
The first two declarations in the body declare two local variables that should be
placed in registers, if available, to speed up the process. The main loop continues
to deposit input characters into the buffer until the line ends, either with a normal
newline or via detection of the **EOF** condition (typically, a **ctrl-d** from the
keyboard). After appending a null character to the buffer, the function normally
returns its argument. However, if the first character read was **EOF**, the function
returns NULL. Notice that a zero-length line (e.g., a single RETURN or ENTER,
from the keyboard) is a perfectly acceptable input.

7.5 Formatted I/O

In order to print the value of a variable on an output device (e.g., the
terminal screen or the printer), that value must be converted into a properly
formatted sequence of characters. Similarly, an input character sequence that
represents the value of a variable must be properly converted from its input
format into the form in which that value is stored internally. For example, the
sequence of 11 characters

$$-123.456E-7$$

whether printed on a display or typed in on a keyboard, is totally different from the form in which that same value is stored internally for processing.

The functions that convert between the external formats of variable values and their internal formats are called *formatted I/O* functions. We have already seen a few elementary instances of such functions. For example, in Problem 3.16, you were asked to accept on faith that the statement

printf ("%d\n", j) ;

prints the value of integer **j** and then starts a new line. Similarly, in Problems 5.8 and 5.10, you were asked to develop functions (**int_to_digits** and **digits_to_int**) to convert between the external representations of integers and their internal representations. In addition, in the introduction that preceded Problem 6.9, you were informed that the function **printf**, when passed a single pointer to a character string, delivers the same result as that provided by the function **put_string** (Problem 5.4), but with the final newline omitted. (Note: We have already renamed the function **put_string** with its standard library name **puts**.)

We now discuss this issue from a more general point of view. Specifically, we will consider two fundamental functions in the standard library, each of which comes in (at least) three variations. These functions are the ones that are employed to perform virtually all of the formatted I/O operations that are required in C programs.

The calls

printf (f), fprintf (fp, f), and sprintf (s, f)

all result in the same formatted *output* function. However, the *destination* of the output character sequence depends on which call is employed. Specifically, **fprintf** directs its output to the file identified by **fp, sprintf** directs its output to the character buffer in memory at location **s**, while **printf** (the one that is most frequently used) directs its output to the standard output device [in which case **printf (f)** is actually a shorthand for **fprintf (stdout, f)**]. The meaning of the argument whose abbreviation is **f**, which is common to all three calls, is the key to understanding the operation of each of these functions. It will be explained in detail below.

Similarly, the calls

scanf (f), fscanf (fp, f), and sscanf (s, f)

all result in the same formatted *input* function. However, the *source* of the input character sequence depends on which call is employed. Specifically, **fscanf** receives its input from the stream identified by **fp**, **sscanf** receives its input from the character buffer in memory at location **s**, while **scanf** (the one most frequently employed) receives its input from the standard input device [in which case **scanf(f)** is actually a shorthand for **fscanf(stdin, f)**]. The meaning of the argument whose abbreviation is **f**, also common to all three calls, is also the key to understanding the operation of each of these functions. We proceed by explaining what abbreviation **f** means.

f stands for a *format control string*—normally a literal character sequence enclosed in double quotes. (A pointer to such a string is, of course, acceptable—but rarely used.) This string contains two kinds of objects: regular characters and *conversion specifications*.

On *output*, regular characters are transmitted to the output destination *verbatim*, while each conversion specification specifies that the next sequence of output characters should be derived instead from a conversion process that is applied to the value of an *argument*. This arguments appears, in a *list* of such arguments, immediately after the format control string. On *input*, ordinary characters must be *received* verbatim, while each conversion specification specifies that the next sequence of *input* characters should undergo a conversion process to derive a value. This value is then stored in the memory location addressed by a corresponding *pointer argument* that also appears, in a list of such arguments, immediately after the format control string.

Thus, as many arguments must appear, in the list that follows the format control string, as there are conversion specifications in the format control string.

Each conversion specification begins with the special character **%** and ends with a special *conversion character*. The conversion character designates the specific *type* of input or output conversion that should take place. For example, the conversion character **d** calls for a *decimal* conversion, while the conversion character **s** calls for a *string* conversion.

We will ignore, for the moment, the fact that special control characters may exist *inside* a conversion specification (i.e., between the leading **%** and the trailing conversion character).

Thus, for example, the format control string

$$\text{"\textbackslash tabc \%d efgh \%s ij\textbackslash n"}$$

contains 15 ordinary characters (including the spaces and the tab and newline escape codes) and two conversion specifications: **%d** and **%s**. Conversion specifications and ordinary characters may be intermixed in any manner, and any parts may be missing. Thus, for instance, the format control string

$$\text{"Prompt message: "}$$

contains no conversion specifications, while the format control string

$$\text{"\%s\%d\%s\%d"}$$

contains four conversion specifications and *no* ordinary characters.

As pointed out earlier, every occurrence of a conversion specification in a format control string must be *matched* by an argument—an appropriate expression supplied immediately following the control string. As many arguments as there are conversion specifications must be given, in the proper order. These arguments must be separated from each other, and from the leading control string, by commas. Thus, a *complete* definition of the abbreviation **f** includes not only the format control string, *but also* any arguments that it calls for. For instance, the first example given above should actually appear as

$$\text{"\textbackslash tabc \%d efgh \%s ij\textbackslash n"}, \quad arg1, \quad arg2$$

where the expression *arg1* will be used to satisfy the **%d** specification, while the expression *arg2* will be used to satisfy the **%s** specification. The second example given above does not need any modification, because it contains no conversion specifications. However, the third example above needs to read, instead, as

$$\text{"\%s\%d\%s\%d"}, \quad arg1, \quad arg2, \quad arg3, \quad arg4$$

where each *arg* expression is designed to satisfy its corresponding conversion specification.

Summarizing, and providing more detail: on *output* (i.e., when calling one of the three **printf** derivatives), each ordinary character in the format control string is delivered to the output destination verbatim, while each conversion specification in the format control string causes a *sequence* of characters to be delivered to the output destination. This sequence is derived by taking the value of the corresponding argument expression and converting it according to the rule specified in the specification. Now we can see, for example, why the call

$$\text{printf ("\%d\textbackslash n", j)}$$

prints the value of integer **j** in decimal form and then appends a newline, or why the call

$$\text{printf ("arbitrary message")}$$

merely prints the message given verbatim, without executing any conversions. Notice that, in this last case, a call to **puts** may be preferable (if the terminating newline that it supplies is acceptable and if the program does not need any *other* format conversions), because, as you might expect, the *size* of the **puts** function is significantly smaller than that of the **printf** function.

Also summarizing, and providing more detail: on *input* (i.e., when calling one of the three **scanf** derivatives), each ordinary character (but *not* a white space character) in the format control string must be received from the input source verbatim, while each white space character in the format control string may be used to match *any arbitrary sequence* of input white space characters. (They are generally employed to separate adjacent input values.) Each conversion specification must be matched by the receipt of an appropriate sequence of input characters (preceded by any amount of white space). This sequence is converted, according to the specification given, into a value that is then stored at the *location* specified by the corresponding argument expression. Thus, we emphasize, again, that each argument expression in a call to one of the **scanf** functions must be a *pointer* of the proper type. For example, the call

scanf ("%d" , &n)

reads a sequence of digits (possibly preceded by a sign) from the standard input device and stores its equivalent decimal value in the location assigned to the integer **n**.

Those conversion characters that are common to the **printf** and **scanf** families are given below. For each one, the conversion that it invokes, between the internal representation of a value and its corresponding external representation, is also specified:

Conversion character	Invokes conversion between	
	Internal form	**External form**
d	Signed integer	Decimal constant notation
o	Unsigned integer	Octal digits
x	Unsigned integer	Hexadecimal digits
u	Unsigned integer	Decimal digits
c	Single character	Single character
s	Character string	Character string
f	Floating-point number	Floating constant notation (of the form [-]aaaa.bbbb)

While it is clear, from the discussion above, that the **printf** and **scanf** families have distinct operational similarities, there are several important differences that should be clarified. We begin by explaining the meaning of all of the control characters that may appear *inside* a format specifier (an alternative name for a conversion specification).

On *output*, a format specifier may have the form

$$\%\text{-m.plX}$$

where **X** is the conversion character, and where each of the internal characters is *optional*. **m** (a digit string) is a *minimum field width*. It constrains the output character string to be appropriately padded with spaces (normally) within a field of that width (to provide for proper vertical alignment, for example). If more space is needed than is specified, it will be used. Normally, the output character sequence is *right-justified* within this field (i.e., spaces are padded on the left). However, if the *minus sign* appears in the format specifier, the output character sequence will be *left-justified* (space padded on the right) instead.

The **.p** portion (**p** is also a digit string) specifies the *precision* of a floating output (the number of digits to be printed to the right of the decimal point—with a default of *six*) or the *maximum* number of characters to be printed from a string. Finally, the **1** indicates that the corresponding data item, normally expected to be an **int**, is to be interpreted instead as a **long**.

Before considering a few examples, we should also point out that the **printf** family of formatted output functions also accepts the conversion characters **e** (to cause floating output to appear in *exponential* form) and **g** (to output a floating value in *either* **e** form *or* **f** form—whichever results in the shortest output length).

To illustrate some of the formatting capabilities in the **printf** family, let us assume the following declarations

```
double num = 123.4567e+3;
char *s = "textfield";
```

Under these assumptions, the following **printf** statements will print the following character sequences (the < and > characters are included as points of reference):

Statement	Output that it generates
`printf("<%9.4f>\n",num);`	`<123456.7000>`
`printf("<%9f>\n",num);`	`<123456.700000>`
`printf("<%9.0f>\n",num);`	`<   123456>`
`printf("<%-9.0f>\n",num);`	`<123456   >`
`printf("<%11.6e>\n",num);`	`<1.234567e+05>`
`printf("<%s>\n",s);`	`<textfield>`
`printf("<%-9.6s>\n",s);`	`<textfi   >`

On *input*, a format specifier may have the form

$$\%*nlX$$

where **X** is the conversion character, and where each of the internal characters is optional. The * causes the specified conversion to be performed on the input string, but *suppresses* the storage of the resulting value. Thus, the * provides a means to effectively *ignore* or *skip* the corresponding input field. **n** (a digit string) specifies a *maximum input field width*, while **l** is used to indicate that a **long** resulting value is desired.

The **scanf** family of functions also accepts the conversion character **h** as calling for conversion to a **short int** output value.

As an example of the use of **scanf**, consider the statement

$$\text{scanf("\%s \%*d \%f", string\_ptr, \&n, \&num);}$$

where it is assumed that **n** is an **int**, while **num** is a **float**. An input of the form

$$\text{Characters 9876 123.45}$$

will store the string **Characters** at the location pointed to by character pointer **string_ptr** (a null character will be automatically appended), will *skip* the input field **9876** (due to the assignment suppression character *), and will store the value **123.45** in the memory location corresponding to floating variable **num**.

You are again reminded that all of the arguments in a **scanf** call *must be pointers*.

A few final points: First, while none of the **printf** functions return useful values, each of the **scanf** functions returns the *number of successfully matched input items*. Such a value may be employed to ensure that the *response* to the **scanf** call for input was proper. Thus, a **scanf** call is frequently embedded in a statement of the form

$$\text{if (scanf}(\ldots)\ ==\ \text{NUM)}\ code$$

where the *code* portion is executed only if the user has provided the proper input values. Second, as you might expect (based on your experience with the \ escape character), if an expected conversion character, following a leading %, is *not* one of those in the accepted set, then it is taken to be an *ordinary* character. Thus, the sequence %% is the way to represent the single regular character %.

Finally, some C systems may provide one or two more **printf** or **scanf** options. You should consult the documentation that is provided with your system to see if any other variations are available.

7.6 Binary Reads and Writes

Much of the discussion, in the preceding sections, placed implicit emphasis on the input and output of conventional text character sequences. For example, all I/O strings were assumed to be null-terminated in storage, meaning that some binary values (specifically, '\0') were assumed *excluded* from the set of possible values being transferred.

We now consider function calls that transfer blocks of data between files and buffers without any regard to the values of the bytes being read or written. Specifically, we will discuss two *read* calls and two *write* calls. The two alternatives in each pair of calls differ primarily in the way in which the file that is to participate in the data transfer is identified. One of the calls employs an integer *file descriptor* argument (i.e., an **fd**), in which case it is considered as a low-level call. The other employs a **FILE** *pointer* argument (i.e., a stream identifier **fp**), in which case it is considered as a standard-level call.

The call

$$\textbf{fread}(\textbf{p}, \textbf{i}, \textbf{n}, \textbf{fp})$$

where **p** will be another abbreviation that we will employ for a *pointer* (of any type—but usually to characters), is a request to transfer **n** data blocks, each of size **i** bytes, from the file identified by **fp**, into the memory buffer at **p**.

Typically, **i** is given as

$$\mathtt{sizeof\,(*p)}$$

assuming that **p** has already been cast as a pointer to objects having the same size of *one* of the data blocks being transferred.

The **fread** call returns the *number* of such blocks actually transferred. This value may be *less than* **n** either because an error was encountered or because the end of the file was reached before the called-for number of data blocks was read. (In Section 7.10, the macros **ferror** and **feof** will be described. They may be used to check for the cause, when the number of data blocks actually transferred is less than the number that was requested.)

The call

$$\mathtt{read\,(fd,p,n)}$$

is a low-level request to read **n** *bytes*, from the file identified by **fd**, into the buffer at **p**. This call also returns the number of bytes actually read—which may be less than that requested, if there is an insufficient number of bytes remaining in the file. Specifically, a returned value of *zero* implies that the end of the file has already been reached. A return of **-1** indicates an error.

The call

$$\mathtt{fwrite\,(p,i,n,fp)}$$

is the companion to **fread**. It appends **n** data items, each of size **i**, to the file identified by **fp**. Again, **p** is normally a pointer to items of this size, in which case the value of **i** is usually **sizeof(*p)**.

This call also returns the number of items actually written, which is less than **n** only if an error condition has been encountered.

Similarly, the call

$$\mathtt{write\,(fd,p,n)}$$

a companion to **read**, writes **n** bytes to the file identified by **fd** from the character buffer at **p**. Again, the number of bytes actually written is returned. An error is indicated if this number is not equal to that requested. A return of **-1** is also an error indication.

As a specific example of the application of the **fread** and **fwrite** functions (and, additionally, of the library functions **atoi** and **exit**—explained further below), consider the following program: It reads an input file containing a series of equal-length data blocks, and writes to an output file only those blocks meeting a specific criterion. Let us assume that the participating file names, and

the criterion, are specified on the command line. One version of the program
might read as follows:

```
#include <stdio.h>
#define MAX_BLOCKS 100
main(argc,argv)
int argc;
char *argv[];
    {
    FILE *in, *out;
    struct data_unit
        {
        int velocity;
        char direction;
            .
            .
            .
        int amplitude;
        } block[MAX_BLOCKS];
    int n, i;
    if ((in = fopen(argv[1],"r")) == NULL)
        err(argv[1]);
    if ((out = fopen(argv[2],"w")) == NULL)
        err(argv[2]);
while((n = fread(block,sizeof(struct data_unit),
                    MAX_BLOCKS,in)) > 0)
        for (i = 0; i < n; i++)
            if (block[i].amplitude > atoi(argv[3]))
                fwrite(&block[i], sizeof(struct data_unit),
                                1, out);
    exit(0);
    }
```

where the routine **err** is defined as follows:

```
    err(name)
    char *name;
        {
        fprintf(stderr, "Can't open %s\n", name);
        exit(1);
        }
```

Notice the declarations of the **FILE** pointers **in** and **out** and the declaration of an arbitrary data structure, whose composition (which is not completely spelled out) is named **data_unit**. The program opens both data files (exiting to the routine **err** if an error is detected) and proceeds to read successive input file segments, each containing **MAX_BLOCKS** (or fewer) data blocks, and to deposit each segment read into the memory array named **block**, until the end of the input file is detected. For each data block in the array of blocks just read, the program then checks a specific criterion (that relies on a value given on the command line) to decide whether or not to include that block in the output file.

The library function **atoi** (short for "ASCII to integer") returns the equivalent integer value of a string of digits (optionally preceded by a minus sign) at the location passed to it as an argument. (Thus, **atoi** is almost the same as the routine **digits_to_int** in Problem 5.10.) In the program above, the last argument on the command line is an integer threshold value that is employed to decide whether or not a specific data block should be copied to the output file.

The library function **exit** terminates program execution in an orderly manner (i.e., it **fclose**s all open files first) and returns its integer argument to the program that initiated the one that is **exit**ing. (The initiating program may be either the operating system or, in an environment that supports the creation of *sub*processes, a corresponding "parent" process.) By convention, a return of *zero* indicates a *normal* return, while any *nonzero* return indicates an *abnormal* return (hence, the return of the value 1 when an error is detected).

Notice that other error-checking code could have been included in the program above. For example, there is presently no check that the number of arguments on the command line is proper. A sequence of statements of the form

```
if (argc != 4)
    {
    puts("Args required: infile outfile threshold");
    exit(1);
    }
```

will abort the program if the number of arguments on the command line is incorrect. Observe that **puts** is preferred to **printf** when no conversions are necessary. Similarly, a preferable form for the **fwrite** line would be

```
if (fwrite(&block[i], sizeof(struct data_unit),
                       1, out) != 1)
    {
    puts("Write error detected");
    exit(1);
    }
```

7.7 Character-Type Macros and Conversions

The idea of a macro having arguments was introduced in Section 4.2, and the specific examples **isdigit**, **isupper**, and **tolower** were first described in Problems 4.4 through 4.6 and later employed in Problem 5.9. We now consider the entire family of related macros. They are all part of the standard C library and are normally defined in a header file named **ctype.h**.

Each of the character-classification macro calls has the format

$$\textbf{is}\,type\,(\textbf{c})$$

where c is a character argument (passed to the macro as an **int**) and *type* is the name of the *property* of c that the macro will test. The macro returns *true* if the argument c *has* the specified property and *false* if it does not. Typically, such a macro call is employed in a relational expression. For example, the solution to Problem 5.10 (implementing the **digits_to_int** function) contains an equivalent of the statement

$$\textbf{while (isdigit(c))} ...$$

which continues to execute the "..." portion of code so long as the character **c** (derived via an expression of the form **c = *ptr++**) remains a digit. Similarly, the statement

$$\textbf{while (isspace(*ptr)) ptr++;}$$

advances the character pointer **ptr** past all white space characters.

The most prevalent of the character testing macros are listed in the table below. (They are also summarized in Appendixes D and E.)

Macro call	Returns TRUE if the argument is:
isalnum(c)	A letter or a digit
isalpha(c)	A letter
isascii(c)	Any ASCII character (value $<=$ 0177)
iscntrl(c)	Any control character
isdigit(c)	A digit
islower(c)	Any lowercase letter
isprint(c)	Any printable character
ispunct(c)	Any punctuation character
isspace(c)	Any white space character
isupper(c)	Any uppercase letter
isxdigit(c)	Any hexadecimal digit

Each macro is normally implemented through use of the conditional operator. For example, the macro definition

```
#define isspace(c)  ((c) == ' ' || (c) == '\n' || (c) == '\t' \
                     ? 1 : 0)
```

defines a macro that returns true if **c** is a space or a newline or a tab character. Since the expression that is the macro argument may be evaluated more than once, it is essential that such an evaluation *not* involve any side effects.

Several C library functions have names developed around the preposition "to" instead of around the verb "is" (like those above). Their names imply *conversions* from one form *to* another.

Two of these functions have already been introduced: **tolower**, in Problems 4.6 and 5.9, and **atoi**, in the previous section. To remind you, the call

tolower(c)

returns **c**, either converted to lowercase, if it was an uppercase letter, or unchanged, if it was not. The companion call

toupper(c)

converts **c** to upper case, if it was a lowercase letter, or leaves it unchanged, if it was not.

These functions may be implemented in macro form, as Problem 4.6 suggests.

A typical use of such a function is to make a section of code *independent* of the case of one or more characters. For example, a good program should not care whether a keyboard response comes in uppercase or in lowercase form. Thus, a construct like

tolower(getchar())

delivers the same value for *either* case.

The function **atof**, like **atoi** (described in the previous section), is passed a pointer to a character sequence. Typically, this sequence has the form

[whitespace] [+|-] digits [. digits] [e|E[+|-] integer]

where each pair of square brackets encloses an *optional* construction. Thus, any of the accepted forms for a *floating* constant are accepted. **atof** returns the equivalent value of the string, as a **double** (which we will henceforth abbreviate as **d**). Like **atoi**, conversion begins with the first non-white-space character and it ends when the first unrecognized character is encountered. (Note: **atof** was briefly referenced in Problem 4.8. Since it returns a noninteger, it should be declared as

double atof();

before it is called.)

7.8 Memory Allocation Functions

As a program runs, the amount of memory that it needs generally varies. Since the total amount of storage space that is available for all purposes is limited, a well-designed program normally varies the amount of space that it is using to suit its current needs. This permits the rest of the storage space to be made available for other purposes. A program varies its use of storage space by making *requests* to the operating system for the space that it needs. When a request is granted, the program receives, in return, a *pointer* to the assigned area. The program retains its portability because its design is independent of the actual location of the storage that is allocated to it. When the program finishes using an assigned area, it normally makes another call to the operating system to *free* or release that space.

Since the total amount of memory that is available for all purposes varies from system to system, a program may be made less machine dependent by adjusting its memory requirements to suit the system on which it is running.

Of all of the memory allocation functions available in a typical C library, the most fundamental are **malloc**, **calloc**, and **free**. The first of these is invoked using the call

malloc(u)

where the unsigned parameter **u** is the size, in bytes, of the space requested. This function returns a character pointer to an area at least as large as that requested. Furthermore, the boundary at which this pointer points is suitably aligned to accommodate all storage requirements. If the requested space is not available, **malloc** returns **NULL**.

Similarly, the call

calloc(n, i)

requests the return of a character pointer to an available space to hold **n** elements, each of size **i** bytes. (**n** and **i** should also be unsigned here.) Again, the returned pointer value is guaranteed to point to an appropriate boundary to suit any use for the assigned storage, and, as you might expect, a NULL is returned if the space requested is not available.

calloc differs from **malloc** not only in the way in which the requested space is defined. The two calls differ primarily in that, while the space delivered by **malloc** is not changed in any way (i.e., it begins containing "garbage"), the space allocated by **calloc** is *cleared* before it is delivered. Thus, the **calloc**-allocated space resembles **static** or "permanent" storage, while the **malloc**-allocated space resembles **auto** or "temporary" storage. In both cases, however, the space remains allocated to the program until it is later **freed**.

Notice, especially, that since both of the above functions return *character* pointers, it is generally necessary to appropriately *cast* their returned values, before using them, to ensure proper scaling of pointer increments and decrements. Furthermore, both of these functions, being non-integer-returning, must be properly *declared* before they are called. (Since they are considered outside of the "standard I/O" library of functions, their declarations do *not* normally appear in the **stdio.h** header file.)

A typical use of **malloc**, then, would appear in the context

```
char *malloc();  /*Non-integer-returning declaration */
int *pi;  /*Pointer to objects that the space is for */
      .
      .
      .
if ((pi = (int *) malloc(NINTS * sizeof(int)))
           == NULL) { ... error code ...}
```

where it is assumed, here, that the space requested will be used to house *integers*. Notice the cast of the value returned by **malloc**, before assignment of that value to the integer pointer **pi**. NINTS is assumed **#defined** earlier. Normally, of course, the *error code* portion is not executed.

A similar request to **calloc** would appear in the context

```
char *calloc();  /*Non-integer-returning declaration*/
struct blk *pb;  /*Ptr to items that space is for*/
      .
      .
      .
if ((pb = (struct blk *) calloc(N, sizeof(struct blk)))
           == NULL) {... error code ...}
```

where the structure tag **blk** and the constant N are assumed defined earlier.

An area of memory that was allocated either by **malloc** or by **calloc** may be released or deallocated (i.e., returned to the pool of available memory space) by use of the call

$$\text{free (p)}$$

where **p** is the same character pointer that was originally returned from the allocation call. In some C environments, **free** does not return a useful value. In others, a preferable realization of **free** exists. It returns a Boolean **b** indicating whether or not the space was properly released (with zero indicating success and **-1** indicating an error). Such a **free** function permits detection of calls to it that are not accompanied by a proper pointer value.

Assuming that **free** does return a success/failure indicator, a call to it would normally appear in the context

$$\text{if (free((char *)ptr) != 0) \{ ... } \textit{error code} ... \}$$

where it is assumed that **ptr** is pointing at the origin of the area to be deallocated. Notice that it is recast back to a character pointer before the call is executed.

7.9 String-Handling Functions

Many of the functions introduced in the problems at the end of Chapter 5 exhibited string-handling properties. Some were quite similar to, if not identical to, functions available in the standard C library. In particular, the Problem 5.5 function **str_len** can now be renamed as the standard library function **strlen**. Similarly, the Problem 5.19 function **str_cmp** can now be renamed as the standard library function **strcmp**.

The family of string-handling functions that is available from one C library may differ from that available in another. We will cover here only those functions that are the most universal.

Many of the functions that we have already discussed process strings in one form or another. We will concentrate here only on those functions that manipulate in-memory, null-terminated character strings.

In addition to **strlen**, we will consider eight other string-handling functions. They are actually subdivided into four *pairs*. First, recall that the call

$$\text{strlen (s)}$$

returns an integer that is the *length* of the string **s**. If **s** points to a *null* string (i.e., the single character '**\0**'), the returned value is zero.

Second, consider the two functions **strchr** and **strrchr**. (In some systems, these functions are known instead by the names **index** and **rindex**, respectively.) Each one *searches* a string for the first occurrence of a specific character and returns a pointer to that character—if it is found. If it is not found (i.e., if the end of the string is reached before the specified character occurs), the function returns **NULL**.

Specifically, the call

$$\textbf{strchr (s, c)}$$

returns a pointer to the *first* occurrence of **c** in **s**, or **NULL** if **c** is not found in **s**. Similarly, the call

$$\textbf{strrchr (s, c)}$$

returns a pointer to the *last* occurrence of **c** in **s**, or **NULL** if **c** is not found in **s**. Thus, **strrchr** begins its search from the *right-hand* end of string **s**.

Notice the similarity between the operation executed by **strrchr** and that executed by the function called **scan** in Problem 5.16. In addition, the operation executed by the function called **index**, in Problem 5.20, bears a distinct resemblance to that of **strchr**.

The other three pairs of string-handling functions that we will cover have the following properties in common: First, one function name in a pair differs from the other only in that it contains an extra letter **n** (e.g., **strcpy** versus **strncpy**). Second, the call of the function whose name contains the inserted **n** has one *extra* call argument, namely, an *integer* **n** that is a character *count*. This count either defines or limits the number of characters that will participate in the specified operation. (For example, **strcat** concatenates two strings, without concern for their lengths, while **strncat** appends *at most* **n** characters of the second string to the first.)

Specifically, the call

$$\textbf{strcmp (s, p)}$$

compares strings **s** and **p**, character by character, and returns the *difference* (first − second) between the character values in the first *mismatching* position. The comparison continues either to the first mismatch or until the null that terminates one (or both) of the strings is encountered. Thus, a return of zero indicates that the two strings are identical, while any other (positive or negative) returned value indicates *which* string is the "greater" (in the ASCII lexicographic sense).

Similarly, the call

$$strncmp(s,p,n)$$

performs exactly the same function, but limits the *number* of characters that will participate in the comparison to **n**. Thus, even though strings **s** and **p** are *not* identical, **strncmp** will still return zero if their first **n** characters are identical.

The call

$$strcpy(s,p)$$

copies the second string to the location specified by the first argument. The copy continues up to, and including, **p**'s null terminator. **strcpy** returns a pointer to the beginning of the just-copied string (i.e., it returns its argument **s**). Thus, for example, the expression

$$atof(strcpy(s,p))$$

not only copies **p** to **s**, but also returns the floating value that is the equivalent of the just-copied string.

Similarly, the call

$$strncpy(s,p,n)$$

copies *exactly* **n** characters from string **p** to the location beginning at **s**. If the length of string **p** is greater than or equal to **n**, the null terminator of **p** will *not* be copied. Otherwise, not only will the null of **p** be copied, but as many *additional nulls* will be padded to the new string **s** to satisfy the requirement that exactly **n** characters be written. **strncpy** also returns its argument pointer **s**.

Finally, the call

$$strcat(s,p)$$

concatenates or appends the string at **p** to the string at **s**. It returns its argument **s**.

Notice that the essence of the **strcat** process (neglecting the issue of returning the proper value) may be realized with the nested call

$$strcpy(s + strlen(s),p)$$

Similarly, the call

$$strncat(s,p,n)$$

appends, at most, **n** characters of **p** to **s**. If the length of string **p** is greater than or equal to **n**, a null terminator will be added to string **s**, immediately after the

n characters of **p** that were copied. On the other hand, if **n** is larger than **strlen(p)**, then **strncat** and **strcat** both supply the same function.

You are reminded that some of the string-handling functions discussed above return *nonintegers*. They must be declared properly before they are called. (In the sequence of problems at the end of Chapter 5, no such declarations were necessary because the *definitions*, of those string-handling functions that were employed, appeared in the source file before they were called.)

7.10 Miscellaneous Library Functions

The functions to be described here round out what we have been calling a "minimal" C library—one that is bound to exist in virtually any environment that supports C. These functions may be subdivided into three classes: those concerned with random positioning within files, those that deal with error detection, and those that might have been added to previous sections, but were postponed, for convenience. We cover the last category first.

The **stdio.h** header file normally includes the definition of a macro that is invoked with the call

$$\textbf{fileno(fp)}$$

This call returns the file descriptor integer **fd** associated with the stream **fp**. Such a call permits the caller to subsequently employ low-level calls to access a file that was originally opened via a call to **fopen**. To demonstrate that a typical library function or macro is not necessarily very complicated, let us write down the definition of **fileno**. It is merely

$$\textbf{\#define fileno(p) (p)->\_file}$$

where you will recall (from Sections 7.2 and 7.3) that every file access control block contains a member, named **_file**, that contains the **fd** value that is associated with that file.

The call

$$\textbf{fflush(fp)}$$

causes the remaining unwritten contents of the buffer associated with the stream **fp** to be written out to its file. While this process is automatically executed on every invocation of **fclose** or **exit** (as previously discussed), there are occasions when it is desirable to flush a buffer *without* closing its file. For example, if a specific function writes to a file, but does not close that file, it is generally good programming practice to ensure that all of the data that should have been written to the file *was* actually written to it, *before* the function in question returns. A call to **fflush** will ensure this.

fflush returns a Boolean **b** indicating whether or not the requested operation was successfully executed (with zero indicating success).

The call

$$\text{unlink(s)}$$

causes the file whose name is string **s** to be removed from the file system. While it is quite common for file removal to be invoked via an appropriate system *command line*, like

$$\textbf{erase filename}$$

which communicates directly with the operating system, it is essential that an equivalent facility be provided to all *programs*. (Actually, the program whose name is **erase**, above, must itself issue the **unlink** call.) Such a facility gives any program the ability not only to create and access files, but also to later *discard* them, making it possible to employ *temporary* files for any of many different purposes. The fact that a program uses temporary files is normally transparent to its user.

Function **unlink** also returns a Boolean **b** indicating whether or not the requested operation was successfully carried out. There are several conditions that will cause an error return. Example: it is an error to ask for the removal of a file that does not exist.

It was pointed out in Section 7.2 that one of the members of a file access control block is a character, named **_flag**, that contains "access control" bits. Some of these bits do indeed indicate the type of access that the associated file is open for (e.g., read, write, read/write). However, other bits in this byte have other purposes. In particular, one flag bit is specifically assigned to indicate whether or not the end of that file has yet been encountered, and a second bit is set whenever any type of access *error* occurs.

Two macros (**feof** and **ferror**) are defined in the **stdio.h** header file to *test* these bits. The call

$$\text{feof(fp)}$$

will return (as an **int**) the state of the end-of-file bit in the file access control block associated with stream **fp**. Similarly, the call

$$\text{ferror(fp)}$$

will return the state of the error bit in this control block.

These calls are available to help clarify the cause of some "exception" return (e.g., when the number of items actually read, as the result of an **fread** call, differs from the number that was requested in the call).

Once either of the end-of-file or error flag bits has been set, it *remains* set until it is explicitly reset. The call

$$\textbf{clearerr(fp)}$$

(also normally implemented as a macro) is specifically provided for the purpose of resetting *both* of the above flags.

At the lowest file access level, a **long** integer (which we will abbreviate as an **l**), called a *file position*, is maintained for every open file. The value of this variable specifies the position of the *current byte* in the file relative to the beginning of the file. Two file positions are fundamental: The byte at position **0L** (notice the **L** to indicate a **long** constant) is the *first* byte in the file, and the byte at position **nL**, where **n + 1** is the total number of bytes in the file, is the *last* byte in the file.

Normally, when a file is opened, the current file position value is set to zero. Reads and writes then proceed from that point on, sequentially. However, when a file is opened in the "append" mode, the current position value is set to the *end* of the file.

The long integer that is the file position may be changed to *any* value between the beginning of the file and the end of the file. Thus, *random access* to any byte position is possible. There are two alternative calls available for this purpose. They differ primarily in the way in which the addressed file is identified. One is a low-level call. It uses an **fd** argument. The other is a standard level call. It employs an **fp** argument. Specifically, the call

$$\textbf{lseek(fd, l, i)}$$

sets the new file position, in the file identified by **fd**, according to the following formula: The integer **i** specifies the *origin* from which the displacement to the new file position will be measured. The following three values are permissible:

i value	Origin or reference position in the file
0	Beginning of the file
1	Position of current byte in the file
2	End of the file

The **long** integer **l** specifies the *offset*, to the new file position, as measured from the origin or reference point that is specified by **i**. Thus, the call

$$\texttt{lseek(fd, 0L, 1)}$$

will not change the current position, while the call

$$\texttt{lseek(fd, 0L, 2)}$$

prepares for appending new information to the *end* of the file. Similarly, the call

$$\texttt{fseek(fp, l, i)}$$

performs the *same* file positioning operation just described—on the file identified by the pointer **fp**. That is, the arguments **l** and **i** have the same interpretations as those given above.

lseek and **fseek** possess one other difference in operation: While **lseek** returns the new current file position, as a **long** (or **-1**, if any error is detected), **fseek** returns a Boolean **b** indicating the success (0) or the failure (-1) of the requested operation.

To compensate for the fact that **fseek** does not return the new file position, another call

$$\texttt{ftell(fp)}$$

is available. It returns, as a **long**, the current byte position in the file identified by **fp**.

Finally, the call

$$\texttt{rewind(fp)}$$

repositions the current file position, in the file identified by **fp**, to the *beginning* of that file. Thus, a **rewind** is equivalent to the call

$$\texttt{fseek(fp, 0L, 0)}$$

In some systems, **rewind** is actually defined, in the **stdio.h** file, as a macro—having the body just spelled out above. Under these conditions, **rewind** returns the same type of value as does the function **fseek**. In other systems, however, **rewind** may be defined differently, in which case it may not return any useful value.

You are reminded that, since **lseek** and **ftell** return nonintegers (a **long** is *not* an **int**), they should be properly *declared* before being called.

Your copy of the **stdio.h** header file may, in fact, already include the declaration

$$\text{long ftell()};$$

To demonstrate how such declarations are normally employed, the following example shows the context in which an **lseek** call is usually found:

```
int fd, ref_point;
long position, offset, lseek();
          .
          .
          .
position = lseek(fd, offset, ref_point);
```

where it is assumed that the "..." portion of code **open**s a file (to get a value for **fd**) and sets the values of the variables **offset** and **ref_point** appropriately.

Problems

7.1 Write a program, called **display**, that takes one command line argument—the name of a file—and prints the contents of that file on the terminal screen. Include appropriate error checks in the program.

7.2 Explain how the two calls

$$\text{gets(s)}$$

and

$$\text{scanf(\%s, s)}$$

differ in operation.

7.3 Using the implementation of **gets**, in Section 7.4, as a model, write an implementation of the function **fputs**.

7.4 Assuming the same initial declarations as those that were used for the **printf** examples in Section 7.5, what will the following **printf** statements generate?

```
a. printf("<%11e>\n", num);
b. printf("<%11.0e>\n", num);
c. printf("<%-11.0e>\n", num);
d. printf("<%20.6s>\n", s);
```

7.5 Assuming that character pointers **weekday** and **month** point to appropriate null-terminated strings (e.g., to "Monday" and "December," respectively), and that integers **day**, **hour**, and **min** have the values 30, 10, and 2, respectively, write a statement that will generate the terminal output

Monday, December 30, 10:02

7.6 What values will be assigned to what variables if the input line

12 34.56E-1 jones

is entered, in response to the statement

scanf("%d %f %s", &j, &y, name);

7.7 What values will be assigned to what variables if the input line

12345 6789 10b98

is entered, in response to the statement

scanf("%2d %f %*d %2s", &j, &y, name);

7.8 Given the existence of the function **atof**, whose description appears in Section 7.7, write an implementation of the function **atoi** (introduced in Section 7.6) that uses **atof**.

7.9 Assuming the existence of all of the *other* character classification and conversion macros, write an implementation of the macro **isxdigit**. (Note: It should recognize the characters **a–f** either in uppercase or in lowercase form.)

7.10 Write an implementation of the function **strcpy**.

SOLUTIONS TO PROBLEMS

Chapter 2

2.1 255, 12774, 255, 19414

2.2

Decimal	Octal	Hexadecimal
12	014	0xC
214	0326	0xD6
672	01240	0x2A0
1999	03717	0x7CF

2.3 1.432565E-1

2.4 \t = \011, \b = \010, \r = \015, \f = \014, \\ = \134

2.5 'a' = 97, '#' = 35, '\t' = 9, 'C' = 67

2.6 String length = 15, number of bytes consumed = 16

2.7 0x3000

2.8 **3_WAY** does not begin with a letter. **NET_$** and **abs val** both contain illegal characters ($ and space).

2.9 a + (b / (–c))

2.10 a = (((b * c) / (–d)) % e)

2.11 a << (b + c)

2.12 a = (b != c)

2.13 a –= ((–(b––))–(––c))

2.14 (a | b) || c

2.15 (!a) ^ (~b)

2.16 (a && b) || c

		Expression value after assignment to			
	char	**int**	**float**	Side effects	Comments
2.17	C	67	67.0	None	
2.18	Z	90	90.0	None	
2.19	J	74	74.0	None	
2.20	i	105	105.0	None	
2.21	2	50	50.0	None	
2.22	\036	30	30.0	None	
2.23	\0	0	0.0	None	
2.24	\001	1	1.0	None	
2.25	\0	0	0.0	None	
2.26	\0	0	0.0	None	
2.27	\036	30	30.0	None	
2.28	\036	30	30.0	None	
2.29	\001	1	1.0	None	
2.30	\005	5	5.0	None	
2.31	\020	16	16.0	None	
2.32	P	80	80.0	None	
2.33	W	87	87.5	None	
2.34	x	120	120.0	None	
2.35	e	101	101.0	None	
2.36	g	103	103.0	None	
2.37	@	64	64.0	None	
2.38	\220	144	144.0	None	
2.39	\201	4225	4225.0	None	
2.40	\002	2	2.0	None	
2.41	\n	10	10.0	None	
2.42	\t	9	9.7468	None	
2.43	i	105	105.0	None	
2.44	K	75	75.0	None	
2.45	#	35	35.0	None	
2.46	E	69	69.0	None	
2.47	#	35	35.0	None	
2.48	V	86	86.0	None	
2.49	b	98	98.0	as[2].m4[0] = 'b'	
2.50	z	122	122.0	as[2].m4[2] = 'z'	
2.51	C	67	67.0	as[2].m4[1] = 'F'	
2.52	\n	10	10.0	ai[0] = 10	
2.53	\017	15	15.0	ai[2] = 90	
2.54	#	35	35.0	ai[1] = 23	
2.55	\003	3	3.5	af[0] = 3.5	
2.56	\010	8	8.5	af[2] = 8.5	
2.57	\006	6	6.0	new af[0] same as old af[0]	
2.58	Z	90	90.0	None	
2.59	x	120	120.0	None	
2.60	A	65	65.0	None	
2.61	\001	1	1.0	None	
2.62	c	99	99.0	as[2].m4[2] = 'B'	
2.63	d	100	100.0	i1 = 11	
2.64	\0	256	256.0	as[2].m2 = ai[0] = 16	

	Expression value after assignment to			Side effects	Comments
	char	**int**	**float**		
2.65	\003	3	3.0	as[2].m3 = 8.5; af[1] = 3.0	
2.66	\0	0	0.0	i2 = 21	
2.67	\001	1	1.0	i1 = 11	
2.68	\0	0	0.0	i2 = ai[1] = 21; pi3 = &ai[2]; ai[2] = 0	
2.69	K	75	75.5	s2.m3 = 4.5; af[0] = 4.5 (assuming that 4.0 is nearer to 4.5 than it is to 5.0); pf3 = &af[1]; af[1] = 75.5	
2.70	\t	9	9.5	aps[0] = &as[2]	
2.71	#	35	35.0	None	
2.72	Z	90	90.0	None	
2.73	\n	10	10.0	i1 = 11	
2.74	\016	14	14.0	i2 = 19	
2.75	\001	1	1.0	None	
2.76	\001	1	1.0	None	
2.77	\0	0	0.0	None	
2.78	\001	1	1.0	None	
2.79	a	97	97.0	s3.m4[1] = 'a'; pc1 = &s3.m4[1]	
2.80	Z	90	90.0	aps[0] = &as[2]	
2.81	\0	0	0.0	None	
2.82	\001	1	1.0	None	
2.83	(	40	40.0	None	
2.84	\003	3	3.0	None	
2.85	\024	20	20.0	c1 = 'B'; i2 = 21	
2.86	\017	15	15.0	api[0] = &ai[1]	
2.87	\002	2	2.5	None	
2.88	\004	4	4.0	f1 = 4.0	
2.89	\005	5	5.0	ai[0] = 5	
2.90	\001	1	1.0	i1 = -10	
2.91	#	35	35.0	i1 = 15; i2 = 25; i3 = 35 pi1 = &ai[2]	
2.92	\017	15	15.0	i1 = 15; ai[0] = 16	
2.93	#	35	35.0	None	
2.94	\005	5	5.4772	None	
2.95	\001	1	1.0	None	
2.96	Z	90	90.0	None	
2.97	\f	12	12.0	None	
2.98	\001	1	1.0	None	
2.99	\341	225	225.0	None	
2.100	\001	1	1.0	None	

[1] The space between the "/" and the "*", in Problem 2.46, is the only one known to be mandatory in all of the expressions in Problems 2.17–2.100. If this space is omitted, the "/*" combination will signal the beginning of a comment, causing the compiler to ignore all subsequent code (until a matching "*/" is later encountered).

Chapter 3

```
3.1 char c1 = 'A', c2 = 'B', c3 = 'C';
    int i1 = 10, i2 = 20, i3 = 30;
    float f1 = 1.5, f2 = 2.5, f3 = 3.5;
3.2 struct mixed {
            char m1;
            int m2;
            float m3;
            char m4[3];
    };
    struct mixed s1 = {'G', 40, 4.5, {'J','K','L'}};
    struct mixed s2 = {'H', 50, 5.5, {'M','N','O'}};
    struct mixed s3 = {'I', 60, 6.5, {'P','Q','R'}};
3.3 char *pc1 = &c1, *pc2 = &c2, *pc3 = &c3;
    int *pi1 = &i1, *pi2 = &i2, *pi3 = &i3;
    float *pf1 = &f1, *pf2 = &f2, *pf3 = &f3;
    struct mixed *ps1 = &s1, *ps2 = &s2, *ps3 = &s3;
3.4 char ac[] = {'D','E','F'};
    int ai[] = { 15, 25, 35 };
    float af[] = { 4.0, 5.0, 6.0 };
    struct mixed as[] = {{'S', 70, 7.5, 'V','W','X'},
                         {'T', 80, 8.5, 'X','Y','Z'},
                         {'U', 90, 9.5, 'A','B','C'}
    };
3.5 char *apc[] = { ac, ac + 1, ac + 2 };
    int *api[] = { ai, ai + 1, ai + 2 };
    float *apf[] = { af, af + 1, af + 2 };
    struct mixed *aps[] = { as, as + 1, as +2 };
3.6 Fc(z) /* given char, if upper—convert to lower,
            * else—leave alone
            */
    int z;
    {
    .
    .
    .
    }
3.7 Fi(z) /* given int arg, return its square */
    int z;
    {
    .
    .
    .
    }
```

```
3.8 double Ff(z) /* given floating arg,
                   * return its square root
                   */
    double z;
    {
    .
    .
    .
    }
3.9 char *Fpc(z,y) /* given 2 chars, search all char
                     * arrays for char1. If found,
                     * replace with char2 and return
                     * ptr to it. Else, return NULL
                     */
    int z;
    int y;
    {
    .
    .
    .
    }
3.10 int *Fpi(z) /* find nearest int in ai, replace it,
                   * and return pointer to it
                   */
     int z;
     {
     .
     .
     .
     }
3.11 float *Fpf(z) /* find nearest float in af, replace
                     * it, and return pointer to it
                     */
     double z;
     {
     .
     .
     .
     }
3.12 struct mixed *Fps(z) /* given char, search m4's of
                            * all structures, and return ptr to
                            * struct of first match or NULL
                            */
     int z;
     {
     .
     .
     .
     }
```

```
3.13 int i;
     fcn1()
     {
     .
     .
     .
     }
     fcn2()
     {
     .
     .
     }
     main()
     {
     fcn1();
     fcn2();
     }
3.14 int i;
     fcn1()
     {
     int j;
     .
     .
     }
     fcn2()
     {
     int k;
     .
     .
     }
     main(){
     fcn1();
     fcn2();
     }
```

3.15 First, convert each function definition's header declaration from the form **fcn1** () [or **fcn2** ()] into the form **char *fcn1** () [or **char *fcn2** ()].If the **main** function is positioned in the source file *after* these function definitions appear (as is the case in the solution given above), no further modifications are necessary. However, if the **main** function is defined *before* the function definitions are encountered, then it too must be modified as follows:

```
main(){
char *fcn1(), *fcn2();
fcn1();
fcn2();
}
```

to ensure that the compiler is aware of the types *returned* by these functions, before their definitions are known.

3.16 3
    2
    1

3.17

	Variables visible

---

file 1
```
  int a;
  static float b;           a
  main(){                   a, b
      short c;              a, b
          .                 a, b, c
          .                 a, b, c
      }                     a, b, c
  funct(d)                  a, b
      int d;                a, b
      {                     a, b, d
      short e;              a, b, d
          .                 a, b, d, e
          .                 a, b, d, e
      }                     a, b, d, e
```
file 2
```
  subr(f)
      float f;
      {                     f
      extern float b;       f
          .                 f, b (from file 3)
          .                 f, b    "    "   "
      }                     f, b    "    "   "
```
file 3
```
  float b;
      {                     b
      int g;                b
          .                 b, g
          .                 b, g
      }                     b, g
```

3.18 First, the values of the arguments must be pushed onto the stack. Each argument expression is evaluated in turn and its value is pushed onto the stack. (A *single* stack is assumed in this example.) The order in which the arguments appear is immaterial, provided that the called routine is able to properly distinguish them. Next, the CALL is executed. The execution of this instruction pushes the *return address* onto the same stack. Next, the called routine begins by *saving* (on the same stack) the values of any processor registers that it will employ in its computation. Thus, before the function's calculation even begins, the stack has grown by the argument values (of varying sizes), which are *under* the return address, which is, in turn, *under* the set of saved register values.

The function's computation uses the values of the arguments that it is expecting. Notice that they are not normally *popped* at this time, because they are not at the *top* of the stack. The called routine knows the *depth* of each argument, however, because it is aware of how much data has been pushed on top of it. In the process of computing its result, the called function may further use, for temporary storage, space on the top of the stack—*above* the saved register area—for automatic variables and for other extra storage that it requires. Finally, when it has computed its result, its returned value (if any) may be passed back to the calling routine in one or more processor registers, specifically allocated for this purpose. (We ignore, in this protocol, the passing back of the result via the same stack.)

Once the returned value has been determined, the called function restores the saved register values, popping them from the stack. It then executes a RETURN instruction, whose execution pops the return address. At this point, the calling function receives control with the arguments that it passed *still positioned* on top of the stack. It must first discard them (by suitably incrementing or decrementing the Stack Pointer) before it may proceed.

3.19

	Automatic	External	static External	static Internal	**register**
Retains value on exiting block		NA	NA	X	
Visible to other functions		X	X		
Available to other files		X			
Zero default value		X	X	X	
Initialized once, at compile time		X	X	X	
Aggregates may be initialized		X	X	X	
May be stored in processor registers					X

NA, not applicable

3.20 `char array_name[];`
`float funct_name();`
`extern int var_name;`

3.21 To a single null character ('\0') in memory.

3.22 `long *lptr;`
`float **a_ptrs[];`
`char *pch = "xxyy";`

3.23 `float vector[10], *fptr = vector;`

3.24 **abc** is a function returning a pointer to an integer. **def** is a pointer to an array of integers. **ghi** is an array of pointers to functions returning integers.

3.25 Both definitions have the same effect.

3.26 `struct node {`

    `char name[5];`

    `int degree;`

    `float weight;`

    `struct node *next;`

  `};`

  `struct node firstnode = { "root", 2, 3.7E4, &othernode };`

3.27 Since **j** is initialized to zero at compile time, the first call will print the value 1. Since **j** *retains* its value from call to call, the next call will print the value 2; the next 3, and so on.

3.28 `int length = sizeof(a_chars);`

3.29 `char *calloc();`

  `int n, *ip;`

  `ip = (int *) calloc( n, sizeof(int));`

3.30 A likely value is 8, assuming that the pointer consumes 2 bytes, the integer consumes 2 bytes, and that the floating quantity consumes 4 bytes. No "holes" appear to be likely in concatenating these objects.

3.31 2 or 4 are the most likely values for the first expression, which is machine dependent. The other values are: 10, 1, 10, and 1.

Chapter 4

4.1 The error is in the **#define** directive, which should not terminate in a semicolon—unless it is specifically required as part of the replacement string. The compiler will not object to the first statement, however, because it terminates in *two* semicolons. The first will be interpreted as the terminator of the statement given, and the second (an isolated semicolon) will be taken as a *null statement*, which does nothing. (Recall its introduction in Section 3.4, during the discussion of the dummy **no_op** function.)

  The compiler will object to the second statement, however, which, after string substitution, appears as

$$x = 35; + y;$$

The portion through the first semicolon will be accepted. The portion after that will cause a "bad syntax" (or some other equivalent) error message. Note: In some cases, there may be a sufficient expression after the first *erroneous* semicolon that the compiler's error message might actually read: "semicolon expected"! (This message is generated whenever the compiler completes the processing of an expression and expects to find its terminator.) Such an error message is particularly surprising when the original statement looks so well-behaved. It is even more surprising when you find out that the actual error is that there is one semicolon *too many*.

4.2 Place the directive

$$\text{#define BELL '\backslash 007'}$$

at the beginning of the program.

4.3 Place the statement

$$\#define \ void \ int$$

at the beginning of the program, or in a "header" file that the program #includes.

4.4 #define isdigit(c) ((c) >= '0' && (c) <= '9' ? 1 : 0)

4.5 #define isupper(c) ((c) >= 'A' && (c) <= 'Z' ? 1 : 0)

4.6 #define tolower(c) (isupper(c) ? ((c) + ('a' - 'A')) : (c))

4.7 The macro expansion yields

$$((p++) \ > \ (q) \ ? \ (p++) \ : \ (q))$$

Evaluation of the condition yields *true*, and a post-increment of **p** to 6. The value of the expression is therefore 6, and the post-increment of **p** during *that* evaluation gives it a final value of 7. **q**'s value remains at 3.

4.8 Include, in the commonly #included header file, which contains all of the common #define directives for the program, a sequence of global function declarations for the set of non-integer-returning standard functions that all of the source modules employ. For example, if this set consists of the function **atof**, which returns a **double**, **calloc** (recall Problem 3.29), which returns a pointer to **char**s, and **index**, which also returns a pointer to **char**s, then the set of declarations

```
double atof();
char *calloc(), *index();
```

in the common header file, ensures that all of the source modules will include the proper declarations. (Each of these library functions is described in detail later in this book.)

4.9 No. The #included file is considered as a part of the file that called for it, in which case the cited function will be callable from any point within the including file.

4.10 If the **basicio.c** file is at all sizable, as it is expected to be—even if it contains only a few key library functions (like **printf**, for example)—the size of the #included module could far outweigh that of the including file. This means that, during development, every time the program is recompiled, most of the compile time is likely to be due to recompiling the same, *unchanged* **basicio.c** source portion. Similarly, once a debugged program has been achieved, it is likely that most of the memory space consumed by the program will be due to the inclusion of the entire library.

It is preferable to *separately compile* all of the library functions and to place the separately derived object modules into an *object* library. The *linking* process will then extract from this library only those functions that are actually referenced in the program. Thus, the CPU time consumed over many recompilations, during program development, is significantly reduced, and so is the amount of memory space ultimately consumed by the program.

4.11 Assuming that each of the function object modules **fcn1** through **fcn5** (as well as any of the function object modules **newfcn1** through **newfcn5**) is available from an object library, let the program under discussion be written with all of its critical I/O references made to the first (or standard) set of functions. When this program is compiled, the *portable* version will be derived. Now construct a header file containing the five directives

```
#define fcn1 newfcn1
                        .
                        .
#define fcn5 newfcn5
```

If this header file is #included at the beginning of the same program, a recompilation will yield the *faster* version.

4.12 Bracket each of the code segments that give the program its *extended* capabilities (even if that code segment is only *one* statement long) with the directives

#ifdef EXTENDED

(before it) and

#endif

(after it). With this arrangement, if nothing else is added to the program, the *basic* version would be compiled. On the other hand, if the directive

#define EXTENDED version

were added to the beginning of the program, a recompilation would yield the *extended* version.

4.13 The initial value of integer **data_length** is 276. It would have been 176 had the replacement string for the identifier **ID_FIELD** been *parenthesized*.

The replacement string in a **#define** directive is treated as a string *constant* (neglecting the issue of macro arguments). Thus, replacement does *not* take place in the *definition* of the macro **ID_FIELD**. Rather, it takes place when the text for this identifier is actually inserted. After substitution, the last statement will read as

```
int data_length = 256 - 30 + 50;
```

which yields a value of 276.

Chapter 5

5.1 The most common expression statements are assignments and function calls. Therefore, the most likely operators in such statements are the assignment operator(s) and the function call operator.

5.2

```
/***** 5.2 Header statements and global data *************/
#include <stdio.h>
#define YES        1        /* True */
#define NO         0        /* False */
#define MAX_WORDS  25        /* Max # input words */
#define MAX_LINE   100        /* Max char array length */
#define MAX_STACK  20        /* Max stack size */
int stack[MAX_STACK], *stack_ptr = stack;
```

5.3

```
/************ 5.3 get_string ***************************
 * Read and store keyboard input character stream
 * (terminated by a \n) in the area pointed to by
 * the input argument. Replace the \n in storage
 * by the null character.
 ************************************************************/
get_string(s)
char *s;
    {
    while ((*s++ = getchar()) != '\n')
        ;
    *--s = '\0';
    }
```

5.4

```
/************ 5.4 put_string ***************************
 * Output the null-terminated string, pointed to
 * by the input argument, to the terminal screen,
 * and append a \n to it.
 ************************************************************/
put_string(s)
char *s;
    {
    while (putchar(*s++))
        ;
    putchar('\n');
    }
```

5.5

```
/************** 5.5 str_len **************************
 * Given a pointer to a null-terminated string,
 * return its length.
 *****************************************************/
str_len(s)
char *s;
    {
    int n;
    for (n = 0; *s++; n++)
        ;
    return (n);
    }
```

5.6

```
/************** 5.6 reverse *************************
 * Given a pointer to a null-terminated string,
 * reverse the contents of that character array
 * in place.
 *****************************************************/
reverse(s)
char s[];
  {
  int i,j;
  char c;
  for (i = 0, j = str_len(s) - 1; i < j; ++i,--j)
        {
        c = s[i];
        s[i] = s[j];
        s[j] = c;
        }
  }
```

5.7

```
/******************* 5.7 reverser *******************
 * Prompt the user, read arbitrary strings, and
 * print them back in reverse order.
 ********************************************************/
reverser()
    {
    char line[MAX_LINE];
    put_string("Reverses all input strings:");
    while (get_string(line), str_len(line))
        {
        reverse(line);
        put_string(line);
        }
    }
```

5.8

```
/*********** 5.8 int_to_digits *********************
 * Given an integer and a char pointer, convert
 * the integer into an equivalent null-terminated
 * character string stored at the specified
 * position. Include a minus sign, if necessary.
 ********************************************************/
int_to_digits(num,str)
int num;
char *str;
    {
    char sign = '\0', *ptr = str;
    if (num < 0) { num = -num; sign = '-'; }
    while (*ptr++ = num % 10 +'0', (num /= 10) > 0)
      ;/* Store remainder digits until none left */
    *ptr++ = sign; /* Digits are in reverse order */
    *ptr = '\0';
    reverse(str);
    }
```

5.9

```
/******** 5.9 macros and character counter ******************/
/* Return true only if argument is a digit. */
#define isdigit(c) ((c) >= '0' && (c) <= '9' ? 1 : 0)
/* Return true only if argument is uppercase letter. */
#define isupper(c) ((c) >= 'A' && (c) <= 'Z' ? 1 : 0)
/* If uppercase, convert to lower. Else, leave alone. */
#define tolower(c) (isupper(c) ? ((c) + ('a'-'A')) : (c))
/**************** counter ***************************************
 * Prompt user, read arbitrary strings, and, for each,
 * output the difference between the number of
 * digits counted and the number of vowels counted.
 ***************************************************************/
counter()
    {
    char line[MAX_LINE];
    put_string("Counts digits and vowels in input strings");
    put_string("and outputs the difference between them:");
    while (get_string(line), str_len(line))
            {
            int count = 0;
            char c, *ptr = line;
            while (c = *ptr++)
                    if (isdigit(c)) count++;
                    else switch (tolower(c))
                        {
                        case 'a':
                        case 'e':
                        case 'i':
                        case 'o':
                        case 'u':
                                count--;
                                break;
                        }
            int_to_digits(count, line);
            put_string(line);
            }
    }
```

5.10

```
/*************** 5.10 digits_to_int ***************************
 * Read the string of digits pointed to by the passed
 * pointer. On the first nondigit, return the
 * (assumed positive) integer equivalent of the string.
 ***********************************************************/
digits_to_int(ptr)
char *ptr;
    {
    int n = 0;
    char c = *ptr++;
    for (; isdigit(c); c = *ptr++)
        n = 10 * n + c - '0';
    return(n);
    }
```

5.11

```
/***************** 5.11 power ********************************
 * Raise the first integer to the power specified
 * by the second integer. Both int's assumed positive.
 ***********************************************************/
power(base, exp)
int base, exp;
    {
    int r = base;
    if (!exp--) return(1);
    while (exp--) r *= base;
    return(r);
    }
```

5.12

```
/*************** 5.12 push *******************************
 * Push the integer given onto the integer stack.
 * stack_ptr points to first available entry. If
 * stack is full, ignore. Return pushed value.
 **********************************************************/
push(num)
int num;
    {
    if (stack_ptr - stack < MAX_STACK)
        return (*stack_ptr++ = num);
    }
```

5.13

```
/*************** 5.13 pop *************************
 * Discard the top stack entry and return it.
 * If stack is empty, return zero.
 **********************************************************/
pop()
    {
    if (stack_ptr > stack) return(*--stack_ptr);
    else return(0);
    }
```

5.14

```
/************* 5.14 calculator ****************************
* Each input line is either a valid operator
* character or a positive integer. Other inputs
* are ignored. Every number entered is pushed on
* the integer stack. Every valid binary operator
* causes an operation on the top two stack entries.
* At each step, the stack's contents are printed.
****************************************************************/
calculator()
   {
   char line[MAX_LINE];
   int *ptr;
   put_string("Enter integers, or any of the binary");
   put_string("operators +,-, *, /, %, # (power) :");
   while (get_string(line), str_len(line))
        {
        switch (line[0])
             {
             case'0':
             case'1':
             case'2':
             case'3':
             case'4':
             case'5':
             case'6':
             case'7':
             case'8':
             case'9': push(digits_to_int(line));
                      break;
             case'+': push(pop() + pop());
                      break;
             case'-': push(pop() - pop());
                      break;
             case'*': push(pop() * pop());
                      break;
             case'/': push(pop() / pop());
                      break;
             case'%': push(pop() % pop());
                      break;
             case'#': push(power(pop(),pop()));
                      break;
             }
        for (ptr = stack_ptr - 1; ptr >= stack; ptr--)
             {
             int_to_digits(*ptr,line);
             putchar(' ');
             put_string(line);
             }
        }
   }
```

5.15

```
/*************** 5.15 border ********************************
 * Given a character and a length, print a horizontal
 * line of that length, using only that character. The
 * last arg specifies whether or not to end with '\n'.
 *********************************************************/
border(c,length, newline)
char c;
int length;
int newline;
     {
     int i;
     for (i = 1; i <= length; i++) putchar(c);
     if (newline) putchar('\n');
     }
```

5.16

```
/*************** 5.16 scan *********************************
 * Given a ptr to a char in a string, and the scan distance,
 * return a pointer to the rightmost space inside that range.
 * At least one space is assumed to exist.
 *********************************************************/
char *scan(start, width)
char *start;
int width;
     {
     start += width;
     while (*start-- != ' ')
          ; /* Stop behind rightmost space */
     return (++start);
     }
```

5.17

```
/*************** 5.17 printer ********************************
* Read a margin value and then arbitrary char strings.
* Print each string, unjustified, in a column of that
* width. Assume that each potential line contains, at
* least, one space, or that it is the final line.
*******************************************************/
printer ()
    {
    char line[MAX_LINE];
    char *start, *end;
    int width, length;
    put_string("Enter a column width, and then strings.");
    put_string("Will print text within column specified:");
    get_string(line);
    width = digits_to_int(line);
    while (get_string(line), length = str_len(line))
        {
        start = line;
        border('-',width,YES); /* Highlight column */
        while (start + width < line + length)
            {
            *(end = scan(start, width)) = '\0';
            put_string(start);
            start = ++end;
            }
        put_string(start); /* Last line */
        border('-',width,YES);
        }
    }
```

5.18

```
/*************** 5.18 swap ************************
* Given two character pointers, exchange the
* characters at which they point.
*****************************************************/
swap(p1,p2)
char *p1, *p2;
    {
    char c;
    c = *p1;
    *p1 = *p2;
    *p2 = c;
    }
```

5.19

```
/***************** 5.19 str_cmp ************************
 * Given two pointers to separate null-terminated
 * strings, return the difference between their
 * first nonmatching ASCII characters.
 ****************************************************/
str_cmp(p1,p2)
char *p1, *p2;
      {
      while (*p1 == *p2) if (p1++,!*p2++) return(0);
      return(*p1 - *p2);
      }
```

5.20

```
/***************** 5.20 index ************************
 * Given two pointers to separate strings, return a
 * pointer to the leftmost match of the first string
 * in the second (assumed longer) string, or NULL—
 * if no match is found.
 ****************************************************/
char *index(p1,p2)
char *p1, *p2;
   {
   char *p = p2 + str_len(p1); /* Null insert position */
   char *limit = p2 + str_len(p2) - str_len(p1);
   char *null = "";
   while (p2 <= limit)
        {
        swap(p,null);
        if (!str_cmp(p1,p2++))
             { swap(p,null); return(--p2); }
        swap(p++,null);
        }
   return(NULL);
   }
```

5.21

```
/************** 5.21 finder *********************************
 * Read long string followed by sequence of shorter
 * strings. For each short string argument, reprint
 * the long string, with the matching sequence
 * replaced by a string of special chars ('*').
 ***********************************************************/
finder ()
      {
      char line[MAX_LINE], test[MAX_LINE];
      char *p1, *p2;
      int length;
      put_string("Finds first match. Enter one long");
      put_string("string, then many short strings:");
      get_string(line);
      while(get_string(test), str_len(test))
            {
            if ((p1 = index(test,line)) != NULL)
                  {
                  for (p2 = line; p2 < p1; p2++)
                        putchar(*p2);
                  border('*', length = str_len(test),NO);
                  put_string(p2 += length);
                  }
            else put_string("Match not found");
            }
      }
```

5.22

```
/****************** 5.22 exchange *************************
 * Given two pointers to pointers to chars, swap the
 * pointers that they point to.
 ***********************************************************/
exchange(p1,p2)
char **p1, **p2;
      {
      char *ptr;
      ptr = *p1;
      *p1 = *p2;
      *p2 = ptr;
      }
```

5.23

```
/****************** 5.23 sort ********************************
 * Given a pointer to an array of pointers to strings,
 * and a number of such strings to process, reorder
 * the pointers so that the strings they point to are
 * ordered lexicographically.
 ***********************************************************/
sort(ptrs,num)
char *ptrs[];
int num;
    {
    int i, j;
    for (i = 0; i < num; i++) /* Pass starting point */
      for (j = i + 1; j < num; j++) /* Scan to right of it */
        if (str_cmp(ptrs[i],ptrs[j]) > 0) /* Of those left, */
           exchange(&ptrs[i],&ptrs[j]); /* choose the smallest */
    }
```

5.24

```
/****************** 5.24 sorter ********************************
 * Read a sequence of words and print them out sorted in
 * ASCII lexicographic order. For simplicity, assume no
 * leading or trailing blanks and only a single space
 * between adjacent words.
 ***********************************************************/
sorter()
    {
    int i, j;
    char line[MAX_LINE], *p, *ptrs[MAX_WORDS];
    put_string("Enter sequences of words to be sorted:");
    while (get_string(line), str_len(line))
        {
        for (i = 0, p = line; ;)
            {
            ptrs[i++] = p; /* Mark beginning of word */
            while(*p >' ') p++; /* Scan to end of word */
            if (*p) *p++ = '\0' ; else break;
            /* At end of each word: either exit, if
            null, or replace the space with a null */
            }
    sort(ptrs,i);
    for (j = 0; j < i; j++) put_string(ptrs[j]);
        }
    }
```

5.25
```
/************** 5.25 main **********************
 * Prompt user with menu of functions and
 * branch to the selected routine.
 ************************************************/
main()
  {
     char line[MAX_LINE];
     for(;;)
       {
       put_string("Select one of the following functions: ");
       put_string("1:reverser 2:counter 3:calculator");
       put_string("4:printer 5:finder 6:sorter");
       put_string("(A NULL input string causes an EXIT");
       put_string("from the current function.)");
       if (get_string(line), !str_len(line)) break;
          switch (line[0])
            {
            case'1': reverser(); break;
            case'2': counter(); break;
            case'3': calculator(); break;
            case'4': printer(); break;
            case'5': finder(); break;
            case'6': sorter(); break;
            }
       }
  }
```

Chapter 6

6.1 The variable named **type** needs to have only three possible values, so a **char** is sufficient for its purposes. The preferred means to *link* **type** and **arg** together is to make them both parts of the same *structure*, which we may name as **data**. Such an arrangement is extendable to an array of many such structures. The declaration of one of these structures would appear as

```
struct {
  union {
        int i;
        float f;
        char string[5];
        } arg;
    char type;
      } data;
```

(The template name has been omitted.) A specific set of values for **type**, corresponding to the three possible data types for **arg**, must be assigned. Assume values 1, 2, and 3, for example. Before any access occurs, the value of **data. type** is checked. Whenever the type of **data. arg** is changed, the value of **data. type** must be correspondingly modified.

6.2 An array of unions is usually employed as a *table* or *stack* of cells, any of which may contain two or more data types (only one at a time). It is particularly useful as part of a symbol table, or as a general data stack, or as any other similar data structure. A union of arrays, on the other hand, is only feasible when only *one* of the *arrays* needs to exist at a time. Under these special conditions, the arrays may *share* the same storage, possibly resulting in significant economies in total area required for data.

6.3 Assuming symbolic constants **STATIC**, **EXTERNAL**, and **KEYWORD** have the values 1, 2, and 4, respectively, the statement

$$\text{flags} \mathrel{|=} \text{STATIC} \mathbin{|} \text{EXTERNAL};$$

sets both of the specified bits, while the statement

$$\text{flags} \quad \&= \quad \sim \quad \text{STATIC} \mathbin{|} \text{EXTERNAL};$$

resets them both.

We may define these bits as fields with the following declaration:

```
struct {
  unsigned is_static : 1;
  unsigned is_external : 1;
  unsigned is_keyword : 1;
  } flags;
```

in which case

$$\text{flags. is\_static} = \text{flags. is\_external} = 1;$$

sets them both, while

$$\text{flags. is\_static} = \text{flags. is\_external} = 0;$$

resets them both.

6.4
```
struct control_block {
    char fname [MAX_FNAME];
    char *buffer;
    int rec_count;
    char *ptr;
    struct control_block *link[3];
};
    struct control_block file[MAX_BLOCKS]  =  {
        { NAME0,  &buffer0,  0,  &buffer0,  &file[1] },
        { NAME1,  &buffer1,  0,  &buffer1,  &file[2] },
        { NAME2,  &buffer2,  0,  &buffer2,  &file[0] },
    };
```

Note: All uninitialized elements (those not covered because of early termination of an initializer) will be initialized to zero, by default.

6.5 The first three lines of the definition must be modified to accommodate one added parameter, namely, a pointer to a function. Therefore, these lines should be changed to read as follows:

```
sort(ptrs,num,comp_fcn)
char *ptrs[];
int num,  (*comp_fcn)();
```

The specific call to **str_cmp** must be modified to name instead the dummy **comp_fcn**. This function name is the one that will be replaced by the function name supplied by the caller. Therefore, the **if** line should be changed to read as follows:

```
if  ((*comp_fcn)(ptrs[i],ptrs[j])  >  0)
```

It is assumed that all new compare functions will be designed (like **str_cmp**) to accept two input string pointers and to return either greater than (positive), equal to (0), or less than (negative).

6.6 sum(num)
```
    int num;
       {
       return (num <= 1 ? 1 : num + sum(num - 1));
       }
```

6.7 ptr must be declared to be a pointer to the same objects that comprise the array **name**. Thus, for the sample definition of **name** given, **ptr** must be defined as

```
char *ptr;
```

row_ptr must be declared as a pointer to one-dimensional arrays of these objects—having the *same size* as one of the *rows* in the array **name**. This will match the *types* of the objects pointed to by pointers **row_ptr** and **name** and will ensure that each increment of **row_ptr** advances it to the beginning of the very *next* row in the array. For the definition of **name** given, this requires the definition

```
char (*row_ptr)[COLUMNS];
```

A test evaluation of the expression in this declaration shows that **row_ptr** is a pointer to arrays of COLUMNS characters.

6.8 typedef char FCH();
     typedef FCH *PFCH;
     typedef PFCH APFCH[];
     typedef APFCH *PAPFCH;

6.9

```
/*************** 6.9 printer ****************************************
 * First argument is a margin value. Other arguments are
 * arbitrary strings. Prints all text, left-justified,
 * in a column of the specified width. No right
 * justification. All word lengths assumed < margin width.
 *****************************************************************/
main(argc,argv)
int argc;
char *argv[];
     {
     int width, i, len, length = 0;
     width = digits_to_int(argv[1]);
     border('-',width,YES); /* Highlight column */
     for (i = 2; i < argc; i++)
          {
          len = str_len(argv[i]);
          if (length + len > width)
               { putchar('\n'); length = 0; }
          /* If past right margin, start a new line */
          printf(argv[i]); /* Print the arg */
          putchar(''); /* Follow with space */
          length += len + 1; /* Accumulate space used */
          }
     putchar('\n');
     border('-',width,YES);
     }
```

6.10

```
/************** 6.10 finder *********************************
 * First argument is the match string. All other args
 * are printed in a column. For each one, the first
 * occurrence of the match string is replaced by a
 * string of special chars ('*').
 *********************************************************/
main(argc,argv)
int argc;
char *argv[];
      {
      char *p1, *p2;
      int i, length = str_len(argv[1]);
      for (i = 2; i < argc; i++)
            {
            if ((p1 = index(argv[1],argv[i])) != NULL)
                {
                for (p2 = argv[i]; p2 < p1; p2++)
                    putchar(*p2); /* Before match */
                border('*', length,NO); /* Match part */
                put_string(p2 + length); /* After match */
                }
            else put_string(argv[i]);
            }
      }
```

6.11

```
/****************** 6.11 sorter *******************************
 * Sort all of the command line arguments, including the
 * program name, and print them out in a column.
 *********************************************************/
main(argc,argv)
int argc;
char *argv[];
      {
      int j;
      sort (argv,argc);
      for (j = 0; j < argc; j++) put_string(argv[j]);
      }
```

Chapter 7

7.1

```
/************ display. c ******************/
/* display filename: terminal print of filename */
#include <stdio.h>
main(argc,  argv)
int argc;
char *argv[];
    {
    FILE *fp;
    int c;
    if (argc != 2)
        {
        puts("Usage: display filename");
        exit(1);
        }
    if ((fp = fopen(argv[1],"r")) == NULL)
        {
        printf("Can't open %s\n", argv[1]);
        exit(1);
        }
    while ((c = getc(fp)) != EOF) putchar(c);
    fclose(fp);
    }
```

7.2 The characters that are entered, in response to a gets(s) call, will continue to be deposited into memory (starting at location s) until the RETURN or ENTER key is depressed (i.e., until a newline is entered). The characters that are entered, in response to a scanf(%s, s) call, will behave similarly. However, the scanf input string will terminate on any white space character—including space, tab ('\t'), and form feed ('\f'). Thus, while these last three characters may *not* be part of an input string responding to scanf, they *may* be part of an input string responding to gets.

7.3

```
/************ fputs ******************************
 * Write string at s onto file identified by fp.
 * Return success/failure indicator.
 ***************************************************/
fputs(s, fp)
register char *s; /* input buffer */
register FILE *fp; /* stream identifier */
    {
    register int c; /* character slot */
    long ftell();    /* If not a valid open file, */
    if (ftell(fp) < 0L) return(-1);/* return failure */
    while (c = *s++) putc(c, fp); /* deposit char's */
    return (0); /* return success */
    }
```

7.4
a. <1.234567e+05>
b. <   1.e+05>
c. <1.e+05   >
d. <   textfi>

7.5

```
        printf("%s, %s %d, %.2d:%.2d", weekday, month,
                                day, hour, min);
```

7.6 **j** gets the value **12**, **y** gets the value **3.456**, and the string "jones" (properly null-terminated) will be placed in storage at location **name**.

7.7 j gets the value **12** and **y** gets the value **345.0**. The input string **6789** is ignored, and the two-character string "10" (properly null-terminated) will be placed in storage at location **name**. The characters **b**, **9**, and **8** will remain in the input buffer to satisfy *subsequent* calls for input. For example, the next **getchar** call will be satisfied by the character **b**.

7.8

```
        atoi(s)/* Convert string at s into integer */
        char *s;
            {
            double atof();
            return(atof(s));/* will be cast into an int */
            }
```

7.9

```
#define isxdigit(c) (tolower(c) >= 'a' && tolower(c) <= 'f'\
                        || isdigit(c) ? 1 : 0)
```

7.10

```
char *strcpy(s, p) /* Copy string at p to location at s */
                   /* Return s */
char *s, *p;
    {
    char *t = s;
    while (*t++ = *p++)
            ; /* Copy all characters including the null */
    return (s);
    }
```

APPENDIX A TABLE OF ASCII CODES

char	dec	oct	hex	char	dec	oct	hex	char	dec	oct	hex
NUL	0	0	00	DLE	16	20	10	space	32	40	20
SOH	1	1	01	DC1	17	21	11	!	33	41	21
STX	2	2	02	DC2	18	22	12	"	34	42	22
ETX	3	3	03	DC3	19	23	13	#	35	43	23
EOT	4	4	04	DC4	20	24	14	$	36	44	24
ENQ	5	5	05	NAK	21	25	15	%	37	45	25
ACK	6	6	06	SYN	22	26	16	&	38	46	26
BEL	7	7	07	ETB	23	27	17	'	39	47	27
BS	8	10	08	CAN	24	30	18	(	40	50	28
HT	9	11	09	EM	25	31	19	)	41	51	29
LF	10	12	0A	SUB	26	32	1A	*	42	52	2A
VT	11	13	0B	ESC	27	33	1B	+	43	53	2B
FF	12	14	0C	FS	28	34	1C	,	44	54	2C
CR	13	15	0D	GS	29	35	1D	−	45	55	2D
SO	14	16	0E	RS	30	36	1E	.	46	56	2E
SI	15	17	0F	US	31	37	1F	/	47	57	2F

(Continued)

char	dec	oct	hex	char	dec	oct	hex	char	dec	oct	hex
0	48	60	30	K	75	113	4B	f	102	146	66
1	49	61	31	L	76	114	4C	g	103	147	67
2	50	62	32	M	77	115	4D	h	104	150	68
3	51	63	33	N	78	116	4E	i	105	151	69
4	52	64	34	O	79	117	4F	j	106	152	6A
5	53	65	35	P	80	120	50	k	107	153	6B
6	54	66	36	Q	81	121	51	l	108	154	6C
7	55	67	37	R	82	122	52	m	109	155	6D
8	56	70	38	S	83	123	53	n	110	156	6E
9	57	71	39	T	84	124	54	o	111	157	6F
:	58	72	3A	U	85	125	55	p	112	160	70
;	59	73	3B	V	86	126	56	q	113	161	71
<	60	74	3C	W	87	127	57	r	114	162	72
=	61	75	3D	X	88	130	58	s	115	163	73
>	62	76	3E	Y	89	131	59	t	116	164	74
?	63	77	3F	Z	90	132	5A	u	117	165	75
@	64	100	40	[	91	133	5B	v	118	166	76
A	65	101	41	\	92	134	5C	w	119	167	77
B	66	102	42	]	93	135	5D	x	120	170	78
C	67	103	43	^	94	136	5E	y	121	171	79
D	68	104	44	_	95	137	5F	z	122	172	7A
E	69	105	45	`	96	140	60	{	123	173	7B
F	70	106	46	a	97	141	61	¦	124	174	7C
G	71	107	47	b	98	142	62	}	125	175	7D
H	72	110	48	c	99	143	63	~	126	176	7E
I	73	111	49	d	100	144	64	DEL	127	177	7F
J	74	112	4A	e	101	145	65				

C KEYWORDS AND THEIR USES

Keyword	Capsule summary of its use
	Keywords that identify data types
char	Shortest integral data element (8-bit byte)
int	Signed integer. Length fits the host processor
short	Either a half-length `int` or the same as an `int`
long	Either a double-length `int` or same as an `int`
unsigned	An `int` having no sign bit. All values positive
float	Floating-point number. Length fits processor
double	Double-precision floating-point number
struct	Employed in all structure declara(defini)tions
union	Employed in all union declarations/definitions

(Continued)

Keyword	Capsule summary of its use

Keywords that identify storage classes

auto	An automatic object (implicit and rarely used)
extern	An object whose definition appears *elsewhere*
static	Permits *internal* variable to retain its value Limits scope of an *external* object to its file
register	Requests CPU register for an **auto** variable

Keywords employed to alter the flow of control

return	Return (possibly with a value) to caller
if	Conditionally execute the following statement
else	Identifies the alternative to an **if**
while	Continue to loop while condition is true
do	Used to develop a special form of a **while**
for	A **while** with initializing and loop-ending portions
break	Exit this loop or **switch**
continue	Skip to the end of this loop pass
goto	Branch to the statement having this label
switch	A multiway branch to the statement whose **case** label value matches that of this expression
case	Used to identify a value-label in a **switch**
default	Identifies the no-other-match statement

Other keywords

sizeof	Gives the length (in bytes) of its argument
typedef	Employed to define a shorthand for a data type

APPENDIX C   OPERATOR PRECEDENCE
TABLE

	Class	Operators
	Primary	() [] −> .
R-L	*Unary*	++ −− ! - − * & (type) sizeof
	Arithmetic	* / %
		+ −
	Bitwise1	>> <<
	Relational1	<= < >= >
		== !=
	Bitwise2	&
		^
		|
	Relational2	&&
		||
R-L	*Conditional*	?:
R-L	*Assignment*	= += −= *= /= %= <<= >>= &= ^= |=
	Comma	,

CAPSULE SUMMARIES OF STANDARD LIBRARY FUNCTIONS

D.1 Notation Employed

Name	Description	Declaration
b	Boolean *truth* value, or success/failure call result indicator	int b;
c	Character value (passed as an int)	int c;
d	Double-precision floating value	double d;
f	Format control string in an [f/s]printf or [f/s]scanf call— *followed by* a list of all of the arguments that it needs	char *f;
fd	Descriptor assigned to an open file	int fd;
fp	Pointer to a FILE structure	FILE *fp;
i	Integer value	int i;
l	Long integer value	long l;
n	Integer value (usually a count)	int n;
p	Pointer to characters (normally)	char *p;
s	Pointer to a null-ending char string	char *s;
u	Unsigned integer value	unsigned u;

D.2 Notes Regarding Returned Values

A. Unless otherwise indicated, a **NULL** returned value for a pointer indicates that an exception was found and that the call could not be serviced normally.

B. A blank in the "returned type" column, in the list below, indicates that no valid value is returned.

C. During all *integer-returning* file I/O operations, a return of -1 (**EOF**) indicates that an error or exception condition (including end-of-file) was detected. If the returned value has no other special meaning, a return of *zero* normally indicates a *successful* operation.

D. An "(M)" notation, at the end of a description, indicates a function normally implemented as a *macro*.

D.3 Function Summaries

Call	Function description		Return
atof(s)	Return equivalent floating value of string **s**		**d**
atoi(s)	Return equivalent integer value of string **s**		**n**
calloc(n,i)	Return pointer to **n** $\times$ **i** cleared bytes		**p**
clearerr(fp)	Clear the error bits for stream **fp**	(M)	
close(fd)	Close the file identified by **fd**		**b**
creat(s,u)	Create & open file **s** in mode **u**		**fd**
exit(i)	Close files, terminate, and pass **i** back		
fclose(fp)	Close the file identified by **fp**		**b**
feof(fp)	Return the **EOF** flag for stream **fp**	(M)	**b**
ferror(fp)	Return the error flag for file **fp**	(M)	**b**
fflush(fp)	Write any buffered output to file **fp**		**b**
fgetc(fp)	Get next character from stream **fp**		**c**
fgets(s,n,fp)	Get max **n** char line from **fp** into **s**		**s**
fileno(fp)	Return descriptor for stream **fp**	(M)	**fd**
fopen(s, "m")	Open file **s** in mode **m** (r/w/a)		**fp**
fprintf(fp,f)	Formatted write to file **fp** based on **f**		
fputc(c,fp)	Write **c** onto file identified by **fp**		**c**
fputs(s,fp)	Write **s** onto file identified by **fp**		**b**
fread(p,i,n,fp)	Read **n** size **i** items from **fp** into **p**		**n**
free(p)	Release [c/m]allocated area at **p**		**b**

Call	Function description		Return
fscanf(fp,f)	Formatted read of file **fp** based on **f**		**n**
fseek(fp,l,i)	Seek in file **fp** to beg/here/end + **l**		**b**
ftell(fp)	Return current offset in file **fp**		**l**
fwrite(p,i,n,fp)	Write **n** size **i** items from **p** onto **fp**		**n**
getc(fp)	Get next character from stream **fp**	(M)	**c**
getchar()	Return next character from **stdin**	(M)	**c**
gets(s)	Read next line from **stdin** into **s**		**s**
isalnum(c)	Return *true* if **c** is alpha or digit	(M)	**b**
isalpha(c)	Return *true* if **c** is alphabetic	(M)	**b**
isascii(c)	Return *true* if **c** <= 0177	(M)	**b**
iscntrl(c)	Return *true* if **c** < 040 ¦¦ **c** == 0177	(M)	**b**
isdigit(c)	Return *true* if **c** is a digit	(M)	**b**
islower(c)	Return *true* if **c** is lowercase	(M)	**b**
isprint(c)	Return *true* if 040 <= **c** <= 0176	(M)	**b**
ispunct(c)	Return *true* if **c** = punctuation char	(M)	**b**
isspace(c)	Return *true* if **c** is whitespace char	(M)	**b**
isupper(c)	Return *true* if **c** is uppercase	(M)	**b**
isxdigit(c)	Return *true* if **c** is a hex digit	(M)	**b**
lseek(fd,l,i)	Seek in file **fd** to beg/here/end + **l**		**l**
malloc(u)	Return pointer to **u** RAM bytes		**p**
open(s,u)	Open file named **s** for mode **u** access		**fd**
printf(f)	Formatted print on **stdout** based on **f**		
putc(c,fp)	Write **c** onto file identified by **fp**	(M)	**c**
putchar(c)	Print **c** on **stdout**	(M)	**c**
puts(s)	Print **s** on **stdout** (appending '\n')		**b**
read(fd,p,n)	Read **n** bytes from file **fd** into **p**		**n**
rewind(fp)	Equivalent to an **fseek(fp,0L,0)**		**b**
scanf(f)	Formatted read from **stdin** based on **f**		**n**
sprintf(s,f)	Formatted print into **s** based on **f**		
sscanf(s,f)	Formatted read from **s** based on **f**		**n**
strcat(s,p)	Append string **p** to string **s**		**s**
strchr(s,c)	Return pointer to *first* **c** in string **s**		**p**
strcmp(s,p)	Return difference at first mismatch		**i**
strcpy(s,p)	Copy string **p** into buffer at **s**		**s**

(Continued)

Call	Function description	Return
strlen(s)	Return length of character string **s**	**n**
strncat(s, p, n)	Append at most **n** characters of **p** to **s**	**s**
strncmp(s, p, n)	**strcmp** (comparing at most **n** characters)	**i**
strncpy(s, p, n)	Copy **n** characters (\0 pad) from **p** to **s**	**s**
strrchr(s, c)	Return pointer to *last* **c** in string **s**	**p**
tolower(c)	Return **c** converted to lower, if upper	**c**
toupper(c)	Return **c** converted to upper, if lower	**c**
ungetc(c, fp)	Push **c** back onto input stream **fp**	**c**
unlink(s)	Delete file named **s** from the system	**b**
write(fd, p, n)	Write **n** bytes from **p** to file **fd**	**n**

STANDARD LIBRARY FUNCTIONS BY CATEGORY

Notes at the beginning of Appendix D apply here.

E.1 Standard File I/O

Call	Function description		Return
clearerr(fp)	Clear the error bits for stream fp	(M)	
fclose(fp)	Close the file identified by fp		b
feof(fp)	Return the EOF flag for stream fp	(M)	b
ferror(fp)	Return the error flag for file fp	(M)	b
fflush(fp)	Write any buffered output to file fp		b
fgetc(fp)	Get next character from stream fp		c
fgets(s,n,fp)	Get max n char line from fp into s		s
fileno(fp)	Return descriptor from stream fp	(M)	fd
fopen(s,"m")	Open file s in mode m (r/w/a)		fp
fprintf(fp,f)	Formatted write to file fp based on f		
fputc(c,fp)	Write c onto file identified by fp		c

(Continued)

Call	Function description		Return
fputs(s,fp)	Write **s** onto file identified by **fp**		**b**
fread(p,i,n,fp)	Read **n** size **i** items from **fp** into **p**		**n**
fscanf(fp,f)	Formatted read of file **fp** based on **f**		**n**
fseek(fp,l,i)	Seek in file **fp** to beg/here/end + **l**		**b**
ftell(fp)	Return current offset in file **fp**		**l**
fwrite(p,i,n,fp)	Write **n** size **i** items from **p** onto **fp**		**n**
getc(fp)	Get next character from stream **fp**	(M)	**c**
putc(c,fp)	Write **c** onto file identified by **fp**	(M)	**c**
rewind(fp)	Equivalent to an **fseek(fp,0L,0)**		**b**
ungetc(c,fp)	Push **c** back onto input stream **fp**		**c**

E.2 Low-Level File I/O

Call	Function description		Return
close(fd)	Close the file identified by **fd**		**b**
creat(s,u)	Create & open file **s** in mode **u**		**fd**
fileno(fp)	Return descriptor for stream **fp**	(M)	**fd**
lseek(fd,l,i)	Seek in file **fd** to beg/here/end + **l**		**l**
open(s,u)	Open file named **s** for mode **u** access		**fd**
read(fd,p,n)	Read **n** bytes from file **fd** into **p**		**n**
unlink(s)	Delete file named **s** from the system		**b**
write(fd,p,n)	Write **n** bytes from **p** to file **fd**		**n**

E.3 Memory Allocation Functions

Call	Function description	Return
calloc(n,i)	Return pointer to **n** × **i** cleared bytes	**p**
free(p)	Release [c/m]allocated area at **p**	**b**
malloc(u)	Return pointer to **u** RAM bytes	**p**

E.4 Formatted File I/O

Call	Function description	Return
fprintf(fp,f)	Formatted write to file fp based on f	
fscanf(fp,f)	Formatted read of file fp based on f	n

E.5 Terminal I/O (Normally)

Call	Function description		Return
getchar()	Return next character from stdin	(M)	c
gets(s)	Read next line from stdin into s		s
printf(f)	Formatted print on stdout based on f		
putchar(c)	Print c on stdout	(M)	c
puts(s)	Print s on stdout (appending '\n')		b
scanf(f)	Formatted read from stdin based on f		n

E.6 String Handling Functions

Call	Function description	Return
atof(s)	Return equivalent floating value of string s	d
atoi(s)	Return equivalent integer value of string s	n
calloc(n,i)	Return pointer to $n \times i$ cleared bytes	p
free(p)	Release [c/m]allocated area at p	b
malloc(u)	Return pointer to u RAM bytes	p
sprintf(s,f)	Formatted print into s based on f	
sscanf(s,f)	Formatted read from s based on f	n
strcat(s,p)	Append string p to string s	s
strchr(s,c)	Return pointer to *first* c in string s	p
strcmp(s,p)	Return difference at first mismatch	i
strcpy(s,p)	Copy string p into buffer at s	s
strlen(s)	Return length of character string s	n
strncat(s,p,n)	Append at most n characters of p to s	s
strncmp(s,p,n)	strcmp (comparing at most n characters)	i
strncpy(s,p,n)	Copy n characters (\0 pad) from p to s	s
strrchr(s,c)	Return pointer to *last* c in string s	p

E.7 Some `<ctype.h>` Character-Type Macros

Call	Function description		Return
`isalnum(c)`	Return *true* if **c** is alpha or digit	(M)	**b**
`isalpha(c)`	Return *true* if **c** is alphabetic	(M)	**b**
`isascii(c)`	Return *true* if **c** $\leq$ 0177	(M)	**b**
`iscntrl(c)`	Return *true* if **c** < 040 ¦¦ **c** == 0177	(M)	**b**
`isdigit(c)`	Return *true* if **c** is a digit	(M)	**b**
`islower(c)`	Return *true* if **c** is lowercase	(M)	**b**
`isprint(c)`	Return *true* if 040 $\leq$ **c** $\leq$ 0176	(M)	**b**
`ispunct(c)`	Return *true* if **c** = punctuation char	(M)	**b**
`isspace(c)`	Return *true* if **c** is whitespace char	(M)	**b**
`isupper(c)`	Return *true* if **c** is uppercase	(M)	**b**
`isxdigit(c)`	Return *true* if **c** is hex digit	(M)	**b**
`tolower(c)`	Return **c** converted to lower, if upper		**c**
`toupper(c)`	Return **c** converted to upper, if lower		**c**

E.8 Character Conversion Functions

Call	Function description	Return
`atof(s)`	Return equivalent floating value of string **s**	**d**
`atoi(s)`	Return equivalent integer value of string **s**	**n**
`tolower(c)`	Return **c** converted to lower, if upper	**c**
`toupper(c)`	Return **c** converted to upper, if lower	**c**

E.9 Miscellaneous Functions

Call	Function description	Return
`exit(i)`	Close files, terminate, and pass **i** back	

E.10 Some <stdio.h> Definitions, Declarations, and Macros

Definitions

Name	Description	Normal value
EOF	End of file indicator	-1
NULL	Pointer value returned to indicate an exception	0
FILE	A structure configured to operate as a *file access control block*. An *array* of such blocks is employed—one for each open file.	
BUFSIZ	Standard buffer size, in bytes	512
stdin	Standard input device **fp**	ptr to **FILE** array[0]
stdout	Standard output device **fp**	ptr to **FILE** array[1]
stderr	Standard error device **fp**	ptr to **FILE** array[2]

Declarations

Non-integer-returning function declarations

FILE *fopen();	**char *fgets();**
long ftell();	**char *gets();**

Macros

Call	Function description		Return
feof(fp)	Return the **EOF** flag for stream **fp**	(M)	**b**
ferror(fp)	Return the error flag for file **fp**	(M)	**b**
fileno(fp)	Return descriptor for stream **fp**	(M)	**fd**
getc(fp)	Get next character from stream **fp**	(M)	**c**
getchar()	Return next character from **stdin**	(M)	**c**
putc(c,fp)	Write **c** onto file identified by **fp**	(M)	**c**
putchar(c)	Print **c** on **stdout**	(M)	**c**

INDEX